CW00767019

C. Gayton Pick

St. Stephe

183

THE

AUTOBIOGRAPHY

OF

DR. WILLIAM LAUD,

ARCHBISHOP OF CANTERBURY, AND MARTYR.

COLLECTED FROM HIS REMAINS.

———

Πνεῦμα Ἅγιον ἄλλον τὴν σωφροσύνην ὑποχεῖσθαι ἄλλον
διδάσκει τὰ περὶ ἐλεημοσύνης· ἄλλον διδάσκει νηστεύειν καὶ
ἀσκεῖν· ἄλλον διδάσκει καταφρονεῖν τῶν τοῦ σώματος πραγμάτων· ἄλλον ἑτοιμάζει πρὸς μαρτύριον· ἄλλον ἐν ἄλλοις.
Αὐτὸ δὲ οὐκ ἄλλο Ἑαυτοῦ. S. Cyrill. Hieros.

———

OXFORD,
JOHN HENRY PARKER.
MDCCCXXXIX.

Br 1862.5.6
Pr 1862.5.6

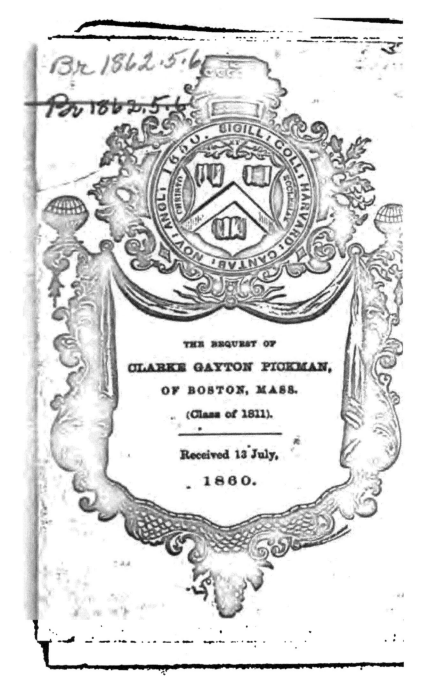

THE BEQUEST OF

CLARKE GAYTON PICKMAN,

OF BOSTON, MASS.

(Class of 1811).

Received 13 July,

1860.

Br 1862.5.6

~~Br 1862.5.6~~

1860, July 13.

Pickman Bequest.

RECD. MAY 17 1911

HARVARD
UNIVERSITY
LIBRARY

BAXTER, PRINTER, OXFORD.

PREFACE.

THIS volume is a compilation from Archbishop Laud's Diary, his History of his Chancellorship of Oxford, and his History of his Troubles and Trial. Very sparing use has been made of his Oxford Letters, and almost none of the Strafford Papers. These alone, to say nothing of the MS. treasures which exist in all probability at Lambeth, and perhaps among the Pococke Papers or elsewhere in the Bodleian, would have swelled the volume to an inconvenient bulk.

Although the materials are so woven together as to make it really an Autobiography throughout, yet the selection and

omission of passages leaves a considerabl
amount of responsibility upon the Editor
He has made his selection mainly with
wish to give the volume an academica
interest. But he has also borne in min
throughout the accusation of a leanin
to Romanism, which has been brough
against Hooker, Andrewes, Laud, Ham
mond, Bull, and Leslie, in company witl
most other sound English Divines, b
those particular schools of theology, whicl
even in our own day represent the conti
nental influence, so disastrous to the Churcl
in the reigns of Edward and Elizabeth.

It may be as well to warn the reader
that the Archbishop begins his year or
the 25th of March, which was the lega
computation in England, till 1751. Th
Gregorian Calendar of 1582 had not ther
been adopted in this country. With re
gard to St. Augustin's day, mentioned ir
page 266, it can only be supposed tha

the Archbishop mistook one day, the 26th of February for the 27th, and also used the Calendar of the English Church, as it was prior to the alterations made in it during the primacy of Cranmer. The 27th of February, though not found in all the old English Calendars, is nevertheless in most marked as "The Feast of St. Augustin, Bishop;" as in Gough Missal, 145. 149. 152. and 206. The Editor has altered very many of the dates, and has spared no pains to be accurate. But among such a profusion of them, not only of years and months, but even days of the week and Church Festivals, a few no doubt, perhaps more than a few, must have escaped his eye.

a. Archbishop Laud has so long suffered, not so much from the abuse of his enemies as from the apologies of his friends, that it seemed very desirable, if possible, that a man, for good or evil so eminent, and the stamp of whose influence is yet visible upon the Church, should be heard for himself. It would of course be out of place here to enter into any detailed vindication of his character. Thus much may be said. He has been vindicated in two ways. The Puritan charges against him have either been contradicted, softened down, and explained away: or acknowledged, lamented, and only excused with much parade of candour and goodnature, on the score of the virtues there are to be set over against his faults[a]. If the first of these ways is consistent with historical truth, it is well enough, however unsatisfactory. But it does not appear that it is consistent with truth, and therefore must be abandoned. The second way is still more unsatisfactory, and leaves the Puritans in fair possession of the field. One

[a] Even Clarendon stands too much on the defensive.

other way remains. To take the Archbishop's bigotry, superstition, narrow-
mindedness, rudeness, and intolerance,
to translate them out of these ungainly
words into Church vocabulary, and
ground our respect and reverence for his
memory on this—that, while he had also
common virtues like common men, he
had as well those higher and nobler and
larger features of an ancient Churchman,
which we first ceased to love, and are
now come scarcely to understand.

β. Archbishop Laud, and the Stuart divines generally, have been charged with an
over-weening reverence for the King, and
an undue and almost servile compliance
with the Court[b]. Whether the view taken
by Laud and others of the King's suprem-

---

[b] In speaking of the Stuart divines, a strong line of
distinction must be drawn between the times of the
first and second Charles. No part of this vindication
is meant to extend to Charles the Second's Bishops.

acy, and the limits by which he would have bounded it in Church matters, was precisely accurate, and whether the attitude in which the Church naturally and of right stands to the State was so intelligible to him as subsequent suffering and revolution have disclosed it to us, is not the question[*]. The charge is brought against him, as a moral defect and meanness, not as an error of judgment or opinion. It is but fair therefore to remember, that, whether right or wrong, the theologians of that day were fully persuaded of the divine right by which kings reign. How a conscientious belief of this would influence their practice in times when widely different notions were stirring

[*] Compare the views taken by Archbishop Whitgift in his Answer to the Admonition, and Hooker, if the Eighth Book is to carry the weight of his name along with it, and Archbishop Laud in some passages of the Conference, with those of Leslie in the Pontificate and Regale: or still more curiously with the new and mixed views of Mr. Gladstone.

among the people, and with such a King, a better than Constantine, in Charles the Martyr, it is not difficult to conceive. The proud doctrine of " public opinion," by which every man is taught to feel himself a part of an irresponsible tribunal at which the actions of sovereign and subject are unreservedly and almost indiscriminately censured, would have been far more difficult of understanding to them, and far less likely to have met with their approval, than the doctrine of divine right among ourselves. At all events, therefore, however unlikely it may be that modesty or a fear of being wrong in such a point will make men backward in despising the political views of our older Bishops, it is but right to shift the accusation from their hearts and feelings, and lay it upon their judgments and opinions. To clear their memories from calumny or harsh mistake is a humble and a pious work. Their wisdom

and teaching are above modern patronage
and vindication.

γ. A religious attention to dreams and possible indications of Providence is another.
point, on which much has been said against
Archbishop Laud, and for the repetition of
which the present volume affords continual
opportunity. He said himself on his trial,
that " dreams are not in the power of him
that hath them, but in the unruliness of
the fancy, which in broken sleeps wanders
which way it pleases, and shapes what it
pleaseth[d]." On this head however, as on
the divine right of kings, being matters
easy to profane, it is well to say little; and
indeed whatever might be said would only
lessen the weight of blame by helping to
bear it. The older English divines, after
they had recovered themselves from the

[d] P. 409, where also he refers to Numbers xii. but
without quoting it—perhaps lest it should seem too much
for him to say.

noise and hurry of the great changes made
in our Church, seem by the help of anti-
quity, and of course in a fainter degree, to
have realized the presence of a spiritual
world, contained within and disclosing
itself through the visible state of things.
They saw in many ways, in the rites and
types of nature, shadows from the inner
Heaven stirring on its earthly counterpart.
Gradually, however, this became less
" open," and even " precious in those
days," until the force of a gross and phy-
sical system of unbelief caused it to re-
appear, under a philosophical veil, in the
school of Bishop Berkeley, " philosopho-
rum religiosissimi." Meanwhile we may
leave Archbishop Laud, supported by a
name " much set by" in the Church, and
little lower than his own. " Although I
am no doter on dreams," says Bishop Bull*,
" yet I verily believe, that some dreams

* Works, i. 295. Oxford.

are monitory, above the power of fancy, and impressed on us by some superior influence. For of such dreams, we have plain and undeniable instances in history, both sacred and profane, and *in our own age and observation.* Nor shall I so value the laughter of sceptics, and the scoffs of the Epicureans, as to be ashamed to profess, that I *myself* have had some *convincing* experiments of such impressions. Now it is no enthusiasm, but the best account that can be given of them, to ascribe these things to the ministry of those invisible instruments of God's providence, that guide and govern our affairs and concerns, namely, the Angels of God."

8. Another charge brought against the Archbishop is, that he treated his brethren the Clergy, and even the Bishops, with roughness and severity, because they were moderate men, and would not go his lengths. Without entering minutely into

the exaggeration which is made of this,
and the overwhelming weight a few facts
are compelled to bear, it may be admitted
that the accusation is true. It is well for
the Church of our day, no less than his, that
Laud was not a moderate man; and, that
he did not sympathize with such, or think
lightly of the mischief they could do, is
evident from his letters. " My Lord," he
writes to Strafford in Ireland, " to speak
freely, you may easily promise more in
either kind than I can perform: for, as for
the Church, it is so bound up in the forms
of the common law, that it is not possible
for me, or for any man, to do that good
which he would, or is bound to do. For
your Lordship sees, no man clearer, that
they which have gotten so much power in
and over the Church, will not let go their
hold; they have, indeed, fangs with a
witness, whatsoever I was once said in
a passion to have. And for the State, in-

deed, my Lord, I am for thorough; but I see that both thick and thin stays somebody, where I conceive it should not; and it is impossible for me to go thorough alone." Again: "As for my marginal note, I see you deciphered it well, and I see you make use of it too—do so still—thorow and thorow. Oh that I were where I might go so too! But I am shackled between delays and uncertainties'." Now it is possible the Archbishop might think in some such way as this. Moderate men, in the popular conversational fallacy of his day as well as ours, no doubt meant—men with right premisses, who, not having moral courage to carry them out, were left by their timidity and love of easiness at some point short of the conclusion: men, who, not being able to think their way down deep enough, to the root of a truth, did not know how far its fibres might extend,

f Life of Strafford, p. 314, 315.

or how much would come with it, if it
was torn up; and therefore had no objection to buy peace with concession. He
had doubtless heard it argued, that people
go into an extreme in religion, and put
entirely out of sight some portion of truth;
then that a reaction comes, and those, who
are the instruments of recovering the forgotten truth, fly off into an equal extreme
the other way; and lastly, that there is
always a party between these two, to
which it is safest to belong, and which
in the end prevails. But he might think
this commentary fitted Church history very
awkwardly. He might from the same history conclude, that the midway place was
popular for the time, because it allowed of
men's timidity, and was not difficult of
access, and constant armed watch was not
kept thereon: and that in uneasy times of
heat and suffering, these middle men melted
away, and subsided into the lower and

easier extreme, and therefore did not pre
vail. And even though they might prevail
he knew that earthly victory was not th
best of arguments for truth. But he migh
remember, that the moderate party i
Arian times was popular, and yet not safe
neither did it prevail. And had he live
forty-four years from his Martyrdom, h
would have seen some of that Churcl
history worked out at home. Moderat
men are not tall enough to throw a shado
over posterity, nor of sufficient intensit
of heart and purpose to project their in
fluence into after-generations.

a. It has been argued too, that in the lif
of Archbishop Laud, there is little or n
trace of his being a religious and spiri
tually-minded man. Now in the sense i
which the objection was probably intended
this may be true. Yet the volume of pri
vate devotions which he has left behind
and which was composed for himself fron

time to time, reveals most clearly that grave inward life which he was living, while common history is telling of his troubled outward life. Thus in his correspondence with Strafford, which is mostly political, there are many quiet disclosures of a thoughtful religious man. Strafford, writing in low spirits about his peerage, mentions, that he is making moral lessons for himself out of Donne's anagrams and Vandyke's shading; the Bishop replies, "If you will but read over the short book of Ecclesiastes, while these thoughts are in you, you will see a better disposition of these things, and the vanity of all their shadows, than is to be found in any anagrams of Dr. Donne's, or any designs of Vandyke. So to the lines there drawn I leave you [s]." Men are always judging others on this point, of which it is im-

[s] Life of Strafford, p. 350.

possible they should form any sure judgment at all.   In religion above all other
things, that of St. Gregory Nazianzen
is true : " What other men say of us,
is no more than what other men dream
of us[b]." This is the great source of un-
kindness among religious friends.   Some
persons, without any sin or ostentation,
are always exhibiting their inward religious feelings by some change or motion
of voice, or countenance, or gesture. They
feel it necessary.   They find that these
changes of outward demeanour are, so to
speak, conditions of the inward feelings ;
a sort of ritual to which they are tied and
bound, and which it would be unsafe for
them to disuse.   As St. Augustine speaks
of praying with our hands stretched out,
the attitude so commonly seen in churches
abroad: et nescio quomodo, cum hi motus

[b] Ap. Bp. Taylor, Duct. Dub. xi. 408.

corporis fieri nisi motu animi præcedente
non possint, eisdem rursus exterius visi-
biliter factis, ille interior invisibilis qui
eos fecit augetur : ac per hoc cordis
affectus, qui ut fierent ista præcessit, quia
facta sunt crescit[1]. Others, on the contrary, without any affected attempt at
concealment, shrink from all this, traiu
their religious emotions with secret nur-
ture, and keep them so close, that they
can only escape and become manifest in
deeds. Orat interior homo, et ante oculos
Dei in secretissimo cubili, ubi compun-
gitur, sternitur. Any outward disclosure
of ascetic ways or holy resolutions, even
though it be unconscious at the time, seems
to scatter and disperse such men's inward
strength : they are like plants that grow
in caves and dark places only, and lose
their green, and languish, in the eye of

[1] De Cur. Gerend. pro Mort. 7. Venet.

day. It is with Archbishop Laud in thi
respect, as with St. Thomas à Becket, o
still more, that great man Innocent th
Third : though perhaps it may not b
thought doing the Archbishop's memor
good service to couple it with these dis
tasteful names. We read the history o
John and his Barons; and, while w
think we are carrying away a clear viev
of the bigoted, haughty, secular Prelate
how unlike the original is the rud
image we have hewn from the coarse ma
terials of Protestant history. He all th
while is at Rome, weighed down witl
care, weary of his greatness, and full o
godly fear lest his height should mak
him proud ; and so, as a penitential safe-
guard, composing a book on the Seven
Penitential Psalms. Thus does he open hi
treatise : " Lest amid occupations mani-
fold and fierce anxieties, which not only
from the care of government, but also from

the badness of the times, I do endure beyond my strength, as though the deep had
altogether swallowed me up—with eager-
ness do I steal some little hours for myself, in the which to revoke and bring
home my spirit to itself, lest from itself it
be sundered and alienated altogether: and
I would meditate somewhat in the Law
of the Lord, which, by His grace Whose
Spirit bloweth where He listeth, may
profit me to this very thing,—that I be not
always so betrayed to other things as that
it shall not be possible to restore me to
myself[b]." Or he may be making in his

---

[b] Innocentii Opera, fol. xcvii. et ccviii. Ne inter
occupationes multiplices et sollicitudines vehementes,
quas non solum ex cura regiminis, verum etiam ex
malitia temporis, patior ultra vires, quasi totus absorbear
a profundo: libenter aliquas horulas mihi furor, quibus
ad revocandum et reducendum spiritum ad seipsum, ne
a seipso dividatur et alienetur omnino, et in lege Domini
aliquid meditetur, quod ad hoc Ipso proficiat inspirante,
Cujus Spiritus ubi vult spirat, ne semper sic sim traditus
aliis, ut nunquam restituar ipse mihi.

careful solitude his earnest and humbl
" Hymn of Christ :"

> Te nuno precor licet reus,
> Miserere mei Deus.
> Miserere Miserator,
> Quia vere sum peccator !

ζ. There is another point which mus
be shortly noticed here: the Archbishop'
claim to the rights and titles of martyi
dom.   However full of childish boastin;
we have been in many things, in increas
ing the number of our Saints we hav
been either singularly humble or negli
gent.   The consciousness seems to hav
been forced upon us, that our sundr
revolutions have not made us much riche
in materials for filling out our Calenda:
England of the nineteenth century has
long way to travel back before it reache
the England proverbially prolific of Saintι
It is a long way to St. David, St. Chad
St. Dunstan, St. Swithun ; to say nothin;

of St. Alban, and the companions of our Augustin. But to our royal Saints, Edmund and Edward and Etheldreda, we have added Charles: and this, being the act of the Church, helps us considerably towards determining the claim of Archbishop Laud. It is curious to observe, that our great struggle with another branch of the Church, with Rome, has left no vestige of itself upon our Calendar. It made no Martyrs. It did not add to our commemorations of the Saints. There is not the shadow of an expression any where upon the Church's countenance to teach us what she feels and thinks, or felt and thought, about the Marian persecution. The whole of that part of our history is as open as any other historical question to the sifting and searching and familiarity of criticism. It is so on both sides. For the Church of Rome herself has hitherto wanted either boldness or

generosity to canonize Cardinal Fisher.
What was done, and what was ruled, is
in a great measure retained. But all
names are dropped, and left at the mercy
of common criticism; which has as yet
been kinder to the sixteenth century than
it has to other and earlier ages, which
may perhaps have deserved as well or
better at its hands. But our second great
struggle, with heretics for the most part
outside the Church, that is to say, the
Puritans, has left traces behind. It added
to our Calendar the only addition that
has been made for some centuries; for
we may except the *recovery* of St. Alban
and the Venerable Bede. The history of
our struggle with the Puritans is thus
not left quite open to Churchmen's criticism. This will be acknowledged as a
great blessing by those who have fairly
studied this portion of history. The vindication of the Martyr Charles by the

Church has closed several painful questions. It has not determined them, nor
imposed a judgment upon us in the particulars. But it has closed them up.
Archbishop Laud has not been vindicated
a Martyr by the Church. Yet she has
come much nearer to it than in any other
case since the changes first began among
us. Every body, however they view it,
and whatever hard names they may give
it, will admit that Laud died for the same
cause, and in the same attitude, as his
royal Master; and the King having been
named a Martyr by authority, we have
fair warrant for extending the same venerable title to the Primate. Now the Church
has given no warrant in any other case,
nor come any way near it. She has not
given the title of Martyr to any who
suffered, however cruelly or unrighte-
ously, at the hands of another Church:
and it is clear that a very great deal

would be involved in such an act. All these sort of canonizations have no higher or more dignified origin than in individual whims and likings, or, historically, in Fox's Book of Martyrs: nor do those who make them seem, for the most part, aware of the many grave questions unconsciously determined in their decision. However, the Church not having made them nor sanctioned them, they are unimportant, and, it is to be hoped, without consequences.

η. It would not be difficult to shew, that the highest characters are for the most part unpopular. The power of pleasing seems in many cases withdrawn, by way of balance, from those men who are sent to stop and save an age. The degree, to which such men as these are misunderstood, is often the only measure we have of their height above ourselves. So it might be shewn, if this were the place, that Archbishop Laud's character was one of these, cast in a mould of proportions that are much above our own, and of stature akin to the elder days of the Church. The features, hard and stedfast, are full of grace in their boldness, and dignified by a scarce kind of beauty, austere and masculine. These are the men vouchsafed to us in the dangers of the Church. Such were his predecessors in the Chair of Canterbury, Lanfranc and the great Anselm. To look at such an one on the mere surface of history is to view him in one posture only: one too which he has not taken up of himself, but which the troubles of high place and a distempered generation have compelled him to assume. It is not so much therefore that Laud's character, *personally*, is harsh and unpleasing; as that we have ceased to sympathize with that *class* of characters at all, or have reverence for the *kind* of greatness by which they are distinguished. There are in many senses " divers orders" in the Church of Christ: " for," says St. Cyril, " one fountain watered the whole of the garden, and one and the same rain comes down upon all the world, yet it becomes white in the lily, and red in the rose, and purple in the violets and pansies, and different and varied in each several kind[1]." It is really quite painful to notice, how persons in these days speak and write of Puritanism. It would be thought wrong, instead of being a duty, to regard it as a hateful and detestable heresy, or rather fearful combination of heresies, and a deadly enmity to Christ's holy Church. Men forget how it began in a hatred and putting down of Episcopacy, whereby, so far as regarded themselves, the Church was destroyed among them, and they were

[1] Oxf. Trans. p. 206.

left unblessed; how the most shocking
notions of the holy Sacraments, such as
would startle even those of our times,
almost universally prevailed: and how
uniformly its career was marked, whether
in its Presbyterian or Independent stages,
by sacrilege and blasphemy; and closed
with the murder of the King. No candid
and fair distinctions, as men call them,
of one school from another, can get rid
of these awful truths. The Presbyterian
form, according to all historians the least
offensive and disgusting, invites from
the most careless reader the application
of the Apostle's words : " Such are false
apostles, deceitful workers, transforming
themselves into the Apostles of Christ.
And no marvel; for Satan himself is transformed into an angel of light. Therefore
it is no great thing if his ministers also
be transformed as the ministers of righ-
teousness; whose end shall be according

to their works[k]." Things must indeed
have come to a fearful pitch, when men
are driven per-force to admire earnest
heretics for their earnestness; when they
should have rather seen in it a sign of
that satanical energy which is the life of
heresy, and its mark. Yet have we been
living all along on Puritan traditions
about Archbishop Laud, without shame
and without reflection. He has come
down to us, as some would vainly make
St. Cyprian come down, a narrow mind
eaten up in the contemplation of his
office: or, like St. Cyril of Alexandria,
to moderns a pattern of nothing but rude
zeal and fierce impatience. Were we to
throw him further back, to lift him above
the age in which his lot was cast, and
give him a niche among the primitive
worthies of the Church, and the stern
upholders of the Faith against the elder

k 2 Cor. xi. 13—15.

heretics, he would beseem it well. Laud was like one of them. Placed on high, apart from all the tenderest relations of society, in a life of austere celibacy and ceaseless labour, between weak friends and strong enemies, in hard and unkind times, and beside all this, with the care of many Churches, a weight of which an Apostle spoke as though it were a great thing even to him, he bore a heavy secret Cross within his Crosier, and went with it stoutly to his Martyrdom.

OXFORD,
, MDCCCXXXIX.

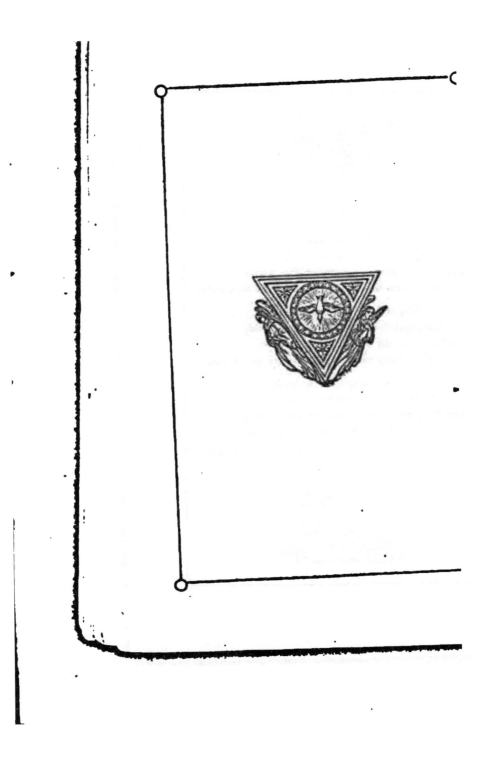

Laud.

Thy spirit in thee strove
To cleanse and set in beauty free
The ancient shrines, mindful of Him whose love
Swept with the scourge His Father's sanctuary.

Thy cloke was burning zeal,
Untaught the worldling s arts to wield,
But innocence thy coat of triple steel,
And Loyalty and Truth thy sword and shield.

Thus arm'd against the tomb,
Thy dauntless course bore on to bind
Thy dying brows with deathless martyrdom,
Unsought by the true soul, but undeclin'd.

THE CATHEDRAL.

INDEX

OF THE YEARS.

INDEX
OF THE LETTERS.

THE DIARY

OF THE

MOST REVEREND FATHER IN GOD

WILLIAM LAUD,

ARCHBISHOP OF CANTERBURY.

———

ANNO 1573. I was born Oct. 7, 1573, at Reading.   In my infancy I was in danger of death by sickness, &c.

1589. I came to Oxford, July.

1590. I was chosen Scholar of St. John's, June.

1593. I was admitted Fellow of St. John's, June.

1594. My father died, April 11, die Mercurii. I proceeded Bachelor of Arts, June.

1596. I had a great sickness.

1597. And another.

1598. I proceeded Master of Arts, July. I was Grammar Reader that year; and fell into a great sickness at the end of it.

1600. My mother died, Nov. 24. I was made Deacon, Jan. 4. *English computation*.

1601. I was made Priest, April 5, being Palm Sunday: both (Orders?) by Dr. Young, Bishop of Rochester.

1602. I read a Divinity Lecture in St. John's College: it was then maintained by Mrs. Maze. I was the last that read it. Queen Elizabeth died at Richmond, Mar. 24. *English computation*.

1603. I was Proctor of the University, chosen May 4. I was made Chaplain to the Earl of Devonshire, Sept. 3. Hope was given to me of A. H. Jan. 1. which after proved my great happiness. I first began to hope it, Jan. 21.

1604. I was Bachelor in Divinity, July 6.

1605. My cross about the Earl of Devon's marriage, Dec. 26, die Jovis.

1606. The quarrel Dr. Ayry picked with
ιe about my sermon at St. Mary's, Oct. 21.

1607. I was inducted into the Vicarage of
tanford in Northamptonshire, Nov. 13.

1608. The Advowson of North Kilworth
ι Leicestershire given to me, April. My
:quaintance with C. W. began. I proceeded
)octor in Divinity in the Act. I was made
haplain to Dr. Neile, then Lord Bishop of
.ochester, Aug. 5. After my unfortunateness
·ith T. (whose death was in July, 1604,) the
rst offer in this kind that I had after was by
ι. Short, June, 1606; then by P. B. not ac-
ϵpted.

1609. My first sermon to King James at
·heobald's, Sept. 17. I changed my Advow-
ϧn of North Kilworth for West-Tilbery in
:ssex; to which I was inducted Oct. 28, to
e near my Lord of Rochester, Dr. Neile.
ly next unfortunateness was with E. M.
)ec. 30, being Saturday. A stay in this.

1610. My Lord of Rochester gave me
uchstone in Kent, May 25. I resigned my
ϵllowship in St. John's College, Oxford,

Oct. 2, and left Oxford the 8th of the same month. I fell sick of a Kentish ague, caught at my benefice, Nov. 5, which held me two months. In the midst of this sickness, the suit about the Presidentship of St. John's began. I left Cuchstone, and was inducted in Norton, Nov. by proxy. The Lord Chancellor Elsmere's complaint against me to the King at Christmas. He was incited against me by Dr. Abbot, Lord Archbishop of Canterbury elect.

1611. My next unfortunateness was by S. B. Feb. 11. It continued long. I was chosen President of St. John's, May 10. The King sat in person three hours to hear my cause about the Presidentship of St. John's at Tichburne, Aug. 29. It was the day of the Decollation of St. John Bapt. The Archbishop of Canterbury was the original cause of all my troubles. I was sworn the King's Chaplain, Nov. 3.

1612. My next unfortunateness was by S. S. June 13. It ended quickly. My next with A. D. which effected nothing, and ended presently. Sept. My great business with E. B. began Jan. 22. It settled, as it could, March 5, *Eng. comput.* It hath had many changes; and what will become of it, God knoweth.

1614. My great misfortune by M. S. began, April 9. A most fierce salt rheum in my left eye, like to have endangered it. Dr. Neile, then Bishop of Lincoln, gave me the Prebend of Bugden, April 18.

1615. Dr. Neile, the Bishop of Lincoln, gave me the Archdeaconry of Huntingdon, Dec. 1.

1616. The King gave me the Deanery of Gloucester, Nov. I resigned my Parsonage of West Tilbery. I set forward with the King toward Scotland, March 14, 1616, *our style:* and returned a little before him, 1617. My acquaintance began with W. Sta. March 5.

1617. . . . . Cum E. B. July 28, die Lunæ, primò. St. John's College on fire under the staircase in the Chaplain's Chamber, by the Library, Sept. 26, die Veneris. Both these days of observation to me. I was inducted to

Ibstock in Leicestershire, August 2, in my return out of Scotland; and left Norton.

1618. *La. Bos.* B. to E. B. May 2. *Et quid ad me?* My ill hap with E. beg. June. The great organ in St. John's Chapel set up: it was begun Feb. 5.

1619. I fell suddenly dead for a time at Wycombe, in my return from London, April 2.

1620. I was installed Prebendary of Westminster, Jan. 22, having had the Advowson of it ten years the November before.

1621. The King's gracious speech unto me, June 3, concerning my long service. He was pleased to say, He had given me nothing but Gloucester, which he well knew was a shell without a kernel.—June 29. His Majesty gave me the grant of the Bishopric of St. David's, being St. Peter's Day. The general expectation in Court was, that I should then have been made Dean of Westminster, and not Bishop of St. David's. The King gave me leave to hold the Presidentship of St. John's College in Oxon. in my Commendam with the Bishopric of St. David's. [But by reason of the strictness of that statute, which I will not violate, nor my oath to it under any colour, I am resolved before my consecration to leave it*.]—Oct. 10. I was chosen Bishop of St. David's. I resigned the Presidentship of St. John's in Oxford, Nov. 17.—I preached at Westminster Nov. 5.—I was consecrated Bishop of St. David's, Nov. 18, at London House Chapel, by the Reverend Fathers, the Lords Bishops of London, Worcester, Chichester, Ely, Llandaff, Oxon. The Archbishop being thought irregular for casual homicide.—Jan. 6. The Parliament, then sitting, was dissolved by proclamation, without any session.—Jan. 14. The King's letters came to the Archbishop, and all the Bishops about London, for a contribution of the Clergy for the recovery of the Palatinate.—Jan. 21. The Archbishop's letters came to me about this business.—Jan. 25. I sent these letters and my own into the Diocese.—Feb. 17. I preached at Westminster. All my former

* This clause is maliciously omitted by Prynne.

sermons are omitted.—March 9. I heard of the death of L. B. He died Jan. 17, between six and seven in the morning.—March 13. Dr. Theodore Price went towards Ireland out of London, about the Commission appointed there.—March 24. I preached at Court: commanded to print.

1622. April 23. The King renewed my Commendam.—April 16. I was with his Majesty and the Prince's Highness, to give notice of letters I received of a treasonable sermon preached in Oxford, on Sunday, April 14, by one Mr. Knight of Broadgates.—April 14. Sunday, I waited at the entertainment of Count Swartzenburg, the Emperor's Ambassador, in the Parliament House.—April 23. Being the Tuesday in Easter week, the King sent for me, and set me into a course about the Countess of Buckingham, who about that time was wavering in point of religion[b].—April 24. Dr. Francis White and I met about this.—May 10. I went to the Court to Green-

[b] All these passages are, for obvious reasons, omitted by Pryune.

wich, and came back in the coach with the
Lord Marquess Buckingham. My promise then
to give his Lordship the discourse he spake
to me for.—May 12, I preached at Westminster.—May 19. I delivered my Lord
Marquess Buckingham the paper concerning
the difference between the Church of England
and Rome, in point of salvation, &c.—May 23.
My first speech with the Countess of Buckingham.—May 24. The conference between
Mr. Fisher a Jesuit, and myself, before
the Lord Marquess Buckingham, and the
Countess his mother. I had much speech
with her after.—June 9. Being Whit-Sunday,
my Lord Marquess Buckingham was pleased
to enter upon a near respect to me. The particulars are not for paper.—June 15. I became
C. to my Lord of Buckingham. And June 16,
being Trinity Sunday, he received the Sacrament at Greenwich.—June 22, &c. I saw two
books in folio of Sir Robert Cotton's. In the
one was all the order of the Reformation in
the time of Henry the Eighth. The original
letters and dispatches under the King's and

the Bishops', &c. own hands. In the other
were all the preparatory letters, motives, &c
for the suppression of the Abbeys : their sup
pression and value, in the originals. A1
extract of both which books I have *pe*
capita.—July 5. I first entered into Wales.—
July 9. I began my first visitation at th
College in Brecknock, and preached.—
July 24. I visited at St. David's, and preached
July 25.—August 6, 7. I visited at Carmarthen
and preached. The Chancellor and my Com
missioners visited at Emlyn, &c. July 16, 17
and at Haverford West, July 19, 20.—Augus
15. I set forwards towards England from
Carmarthen.—Sept. 1. My answer given to
his Majesty about nine articles delivered in
a book from Mr. Fisher the Jesuit. These
articles were delivered me to consider of
August 28. The discourse concerning then
the same night at Windsor, in the presence o
the King, the Prince, the Lord Marques
Buckingham, his lady, and his mother.—
Sept. 18. *aut circiter.* There was notice given
me, that Mr. Fisher had spread certain copie

of the conference had between him and me, May 24, into divers recusants' hands.—October. I got the sight of a copy, &c. in October; made an answer to it.—Oct. 27. I preached at Westminster.—Dec. 12. My ancient friend, Mr. R. Peashall, died, at six in the morning. It was Thursday, and *Sol in Capri. Lucia Virgo* in some Almanacks a day before, in some a day after it.—Dec. 16. My Lord Marquess Buckingham's speech to me about the same key.—Dec. 25. I preached at St. Giles without Cripplegate. I was three times with the King this Christmas; and read over to him the answer which I had made to Fisher; which he commanded should be printed: and I desired it might pass in a third person, under the name of R. B.

1622. Jan. 11. My Lord of Buckingham and I in the inner chamber at York House. *Quod est Deus Salvator noster Christus Jesus.*— Jan. 17. I received a letter from E. B. to continue my favour, as Mr. R. P. had desired me.—Jan. 19. I preached at Westminster.— Jan. 27. I went out of London about the

Parsonage of Creeke, given me into my Commendam.—Jan. 29. I was instituted at Peterborough to the Parsonage of Creeke.—Jan. 31. I was inducted into Creeke.—Feb. 2. Being Sunday and Candlemas Day, I preached and read the Articles at Creeke.—Feb. 5. Wednesday, I came to London. I went that night to his Majesty, hearing he had sent for me. He delivered me a book to read and observe. It was a Tract of a Capuchin, that had once been a Protestant. He was now with the French Ambassador. The Tract was to prove, that Christ's Body was in two places at once, in the apparition to St. Paul, Acts ix.—Feb. 9. I gave the King an account of this book. I ordained Edmund Provant, a Scot priest. He was my first-begotten in the Lord.—Feb. 17. Monday, the Prince and the Marquess Buckingham set forward very secretly for Spain.—Feb. 21. I wrote to my Lord of Buckingham into Spain.—Feb. 22. Saturday, I fell very ill; and was very suddenly plucked down in four days. I was put into the Commission of Grievances. There were in the Commission the Lord Marquess Buckingham, Lord Arundel, Lord Pembroke, Bishop of Winchester, and myself. The Proclamation came out for this, Feb. 24.—March 9. I ordained Thomas Owen, Bachelor of Arts, Deacon.— March 10. I ordained him and John Mitchell, Priests.—March 23. I preached at Whitehall.

1623. March 31. I received letters from my Lord of Buckingham out of Spain.—April 9. I received letters from my Lord of Buckingham out of Spain.—April 13. Easter Day, I preached at Westminster.—April 16. I ordained John Burraigh, Master of Arts, Deacon and Priest.—May 3 and 16. My speech with B. E. and the taking off my jealousies about the great business.—June 1. Whit-Sunday, I preached at St. Bride's.—June 13. I received letters from the Duke of Buckingham out of Spain.—June 15. R. B. died at Stony Stratford; which, what it will work with B. E. God in Heaven knoweth; and be merciful unto me. — July 6. I preached at Westminster.—July 15. St. Swithin: a very fair day till towards 5 at night; then great extremity of thunder and lightning. Much hurt done. The lanthorn at St. James's House blasted: the vane bearing the Prince's arms beaten to pieces. The Prince then in Spain. It was Tuesday, and their St. James's day, *new style.*—Aug. 17. I received letters from the Duke of Buckingham out of Spain.—Aug 31. I preached at Sunninge with my Lord of Bristol.—Sept. 8. I was at Bromley; and heard of the unfortunate passage between my friends there.—Oct. 3. Friday, I was with my Lord Keeper; to whom I found some had done me very ill offices. And he was very jealous of L. B.'s favour.—Oct. 5. The Prince and the Duke of Buckingham landed at Portsmouth from Spain.—Oct. 6. Monday, they came to London. The greatest expression of joy by all sorts of people that ever I saw.—Oct. 20. I ordained Thomas Blakiston, Bach. of Arts, Deacon.—Oct. 26. The fall of an house, while Drewrye the Jesuit was preaching, in the Black Fryars. About 100 slain. It was in their account November 5.—

Oct. 31. I acquainted my Lord Duke of Buckingham with that which passed between the Lord Keeper and me.—Nov. 12. Wednesday night, a most grievous fire in Bread Street, in London. Alderman Cocking's house, with others. burnt down.—Nov. 18. Tuesday night, the Duke of Buckingham entertained the two Spanish Ambassadors, Don Diego de Mendoza the Extraordinary, and Don Carolos Columnas the Ordinary, and Mexia (I think his name was), Ambassador from the Archdukes. One of the Extraordinary Ambassadors of Spain, Marquess Iniioca, came not, because Mendoza and he could not agree upon precedency. His Majesty and the Prince were there. The Bishop of London and myself waited upon the King.—Dec. 14. Sunday night, I did dream that the Lord Keeper was dead: that I passed by one of his men, that was about a monument for him: that I heard him say, his lower lip was infinitely swelled and fallen, and he rotten already. This dream did trouble me.—Dec. 15. On Monday

morning, I went about business to my Lo:
Duke of Buckingham. We had speech :
the Shield Gallery at Whitehall. There
found, that the Lord Keeper had strange:
forgotten himself to him; and I think w:
dead in his affections.—Dec 21. I preache
at Westminster.—Dec. 27. St. John's Da:
I was with my Lord Duke of Buckinghan
I found, that all went not right with th
Lord Keeper, &c. He sent to speak with m
because he was to receive the next day.-
Dec. 30. I adventured to tell my Lor
Duke of Buckingham, of the opinion gen:
rally held touching the Commission of send
ing Sir Edward Coke and some others int
Ireland, before the intended Parliament.-
Jan. 3. I received my writ to appear i
Parliament, Feb. 12, following.—Jan. 10.
received a command under seal from m
Lord of London, to warn for the Convocatio:
I was with my Lord Duke of Buckingham
and shewed him the state of the boo:
printed about the *Visitation of the Church*
and what was like to ensue upon it.—Jan. 1:

I was with his Majesty, to shew him the
Epistle, that was to be printed before the Con-
ference between me and Fisher the Jesuit,
May 24, 1622, which he was pleased to ap-
prove. The King brake with me about the
Book printed then of the *Visitation of the
Church.* He was hard of belief, that A. B. C.
(Abbot) was the author of it. My Lord Keeper
met with me in the withdrawing chamber, and
quarrelled with me gratis.—Jan. 12. I sent the
summons down into the country to the Clergy,
for their appearance at the Convocation.—
Jan. 14. I acquainted my Lord Duke of
Buckingham with that which passed on the
Sunday before, between the Lord Keeper and
me.—Jan. 16. I was all day with Dr. W.
(White) about my papers of the Conference;
and making them ready for the press.

Here is left a large void space in the original, to
insert the occurrences of the eight following days:
which space was never filled up.

Jan. 25. It was Sunday. I was alone, and
languishing with I know not what sadness.

I was much concerned at the envy and undeserved hatred borne to me by the Lord Keeper. I took into my hands the Greek Testament, that I might read the portion of the day. I lighted upon the thirteenth chapter to the Hebrews; wherein that of David, Psalm lvi. occurred to me, then grieving and fearing: *The Lord is my helper: I will not fear what man can do unto me.* I thought an example was set to me; and who is not safe under that Shield? Protect me, O Lord my God.

Jan. 31. A Commission, passed under the Broad Seal of England, constituted me, among others, a Judge Delegate in a suit of dilapidation, between the Rev. Father in God, Richard Neile, Lord Bishop of Durham, and Francis James, son and heir of his predecessor. I attended the execution of this Commission from two to five 'o'clock in the afternoon on Saturday, in the great chamber of Doctors' Commons.

Feb. 1. Sunday. I stood by the most illustrious Prince Charles at dinner. He was then very merry; and talked occasionally of many things with his attendants. Among other things, he said, that if he were necessitated to take any particular profession of life, he could not be a lawyer; adding his reasons. *I cannot* (saith he) *defend a bad, nor yield in a good cause.* May you ever hold this resolution, and succeed (most serene Prince) in matters of greater moment, for ever prosperous!

Feb. 4. Wednesday, my conference held with Fisher the Jesuit, May 24, 1622, and put in writing at the command of King James, having been before read to the King, was this day put into the press; being licensed by the Bishop of London. I had not hitherto appeared in print. I am no controvertist. May God so love and bless my soul, as I desire and endeavour, that all the never to be enough deplored distractions of the Church, may be composed happily, and to the glory of His Name!

This day I waited on the Duchess of Buckingham. That excellent lady, who is goodness itself, shewed me a form of devotions, which another woman, unknown to me, had put into her hands. I read it. All was mean in it: nothing extraordinary; unless that it was more like to poetry.

Feb. 6, Friday. My Lord Duke of Buckingham told me of the reconciliation the day before made with the Lord Keeper.—Feb. 10. Shrove Tuesday at the Commons; Sentence in my Lord of Durham's case.—Feb. 12. Thursday the Parliament was to begin; but was put off to Monday, the 16th of Feb.— Feb. 15, Sunday. I assisted at the consecration of Dr. Harmer, Bishop of St. Asaph.— Feb. 16, Monday. The Duke of Richmond, being seized suddenly with the palsy, died. This accident put off the Parliament to the 19th of February. — Feb. 18, Wednesday. My Lord Duke of Buckingham told me of the reconciliation and submission of my Lord Keeper; and that it was confessed unto him, that his favour to me was a chief cause. *Invidia quo tendis?* &c. *At ille de novo fœdus pepigit.*—Feb. 19, Thursday. The Parliament began.—Feb. 20, Friday. The Con-

vocation began.—Feb. 22. Will. Fulwell,
Master of Arts of Queen's Coll. in Cambridge,
made Deacon.—Feb. 24, Tuesday. The Duke
of Buckingham's relation of the negociation
with Spain about the Prince's Marriage, to
both Houses of Parliament.—Feb. 29, Sunday.
In the evening, the Duke of Buckingham's
coach overthrown between Exeter House and
the Savoy. The Spanish Ambassador lay
there. No omen, I hope, more than that they
thought to soil him. Secretary Conway was
in the coach with him. Mr. Bond came in
to the help, and told it me.—March 7, Midlent
Sunday. I preached at Whitehall.—March 14,
Passion Sunday. I preached at Westminster.—
March 17. The Lord Keeper his compli-
menting with me. Will. Fulwell made Priest.
—March 22, Monday. Dismal day. The
accident of my Lord of Rutland giving *not
content* to the form consented to in the Parliament house, being the only voice dissenting.—
March 23, Tuesday. The censure of Morley,
Waterhouse, and the Printer, about the petition against my Lord Keeper. That after-

noon the King declared to the Committee, that he would send a messenger presently into Spain, to signify to that King, that his Parliament advised him to break off the Treaties of the match and the Palatinate, and to give his reasons of it; and so proceed to recover the Palatinate as he might. Bonfires made in the city by the forwardness of the people, for joy that we should break with Spain. *O quoties tenuit me illud*, Psalm lxvii. 30. *Dissipa gentes quæ bella nolunt. Sed spero quia coacti.*—March 24, Wednesday. *Initium regis Jacobi.* The Earl of Oxford, practising a tilt, fell and brake his arm. That night, between the hours of six and seven, a great eclipse of the moon.—March 25, Thursday. The recess of the Parliament for a week.

1624. March 26, Good Friday. Viscount Mansfield, running at tilt to practise, with the shock of the meeting, his horse, weaker or resty, tumbled over and over, and brake his own neck in the place ; the Lord had no great harm. Should not this day have other employment?—March 27, Saturday, Easter Even. My speech with my Lord Duke of Buckingham about a course to ease the Church in times of payment of the subsidy now to be given. His promise to prepare both the King and the Prince.—March 28, Easter Day. Richard Earl of Dorset died, being well and merry in the Parliament House on Wednesday the 24th. *Quam nihil est vita hominis? Miserere nostri Deus!* His grandfather, Thomas Earl of Dorset, died suddenly at the Council Table. His grandmother rose well, and was dead before dinner. His father Robert lay not above two days. And now this man. Sir Edward Sackville.....

March 29, Easter Monday. I went and acquainted my Lord Keeper with what I said to my Lord Duke. He approved it, and said it was the best office that was done for the Church this seven years. And so said my Lord of Durham. They persuaded me to go and acquaint my Lord's Grace (of Canterbury) with what I had done. I went. His Grace was very angry. Asked, what

I had to do to make any suit for the Church.
Told me, never any Bishop attempted the
like at any time, nor would any but myself
have done it.   That I had given the Church
such a wound, in speaking to any Lord of
the Laity about it, as I could never make
whole again.   That, if my Lord Duke did
fully understand what I had done, he would
never induce me to come near him again.
I answered, I thought I had done a very
good office for the Church; and so did my
betters think. If his Grace thought otherwise,
I was sorry I had offended him. And I
hoped, being done out of a good mind, for
the support of many poor Vicars abroad in
the country, who must needs sink under three
subsidies a year, my error (if it were one)
was pardonable. So we parted. I went to
my Lord Duke, and acquainted him with it;
lest I might have ill offices done me for it, to
the King and the Prince. So may God bless
me His servant, labouring under the pressure
of them, who alway wished ill to me.

April 16, Friday. My Conference with

Fisher the Jesuit printed, came forth.—April 18, Sunday. I preached at Paul's Cross.—April 27, Tuesday. My very good friend Dr. Linsell, cut for the stone, about nine o'clock in the forenoon.—May 1, Saturday. E. B. married. The sign in *Pisces*.—May 5, Wednesday. Ascension Eve. The King's speech in the Banquetting House at Whitehall, to the Upper House of Parliament, concerning the hearing of the Lord Treasurer's cause, which was to begin the Friday following. This day my Lord Duke of Buckingham came to town with his Majesty sick, and continued ill till Saturday, May 22.—May 13, Thursday. Lionel, Earl of Middlesex, Lord Treasurer of England, and Master of the Wards, censured in Parliament for bribery and extortion, and deceiving the King, &c. To lose his offices, to be ever disenabled to bear any, fined to the King in £50,000, imprisoned in the Tower during the King's pleasure, never to sit again as a peer in Parliament, not to come within the verge of the Court.—May 15, Saturday, Whitsun Eve.

The Bill passed in Parliament for the King to have York House in exchange for other lands. This was for the Lord Duke of Buckingham.—May 16, Whitsunday night. I watched with my Lord Duke of Buckingham. This was the first fit that he could be persuaded to take orderly.—May 18, Tuesday night. I watched with my Lord Duke of Buckingham. He took this fit very orderly.—May 19, Wednesday. The Bishop of Norwich, Samuel Harsnet, was presented by the House of Commons to the Lords. His cause was referred by the House to my Lord's Grace of Canterbury and the High Commission.—May 22, Saturday. My Lord Duke of Buckingham missed his fit.—May 26, Wednesday. He went with his Majesty to Greenwich.

May 28, Friday. E. B. came to London. He had not leisure to speak with me (though I sent and offered to wait all opportunities) till June 16, being Wednesday.—May 29, Saturday. The first Session of Parliament ended: and the prorogation was to the second of November.—June 6, Second Sunday after Trinity.

I preached at Westminster.—June 8, Tuesday. I went to New Hall to my Lord Duke of Buckingham, and came back to London on Friday, June 11.—June 16, Wednesday. I took my lasting leave of E. B. The great dry summer. My dream June 4, Wednesday night, 1623. In this dream was all contained, that followed in the carriage of E. B. towards me; and that night R. B. sickened to the death.—May 29, Saturday night, 1624. I was marvellously troubled with E. B. before they came to London. That there was much declining to speak with me; but yet at last, I had conference, and took my lasting leave. And this so fell out. See May 28.

July 7, Wednesday night. My Lord of Durham's quarrel about the trifling business of Fr. N.—July 23, Friday. I went to lie and keep house, and preach at my Livings, held in Commendam, Creeke and Ibstock. That Friday night, at St. Alban's, I gave R. R. my servant, his first interest in my businesses of moment.—July 27. This I confirmed unto him, the Wednesday morning following, at

Stanford.—Aug. 7, Saturday. While I was at Long Whatton with my brother, my passion by blood, and my fear of a stone in my bladder.—Aug 8, Sunday. I went and preached at my parsonage at Ibstock, and set things in order there.—Aug. 26, Thursday. My horse trod on my foot, and lamed me: which stayed me in the country a week longer than I had intended.—Sept. 7, Tuesday. I came to London.—Sept. 9, Thursday. My Lord of Buckingham consulted with me about a man, that offered him a strange way of cure for himself and his brother. At that time I delivered his Grace the copies of the two little books which he desired me to write out.

Sept. 16, Thursday. Prince Charles his grievous fall, which he had in hunting.— Sept. 25, Saturday. My Lord Duke's proposal about an army, and the means, and whether Sutton's Hospital might not, &c.— Oct. 2, Saturday. In the evening at Mr. Windebank's, my ancient servant Adam Torless fell into a swoon; and we had much ado to

recover him; but I thank God we did.—
Oct. 10, Sunday. I fell at night in pas-
sionem iliacam; which had almost put me
into a fever. I continued ill fourteen days.—
Oct. 13, Wednesday. I delivered up my
answer about Sutton's Hospital.—Nov. 21,
Sunday. I preached at Westminster.—Dec. 6,
Monday. There was a referment made from
his Majesty to my Lord's Grace of Canterbury, my Lords of Durham and Rochester,
and myself, to hear and order a matter of
difference in the Church of Hereford, concerning a Residentiaryship, and the Lecturer's
place; which we that day ordered.

Dec. 13, Monday. I received letters from
Brecknock, that the saltpetre man was dead,
and buried the Sunday before the messenger
came. This saltpetre man had digged in
the College-Church for his work, bearing
too bold upon his commission. The news of
it came to me to London, about Nov. 26. I
went to my Lord Keeper, and had a messenger sent to bring him up to answer that
sacrilegious abuse. He prevented his punish-

ment by death.—Dec. 21, Tuesday. *Fest.
Sancti Thomæ.* Mr. Crumpton had set out
a book, called *St. Augustin's Summe.* His
Majesty found fault with divers passages in it.
He was put to recal some things in writing.
He had dedicated this book to my Lord Duke
of Buckingham. My Lord had sent him to me
to overlook the articles, in which he had recalled and explained himself, that I might see
whether it were well done, and fit to shew the
King. This day Mr. Crumpton brought his
papers to me.—Dec. 23, Thursday. I delivered
these papers back to Mr. Crumpton. The same
day at York House, I gave my Lord Duke
of Buckingham my answer, what I thought
of these papers. The same day I delivered
my Lord a little tract about *Doctrinal Puritanism,* in some ten heads; which his Grace had
spoken to me that I would draw for him, that
he might be acquainted with them.—Dec 31
Friday. His Majesty sent for me, and delivered unto me Mr. Crumpton's papers, the
second time, (after I had read them over to
himself,) and commanded me to correct them

as they might pass in the doctrine of the Church of England.—Jan. 3, Monday. I had made ready these papers, and waited upon my Lord Duke of Buckingham with them; and he brought me to the King. There I was about an hour and a half, reading them, and talking about them, with his Majesty and my Lord Duke. After this, I went to visit my sister, who lay then sick at London.

Jan. 5, Wednesday. My Lord Duke of Buckingham shewed me two letters of, &c. the falsehood of, &c. That day, as I waited to speak with my Lord, Secretary Calvert fell in speech with me about some differences between the Greek and the Roman Church. Then also and there, a young man, that took on him to be a Frenchman, fell into discourse about the Church of England. He grew at last earnest for the Roman Church; but *Tibi dabo claves*, and *Pasce oves*, was all he said; save that he would shew this proposition in St. Augustin, *Romana Ecclesia facta est caput omnium Ecclesiarum ab instante mortis Christi.* I believe he was a Priest; but he wore a

lock down to his shoulders. I heard afte
that he was a French gentleman.

Jan. 15, Saturday. The speech which
had with my Lord Duke at Wallingfor
House.—Jan. 21, Friday. The business o
my Lord Purbeck, made known unto me b
my Lord Duke.—Jan. 23, Sunday night
The discourse which my Lord Duke ha
with me about witches and astrologers.—
Jan. 25, Tuesday night. I acquainted m
Lord Duke with my hard hap in my busines
with L. C. D. for which I had been so ofte
blamed.—Jan. 28, Friday. I took my leav
of my Lord Duke. His wish that he ha
known K. L. sooner, but, &c.

Jan. 30, Sunday night. My dream of m
Blessed Lord and Saviour Jesus Christ. On
of the most comfortable passages that eve
I had in my life.

Feb. 12, Saturday. I ordained Mr. Thoma
Atkinson, of St. John's, Deacon.—Feb. 13
Sunday. I preached at Westminster.—
March 5, Saturday. The High Commissio
sat first about Sir R. H. &c.—March 6,

Sunday, the first in Lent. I preached at the Temple, at the Reader's solemnity. The Duke of Buckingham and divers other Lords there.—March 13, Sunday, second in Lent. I ordained Robert Rockell, Priest, Eleazar Dunkon and Edward Quarles, Deacons. They were Masters of Arts of Pembroke Hall in Cambridge.

1625. March 27, Midlent Sunday. I preached at Whitehall. I ascended the pulpit much troubled, and in a very melancholy moment, the report then spreading, that his Majesty King James, of most sacred memory to me, was dead. Being interrupted with the dolours of the Duke of Buckingham, I broke off my sermon in the middle. The King died at Theobald's, about three quarters of an hour past eleven in the forenoon. He breathed forth his blessed soul most religiously, and with great constancy of faith, and courage. That day, about five o'clock, Prince Charles was solemnly proclaimed King. God grant to him a prosperous and happy reign! The King fell sick, March 4, on Friday. The disease appeared to be a tertian ague. But I fear it was the gout, which, by the wrong application of medicines, was driven from his feet to his inward vital parts.

April 1, Friday. I received letters from the Earl of Pembroke, Lord Chamberlain to the King, and therein a command from his Majesty King Charles, to preach a sermon before himself and the House of Peers in the Session of Parliament, to be held on the 17th day of May next following.—April 3, Sunday. I delivered into the Duke of Buckingham's hands my short annotations upon the life and death of the most august King James; which he had commanded me to put in writing.— April 5, Tuesday. I exhibited a schedule, in which were wrote the names of many Churchmen, marked with the letters O and P. The Duke of Buckingham had commanded to digest their names in that method; that (as himself said) he might deliver them to King Charles.—April 9, Saturday. The Duke of Buckingham, whom upon all accounts I am bound for ever to honour, signified to me, that a certain person, moved through I know not what envy, had blackened my name with his Majesty King Charles; laying hold for that purpose of the error, into which, by I know not what fate, I had formerly fallen in the business of Charles Earl of Devonshire, 1605, Dec. 26. The same day I received in command, to go to the Right Reverend the Bishop of Winchester, and learn from him, what he would have done in the cause of the Church; and bring back his answer, especially in the matter of the *Five Articles*, &c.

April 10, Sunday. After sermon was done, I went to the Bishop, who was then in his chamber at Court. I acquainted him with what I had received in command. He gave to me his answer. From thence we went together to hear prayers in Somerset House. Having heard prayers, we afterwards saw there the body of the late King James; which rested there till the day of his funeral rites.—April 13, Wednesday. I brought back to the Duke of Buckingham the answer of the Bishop of Winchester. At the same time, the Duke made known to me, what the King had determined concerning his Clerk of the Closet, the Right Reverend the Bishop of Durham, and about his successor in that office.—April 17, Easter Day. The Bishop of Durham being sick, I was appointed (but at the desire of the said Bishop) by the Right Honourable the Earl of Pembroke, Lord Chamberlain of the Household, to wait upon his Majesty in the quality of Clerk of the Closet; which place I executed till the first of May.—April 23. Burton presented his paper to the King.

May 1. The marriage was celebrated at Paris, between his Majesty King Charles, and the most illustrious Princess Henrietta Maria of France, daughter of Henry IV.—May 7, Saturday. We celebrated the funeral of King James.—May 11. Early in the morning, the Duke of Buckingham went towards the sea-side, to pass over into France to meet the Queen Mary. I wrote letters to the Duke that day, which might follow after him; for

tinued, until they had entered Whitehall; and then ceased.

June 18, Saturday. The first Parliament of King Charles, which had been so often put off, now began. There were present at the opening of it, the Duke of Shiverus, with other French noblemen; a Bishop also, who attended the Queen. For fear of the pestilence, which then began to be very rife, the King omitted the pomp usual upon that day, lest the great conflux of people should be of ill consequence. And the Sermon, which had been imposed upon me to be preached in Westminster Abbey at the beginning of this Session, was put off to the next day, that is, to June 19, First Sunday after Trinity. On which day I preached it in the Chapel at Whitehall.—June 20. The Convocation began.—June 24, was the Feast of St. John Baptist. The King commanded the Archbishop of Canterbury, with six other Bishops, whom he then named, to advise together concerning a public Fast, and a Form of Prayer, to implore the Divine mercy, now that the pestilence began to spread, and the extraordinary wet weather threatened a famine; and also to beg the Divine blessing upon the fleet, now ready to put to sea. The Bishops were, London, Durham, Winchester, Norwich, Rochester, St. David's. This was done.—June 25, Saturday. All the Bishops, who were then in town, were introduced together, that they might wait upon Queen Mary, and kiss her hand. She received us very graciously.—July 2, Saturday. The Fast was kept by both Houses of Parliament, to set an example therein to the whole kingdom.

July 3, Sunday. In my sleep, his Majesty King James appeared to me. I saw him only passing by swiftly. He was of a pleasant and serene countenance. In passing he saw me, beckoned to me, smiled, and was immediately withdrawn from my sight.

July 7, Thursday. Richard Montague was brought into the lower House of Parliament, &c.—July 9, Saturday. It pleased his Majesty King Charles to intimate to the House of Commons, that what had been there said and resolved, without consulting him, in Montague's cause, was not pleasing to him.—July 11, Monday. The Parliament was prorogued to Oxford against the first day of August.—July 13, Wednesday. There having died in the former week at London 1222 persons, I went into the country to the house of my good friend Francis Windebank. In going thither, Richard Montague met me by chance. I was the first who certified him of the King's favour to him.—July 15, Friday. I went to Windsor; and performed some businesses committed to my trust by the Right Reverend Bishop of Durham. I returned that night. The Court was there at that time.—July 17, Sunday. I went again to Windsor. I stood by the King at dinner time. Some matters of philosophy were the subject of discourse. I dined. Afterwards I sat in the house of the Bishop of Gloucester. Baron Vaughan was there present with his eldest son. The next day, one of the Bishop's servants, who had waited at table, was seized with the plague. God be merciful to me and

the rest! That night I returned, being become
lame on the sudden, through I know not
what humour falling down upon my left leg,
or (as R. An. thought) by the biting of bugs.
I grew well within two days.

July 20, Wednesday. A public Fast was
held throughout all England. I preached in
the parish of Hurst, where I then abode with
Master Windebank.—July 21, Thursday. I
visited Sir Richard Harrison, and returned.—
July 24, Sunday. I preached in the parish
of Hurst.—July 29, Friday. I entered into
Oxford.—July 31, Sunday. I fell down, I
know not how, in the parlour of the President's lodging at St. John's College, and hurt
my left shoulder and hip.—Aug. 1, Monday.
The Parliament began at Oxford. Presently
after the beginning of it, a great assault was
made against the Duke of Buckingham.—
Aug. 12, Friday. The Parliament was dissolved; the Commons not hearkening, as was
expected, to the King's proposals.—Aug. 15.
My relapse. I never was weaker, in the
judgment of the physician. It was Mond

The same day I began my journey towards Wales.—Aug. 21, Sunday. I preached at Brecknock: where I stayed two days, very busy in performing some business. That night, in my sleep, it seemed to me, that the Duke of Buckingham came into bed to me; where he behaved himself with great kindness towards me, after that rest, wherewith wearied persons are wont to solace themselves. Many also seemed to me to enter the chamber, who saw this. Not long before, I dreamed that I saw the Duchess of Buckingham, that excellent lady, at first very much perplexed about her husband, but afterwards cheerful and rejoicing, that she was freed from the fear of abortion, so that in due time she might be again a mother.

August 24, Wednesday. The Festival of St. Bartholomew. I came safely (thanks be to God) to my own house at Aberguille, although my coach had been twice that day overturned between Aber-markes and my house. The first time I was in it; but the latter time it was empty.—August 20, Sunday.

I consecrated the chapel, or oratory, which I had built at my own charge in my house, commonly called Aberguilly House. I named it the chapel of St. John Baptist, in grateful remembrance of St. John Baptist's College in Oxford, of which I had been first Fellow, and afterwards President. And this I had determined to do. But another thing intervened, (of no ill omen as I hope,) of which I had never thought. It was this. On Saturday, the evening immediately preceding the consecration, while I was intent at prayer, I know not how, it came strongly into my mind, that the day of the Beheading of St. John Baptist was very near. When prayers were finished, I consulted the Calendar. I found that day to fall upon Monday, to wit, the 29th of August, not upon Sunday. I could have wished it had fallen upon that same day, when I consecrated the chapel. However, I was pleased that I should perform that solemn consecration at least on the eve of that Festival. For upon that day, his Majesty King James heard my cause about

the election to the Presidentship of St. John's
College in Oxford, for three hours together
at least; and with great justice delivered me
out of the hands of my powerful enemies.

Sept. 4, Sunday. The night following I
was very much troubled in my dreams. My
imagination ran altogether upon the Duke of
Buckingham, his servants, and family. All
seemed to be out of order: that the Duchess
was ill, called for her maids, and took her bed.
God grant better things!—Sept. 11, Sunday.
I preached at Carmarthen, the Judges being
then present. The same night I dreamed,
that Dr. Theodore Prince admonished me
concerning Ma. S. and that he was unfaithful
to me, and discovered all he knew: and that
I should therefore take heed of him, and
trust him no more, &c. Afterwards I dreamed
of Sackville Crow, that he was dead of the
plague, having not long before been with the
King.—Sept. 24. One only person desired
to receive Holy Orders from me; and he
found to be unfit, upon examination.—Sept.
25. I sent him away with an exhortation, not

ordained. It was then Saturday.—Sept. 26, Sunday. That night I dreamed of the marriage of I know not whom at Oxford. All that were present were clothed with flourishing green garments. I knew none of them but Thomas Flaxnye. Immediately after, without any intermission of sleep, (that I know of,) I thought I saw the Bishop of Worcester, his head and shoulders covered with linen. He advised and invited me kindly to dwell with them, marking out a place, where the Court of the Marches of Wales was then held. But not staying for my answer, he subjoined, that he knew I could not live so meanly, &c.

Oct. 8, Saturday. The Earl of Northampton, President of Wales, returned out of Wales, taking his journey by sea.—Oct. 9, Sunday. I preached at Carmarthen.—Oct. 10, Monday. I went on horseback up to the mountains. It was a very bright day for the time of year, and so warm, that, in our return, I and my company dined in the open air, in a place called Pente-Cragg, where my Registrary had his country house.—Oct. 30, Sunday. Sir Thomas Coventry made Lord Keeper.—Nov. 11, Friday. I began my journey to return into England.—Nov. 17, Thursday. Charles, the Duke of Buckingham's son, was born.—Nov. 20, Sunday. I preached at Honye-Lacye in Herefordshire.—Nov. 24, Thursday. I came to the house of my great friend Fr. Windebank, at Hains-Hill. There the wife of my friend, (for himself was then at Court,) immediately as soon as I came told me, that the Duke of Buckingham (then negociating for the public in the Low Countries) had a son born; whom God bless with all the good things of heaven and earth.—Dec. 4, Sunday. I preached at Hurst. I stayed there in the country until Christmas.—Dec. 14, Wednesday. I went to Windsor; but returned the same day.—Dec. 25, Sunday. I preached at Hurst upon Christmas Day.—Dec. 31, Saturday. I went to the Court, which was then at Hampton Court. There, Jan. 1, Sunday, I understood that I was named among other Bishops, who were to consult together on Wednesday following at Whitehall, concerning the Ceremonies of the Coronation. I was also at the same time informed, that the bigger part of the Bishop of Durham's house was appointed for the residence of the Ambassador Extraordinary of the King of France.—Jan. 2, Monday. I returned to Hains-Hill. For there, not then knowing any thing of these matters, I had left my necessary papers with my trunk. When I had put these in order, I went to Sir Richard Harrison's house, to take leave of my friends. There (if I mistake not) I first knew what F. H. thought of me. I told my mind plainly, &c. I returned.

Jan. 3, Tuesday. I came to London, and fixed myself at my own house at Westminster. For the week before Christmas I had sent my servant, who had brought all my things out of the house of my good friend the Bishop of Durham (with whom I had abode as a guest for four years complete) to my own house, save only my books; the removal of which I unadvisedly put off till my own coming. For

the coming of the French Ambassador forced
me to make over-much haste; and the multitude of business then laying upon me, made
it requisite that I should have my books
at hand. In the evening, I visited the Duke
of Buckingham.—Jan. 4, Wednesday. We
met at Whitehall to consult of the Ceremonies
of the Coronation. I sent my servant to
bring my books, who brought them. That
night I placed them in order in my study.
And it was high time. For while we were
in consultation about the Ceremonies, the
Right Honourable the Earl of Pembroke,
Lord Chamberlain of the Household to his
Majesty, came from the King to us, and
delivered to me the King's order, to be ready
against the sixth day of February, to preach
that day at the opening of Parliament.—Jan. 6,
Friday, Epiphany Day. We met again to
consult concerning the Ceremonies; and gave
up our answer to the King.—Jan. 16. The
Archbishop of Canterbury made known to me
the King's pleasure, that at the Coronation I
should supply the place of the Dean of West-

minster. For that his Majesty would not
have the Bishop of Lincoln, then Dean, to be
present at the Ceremony. It was then Monday. The same day, by the King's command, a consultation was held, what was to
be done in the cause of Richard Montague.
There were present, the Bishops of London,
Durham, Winchester, Rochester, and St.
David's.

Jan. 17, Tuesday. We gave in our answer
in writing, subscribed this day. This day
also, the Bishop of Lincoln deputed me, under
his hand and seal, to supply the place for him,
which he, as Dean of Westminster, was to
execute in the Coronation of King Charles.—
Jan. 18, Wednesday. The Duke of Buckingham brought me to the King, to whom I
shewed my notes, that if he disliked any thing
therein, &c. The same day by the King's
command, the Archbishop of Canterbury,
and the Bishops of London, Durham, Winchester, Rochester, and St. David's, consulted
together concerning a Form of Prayer, to give
thanks for the decrease of the plague.—

Jan. 23. I had a perfect book of the Ceremonies of the Coronation made ready, agree-
ing in all things with the King's Book. It
was Monday.

Jan. 29, Sunday. I understood what D. B.
had collected concerning the cause, book, and
opinions of Richard Montague, and what R. C.
had determined with himself therein. Methinks I see a cloud arising, and threatening
the Church of England. God of His mercy
dissipate it.

[As the Archbishop regarded Mr. Montague's case
of such great importance, it may be well here to
insert a letter which has reference to this matter.
Mr. Montague, Bishop of Norwich, was an Etonian,
and afterwards Fellow of King's. He first came
into notice by a successful attack upon Selden's
History of Tithes : which gained him the favour of
King James. In 1624, he was very much annoyed
in his parish of Stamford Rivers in Essex, by some
Jesuits making converts there. In the course of
controversy with them, he managed to exasperate
the ultra-Protestant party, who accused him of
Arminianism before the House of Commons. His
chief offence, according to Heylin, was his having

presumed to speak disrespectfully of the Synod of
Dort. However, the House of Commons, thinking
itself as competent to take spiritual as well as
temporal matters under its protection, had him
arrested, reprimanded by the Speaker, and com
mitted to the custody of the Serjeant-at-Arms, till
he could find security for his appearance in £2000.
His famous book, "Appello Cæsarem," was the
more obnoxious to them, because of the favour it
had found in the eyes of King Charles. Mon
tague, however, was subsequently raised to the see
of Chichester, and afterwards translated to Nor
wich. Among his other works, he wrote a Com
mentary on the Epistles of Photius, and had some
share in bringing out Sir Henry Savile's edition of
St. Chrysostom in 1613; he being at that time a
Fellow of Eton. Laud, with the Bishops of Ro
chester (John Buckeridge, who preceded him as
President of St. John's) and Oxford, (John How
son, Canon of Christ Church,) foreseeing the evil
which might fall upon the Church from this conduc
of the House of Commons, wrote a joint letter to
the Duke of Buckingham; of which a copy is given
in Heylin's Cyprianus Anglicus.]

May it please your Grace,

We are bold to be suitors to you in behalf
of the Church of England, and a poor member

of it, Mr. Mountague, at this time not a little distressed. We are not strangers to his person, but it is the cause which we are bound to be tender of. The cause we conceive (under correction of better judgment) concerns the Church of England nearly; for that Church, when it was reformed from the superstitious opinions broached or maintained by the Church of Rome, refused the apparent and dangerous errors, and would not be too busy with every particular school-point. The cause why she held this moderation was, because she could not be able to preserve any unity amongst Christians, if men were forced to subscribe to curious particulars disputed in schools. Now may it please your Grace, the opinions which at this time trouble many men in the late book of Mr. Mountague, are some of them such as are expressly the resolved doctrine of the Church of England, and those he is bound to maintain. Some of them are such as are fit only for schools, and to be left at more liberty for learned men " to abound in their own sense," so they keep themselves peaceable, and distract not the Church.   And therefore to make any man subscribe to school opinions, may justly seem hard in the Church of Christ, and was one great fault of the Council of Trent.   And to affright them from those opinions in which they have (as they are bound) subscribed to the Church, as it is worse in itself, so may it be the mother of greater danger.

May it please your Grace farther to consider, that when the Clergy submitted themselves in the time of Henry the Eighth, the submission was so made, that if any difference doctrinal or other fell in the Church, the King and the Bishops were to be judges of it in the national Synod or Convocation; the King first giving leave under his Broad Seal to handle the points in difference.   But the Church never submitted to any other judge, neither indeed can she though she would. And we humbly desire your Grace to consider, and then to move his most gracious Majesty, (if you shall think fit,) what dangerous consequences may follow upon it. For first, if any other judge be allowed in matter of doctrine, we shall depart from the ordinance of Christ, and the continual cause and practice of the Church. Secondly, If the Church be once brought down beneath herself, we cannot but fear what may be the next stroke at it. Thirdly, It will someway touch the honour of his Majesty's dear father, and our most dread Sovereign of glorious and ever-blessed memory, King James, who saw and approved all the opinions of this book. And he in his rare wisdom and judgment would never have allowed them, if they had crossed with truth and the Church of England. Fourthly, we must be bold to say, that we cannot conceive what use there can be of civil government in the Commonwealth, or of preaching, or external ministry in the Church, if such fatal opinions, as some which are opposite and contrary to these delivered by Mr. Mountague are, shall be publicly taught and maintained. Fifthly, we are certain that all or most of the contrary opinions were treated of at Lambeth, and ready to be published, but then Queen Elizabeth of famous memory, upon notice given, how little they agreed with the practice of piety, and obedience to all government, caused them to be suppressed. And so they have continued ever since, till of late some of them have received countenance at the Synod of Dort. Now this was a Synod of that nation, and can be of no authority in any other national Church, till it be received there by public authority. And our hope is, that the Church of England will be well advised, and more than once over, before she admit a foreign Synod, especially of such a Church as condemneth her discipline and manner of government, to say no more.

And further, we are bold to commend to your Grace's wisdom this one particular. His Majesty (as we have been informed) hath already taken this business into his own care, and most worthily referred it in a right course to Church consideration. And we well hoped, that without further trouble to the State, or breach of unity in the Church, it might so have been well and orderly composed, as we still pray it may.   These things considered, we have little to say for Mr Mountague's person: only thus much we know. He is a very good scholar, and a right honest man : a man every way able to do God, his Majesty, and the Church of England, great service. We fear he may receive discouragement, and (which is far worse) we have some cause to doubt this may breed a great backwardness in able men to write in the defence of the Church of England, against either home or foreign adversaries, if they shall see him sink in fortunes, reputation, or health, upon occasion of his book.   And this we most humbly submit to your Grace's judgment, and care of the Church's peace and welfare.   So commending your Grace to the protection of Almighty God,

   We shall ever rest at your Grace's service,
        Jo. Roffens. Jo. Oxon. Guil. Meneven.
Aug. 2, 1625.[d]

   [d] The day after Parliament met at Oxford. *Ed.*

Jan. 31, Tuesday.   The Bishops and other Peers, before nominated by the King to consult of the Ceremonies of the Coronation, that the ancient manner might be observed, by his Majesty's command, went together to him. The King viewed all the Regalia; put on St. Edward's tunics; commanded me to read the Rubrics of direction.   All being read, we carried back the Regalia to Westminster Church, and laid them up in their place.

Feb. 2, Thursday and Candlemas Day. His Majesty King Charles was crowned.   I then officiated in the place of the Dean of Westminster.   The King entered the Abbey Church a little before ten o'clock; and it was past three before he went out of it.   It was a very bright sunshining day.   The solemnity being ended, in the great Hall at Westminster, when the King delivered into my hands the Regalia, which are kept in the Abbey Church of Westminster, he did (which had not before been done) deliver to me the Sword called Curtana, and two others, which had been carried before the King that day, to be kept in the Church, together with the other Regalia. I returned, and offered them solemnly at the Altar in the name of the King, and laid them up with the rest. In so great a ceremony, and amidst an incredible concourse of people, nothing was lost, or broke, or disordered. The theatre was clear, and free for the King, the Peers, and the business in hand; and I heard some of the nobility saying to the King in their return, that they never had seen any solemnity, although much less, performed with so little noise, and so great order.

[We learn from Heylin, that the King himself had appointed the Feast of the Purification of the Blessed Virgin, vulgarly called Candlemas Day. The reason why so much consultation took place about the Ceremonies, was this; Edward VI. and Elizabeth had been crowned according to the Rites of the Roman Pontifical; and the arrangements at King James's Coronation had been very hasty and incomplete. Among other alterations were these; that the unction should be made in the form of a Cross: that the following address should be made to the King after the unction: " Stand, and hold fast from henceforth the place to which you have been heir by the succession of your forefathers, being now delivered to you by the authority of Almighty God, and by the hands of us and all the Bishops, and servants of God: and as you see the Clergy to come nearer to the Altar than others, so remember that in place convenient you give them greater honour; that the Mediator of God and man may establish you in the kingly throne, to be the mediator between the Clergy and the Laity, that you may reign for ever with Jesus Christ, the King of kings, and Lord of lords, Who, with the Father and the Holy Ghost, liveth and reigneth for ever. Amen:" and, lastly, a prayer was revived which had been disused since Henry the Sixth's time, as being conceived by the Church of Rome to give too much ecclesiastical jurisdiction to the King: " Let him obtain favour for the people, like Aaron in the tabernacle, Elisha in the waters, Zacharias in the temple: give him Peter's key of discipline, and Paul's doctrine."]

Feb. 6, Monday. I preached before King Charles and the House of Peers, at the opening of the Parliament. [He preached on the 3d, 4th, and 5th verses of Psalm cxxii: and his Sermon contains this solemn and prophetic warning. He reminds them of the words of Tacitus; "That nothing gave the Romans (powerful enemies as they were) more advantage against the ancient Britons, than this; *quod factionibus et studiis trahebantur;* that they were broken into factions, and would not so much as take counsel and advice together; and they smarted for it. But, I pray, what is the difference for men not to meet in council, and to fall to pieces when they meet? If the first were our forefathers' error, God of His mercy grant this second be not ours. And for the Church, that is, as the city too, just so; doctrine and discipline are the walls and towers of it. But be the one never so true, and the other never so perfect, they come both short of preservation, if that body be not at unity in itself. The Church, take it Catholic, cannot stand well, if it be not compacted together into an holy unity with faith and charity. And as the whole Church is in regard of the affairs of Christendom, so is each particular Church in the nation and kingdom in which it sojourns.

If it be not at unity in itself, it doth but invite malice, which is ready to do hurt without any invitation: and it ever lies with an open side to the Devil and all his batteries. So both Church and State, then happy, and never till then, when they are at unity within themselves, and one with another. Well, both State and Church owe much to unity; and therefore very little to them that break the peace of either. " Father, forgive them, for they know not what they do." But, if unity be so necessary, how may it be preserved in both? How? I will tell you. Would you keep the State in unity? In any case, take heed of breaking the peace of the Church. The peace of the State depends much upon it. For divide Christ in the minds of men, or divide the minds of men about their hopes of salvation in Christ, and tell me what unity there will be.]

Feb. 11, Saturday. At the desire of the Earl of Warwick, a conference was held concerning the cause of Richard Montague, in the Duke of Buckingham's house, [between

Dr. Morton and Dr. Preston on the one side, and Dr. White on the other.]—Feb. 17, Friday. The foresaid conference was renewed in the same place, many of the nobility being present.—Feb. 21, Shrove Tuesday. The Duke of Buckingham sent for me to come to him; and then gave me in command that, &c.—Feb. 23, Thursday. I sought the Duke at Chelsea. There I first saw his son and heir, Charles, lately born. I found not the Duke. Returning, I found his servant, who was seeking me. I went immediately with him, and found the Duke at Court. I related to him what I had done.—Feb. 24, Friday, and St. Matthias's Day. I was with the Duke in his house almost three' hours; where, with his own hand, &c. he commanded me to add somewhat. I did so, and brought it to him next day, Feb. 25.—Feb. 26, First Sunday in Lent. In the evening I presented to his Majesty King Charles my Sermon, which I had preached at the opening of the Parliament, being now printed by his Majesty's command.—Feb. 27, Monday. The danger which happened to King Charles from his horse; which, having broken the two girths of the saddle, and the saddle together with the rider fallen under his belly, stood trembling, until the King, having received no hurt, &c.

March 1, Wednesday, and the Festival of St. David. A clamour arose in the House of Commons against the Duke of Buckingham, more particularly for stopping a ship, called the St. Peter of Newhaven, after sentence pronounced. From that day there were perpetual heats in the House.—March 6. I resigned the Parsonage of Ibstock, which I held in Commendam.—March 11. Dr. Turner, a physician, offered in the House seven queries against the Duke of Buckingham; yet grounded upon no other foundation, than what he received from public fame: as himself confessed. It was then Saturday.—March 16, Thursday. A certain Dutchman, named John Oventrout, proposed to shew a way how the West Indies might shake off the yoke of Spain, and put themselves under the subjection of our King Charles. The matter was referred to be disclosed to the Earl of Totness, the Lord Conway, Principal Secretary, and, because he said that his stratagem did depend in a great measure upon religion, I was added to them. The old man proposed somewhat about the taking of Arica: yet shewed not to us any method, how it might be taken; unless it were, that he would have the minds of the inhabitants to be divided in the cause of religion, by sending in among them the Catechism of Heidelberg. We dismissed the man, and returned not a whit the wiser.

1626. March 26, Sunday. D. B. (D. of Buck.?) sent me to the King. There I gave to the King an account of those two businesses, which, &c. His Majesty thanked me.—March 29. King Charles spoke to both Houses of Parliament, (but directed his speech chiefly to the lower House,) both by himself, and by the Right Honourable the Lord Keeper of the Great Seal, in the palace at Whitehall. He also added much concerning the Duke of Buckingham, &c. In the

Convocation held that day, there was much
debating concerning the Sermon which
Gabriel Goodman[a], Bishop of Gloucester,
had preached before the King on the
Sunday preceding, being the fifth Sunday
of Lent.

April 5, Wednesday. The King sent in
the morning, commanding the Bishops of
Norwich [Sam. Harsnet], Litchfield [Thos.
Morton], and St. David's to attend him. I
and the Bishop of Litchfield waited upon
him; the Bishop of Norwich being gone into
the country. We received the King's commands about, &c. and returned.—April 12,
Wednesday. At nine in the forenoon, we
met together, *viz.* the Archbishop of Canter-

[a] The Archbishop seems to have mistaken Bishop
Goodman's Christian name, which was Godfrey, not
Gabriel; as may be seen from his signature to the
Bishops' Protestation in Lord Clarendon, sub an. 1641.
See also Godwin's Præsul. The Sermon in question
was to assert the high view of the Sacraments; and
was supposed to favour the Corporal Presence of
Christ's Body in the Sacrament of the Altar.

bury [G. Abbot], Winchester [Lanc. Andrewes], Durham [Rich. Neile], and St. David's; being commanded by the King to consult together concerning the Sermon which Dr. Goodman, the Bishop of Gloucester, had preached before his Majesty on the fifth Sunday in Lent last past. We advised together, and gave this answer to the King; That some things were therein spoken less cautiously, but nothing falsely; that nothing was innovated by him in the doctrine of the Church of England: that the best way would be, that the Bishop should preach the Sermon again, at some time to be chosen by himself, and should then shew how and wherein he was misunderstood by his auditor. That night, after nine o'clock, I gave to the King an account of what I had received in command on the fifth of April, and of other things relating thereto. Among the rest, concerning restoring Impropriations. The King spoke many things very graciously therein; after I had first discoursed of the manner of effecting it.

April 14, Friday. The Duke of Buckingham fell into a fever.—April 19, Wednesday. The petition of John Digby, Earl of Bristol, against the Duke of Buckingham, was read in the House of Lords. It was very sharp, and such as threatens ruin to one of the parties.—April 24, Friday. King Charles referred the cognizance of that whole matter, as also of the petition of the Earl Digby, to the House of Parliament.—April 21, Saturday. The Duke of Buckingham sent to me to come to him. There I first heard what Sir John Cooke the King's Secretary had suggested against me to the Lord Treasurer, and he to the Duke. Lord, be merciful to me Thy servant!—April 22, Sunday. The King sent for all the Bishops to come to him at four o'clock in the afternoon. We waited upon him, fourteen in number. Then his Majesty chid us, that in this time of Parliament we were silent in the cause of the Church, and did not make known to him what might be useful, or was prejudicial to the Church; professing himself ready to promote the cause of the Church.

He then commanded us, that in the causes of the Earl of Bristol and Duke of Buckingham, we should follow the direction of our own consciences, being led by proofs, not by reports.—April 30, Sunday. I preached before the King at Whitehall.

May 1, Monday. The Earl of Bristol was accused in Parliament of high treason, by the King's Attorney, Sir Robert Heath; the Earl then and there preferred twelve articles against the Duke of Buckingham, and therein charged him with the same crime; and other articles also against the Lord Conway, Secretary of State. The Earl of Bristol was committed to the custody of James Maxwell, the officer in ordinary of the House of Peers.—May 4, Thursday. Arthur Lake, Bishop of Bath and Wells, died at London.—May 8, Monday. At two o'clock in the afternoon, the House of Commons brought up to the House of Peers a charge against the Duke of Buckingham, consisting of thirteen articles.—May 11, Thursday. King Charles came into the Parliament House, and made a short

speech to the Lords, concerning preserving
the honour of the nobility against the vile and
malicious calumnies of those in the House of
Commons, who had accused the Duke, &c.
They were eight who in this matter chiefly
appeared. The Prologue, Sir Dudley Digges,
the Epilogue, John Elliott, were this day by
the King's command committed to the Tower.
They were both dismissed thence within few
days.—May 25, Thursday. The Earl of
Arundel not being sent back to the House,
nor the cause of his detainment made known,
the House of Peers began to be jealous of
the breach of their privileges; and resolved
to adjourn the House to the next day. On
which day, May 26, they adjourned again
to June 2, resolving to do nothing until the
Earl should be set free, or at least a cause
given, &c.—May 25. On which day these
troubles first began, was the Feast of Pope
Urban; and at this time Urban VIII. sitteth
in the Papal Chair; to whom and to the
Spaniard, if they, who most desire it, would
do any acceptable service; I do not see, what

they could better devise in that kind, than to divide thus into parties the great Council of the kingdom.

June 15, Thursday. After many debates and strugglings, private malice against the Duke of Buckingham prevailed, and stopped all public business. Nothing was done; but Parliament was dissolved.—June 20, Tuesday. His Majesty King Charles named me to be Bishop of Bath and Wells: and at the same time commanded me to prepare a Sermon for the public Fast; which he had by proclamation appointed to be kept on the 5th of July following.—July 5. A solemn Fast appointed, partly upon account of the pestilence yet raging in many parts of the kingdom, partly on account of the danger of enemies threatening us. I preached this day, before the King and nobility, at Whitehall. It was Wednesday.—July 8. The King commanded me to print and publish the Sermon. It was Saturday.—July 16. I presented that Sermon, which was now printed, to his Majesty; and returned.—July 26, Wednesday. The King

signed the congé d'élire, empowering the
Dean and Chapter to elect me Bishop of Bath
and Wells.—July 24, Thursday. In the morning, Dr. Field, Bishop of Llandaff, brought to
me certain letters from the most illustrious
Duke of Buckingham. The letters were
open, and wrote partly in characters. The
Duke sent them to me, that I should consult
one named Swadlinge, mentioned in those letters, as one who could read the characters. I
was also named in them, as to whom that
Swadlinge was known, having been educated
in St. John's College in Oxford, at what time
I was President of that College.

Aug. 1. Thomas Swadlinge came to me,
whom, from his leaving College to that day,
for almost eight years, I had not once seen. He
bestowing some pains, at length read the characters, and Aug. 4, Friday, I and he went
to the Duke. He read them: they were certain malicious things. The Duke, as was fit,
despised them. We returned.—Aug. 16. I
was elected Bishop of Bath and Wells, being
Wednesday, the letter D.—Aug. 25, Friday.

Two robin-redbreasts flew together through the door into my study, as if one pursued the other. That sudden motion almost startled me. I was then preparing a Sermon on Ephes. iv. 30. and studying.

Sept. 14, Thursday evening. The Duke of Buckingham willed me to form certain instructions, partly political, partly ecclesiastical, in the cause of the King of Denmark, a little before brought into great straits by General Tilly, to be sent through all parishes. He would have them made ready by Saturday following.—Sept. 16. I made them ready, and brought them at the appointed hour. I read them to the Duke. He brought me to the King. I, being so commanded, read them again. Each of them approved them.— Sept. 17, Sunday. They were read (having been left with the Duke) before the Lords of the Privy Council; and were (thanks be to God) approved by them all.

[It may not be amiss to subjoin these instructions from Heylin, sub an. 1626.]

Most Reverend Father in God, right trusty
and right well-beloved Counsellor, we
greet you well.

We have observed that the Church and the
State are so nearly united and knit together,
that though they may seem two bodies, yet
indeed in some relation they may be accounted but as one, inasmuch as they both
are made up of the same men, which are
differenced only in relation to spiritual or
civil ends. This nearness makes the Church
call in the help of the State, to succour and support her, whensoever she is pressed beyond
her strength. And the same nearness makes
the State call in for the service of the Church,
both to teach that duty which her members
know not, and to exhort them to, and encourage them in, that duty which they know.
It is not long since we ordered the State to
serve the Church, and by a timely proclamation settled the peace of it. And now the State
looks for the like assistance from the Church,
that she and all her ministers may serve God

and us, by preaching peace and unity at home, that it may be the better able to resist foreign force uniting and multiplying against it. And to the end that they to whom we have committed the government of the Church under us, may be the better able to dispose of the present occasions, we have, with the advice of our Council, thought fit to send unto you these instructions following, to be sent by you to the Bishops of your province, and such others whom it may concern, and by them and all their officers directed to all the ministers throughout the several dioceses, that according to these punctually they may instruct and exhort the people to serve God and us, and labour by their prayers to divert the dangers which hang over us. The danger in which we are at this time is great. It is increased by the late blow given our good uncle the King of Denmark, who is the chief person in those parts that opposed the spreading forces of Spain. If he cannot subsist, there is little or nothing left to hinder the House of Austria from being lord and master

of Germany : and that is a large and mighty
territory, and such as, should it be gotten,
would make an open way for Spain to do
what they pleased in all the west part of
Christendom. For besides the great strength
which Germany once possessed would bring
to them, which are too strong already, you
are to consider, first, how it enables them by
land, in that it will join all or the most part
of the Spaniard's now distracted territories,
and be a means for him safely and speedily
to draw down forces against any other kingdom that shall stand in his way. Nor can it
be thought that the Low Countries can hold
out longer against him if he once become
lord of the upper parts. And secondly, you
are to weigh how it will advantage him by
sea, and make him strong against us in our
particular, which is of easy apprehension to
all men. And besides, if he once get Germany, he will be able, though he had no gold
from India, to supply the necessity of those
wars, and to hinder all trade and traffic of the
greatest staple commodities of this kingdom,

cloth and wool, and so make them of little or no value.

You are to know therefore, that to prevent this, is the present care of the King and State, and there is no probable way left but by sending forces and other supplies to the said King of Denmark, our dear uncle, to enable him to keep the field, that our enemies be not masters of all on the sudden. You are further to take notice, how both we and the whole State stand bound in honour and conscience to supply the present necessity of the King of Denmark. For this quarrel is more nearly ours, the recovery of the ancient inheritance of our dear sister and her children. The King of Denmark stands not so near in blood unto her, as we do. Yet for her and our sakes, that brave and valiant King hath adventured into the field, and in that engagement hath not only hazarded his person, but, as things go now, it may turn to some danger to his own kingdom and posterity, should he not receive aid and succour from us without delay: which should it happen, (as God for-

bid,) will be one of the greatest dishonours
that ever this kingdom was stained withal.
Nor is danger and dishonour all the mischief
that is like to follow this disaster.   For if it
be not presently relieved, the cause of religion
is not only likely to suffer by it in some one
part, (as it hath already in a fearful manner
in the Palatinate,) but in all places where it
hath gotten any footing.   So that if we supply
not presently our allies and confederates in
this case, it is like to prove the extirpation
of true religion, and the replanting of Romish
superstition in all the neighbouring parts
of Christendom.   And the coldness of this
State shall suffer in all places as the betrayer
of that religion elsewhere, which it professeth
and honoureth at home, which will be an
imputation never to be washed off.   And
God forbid this State should suffer under it.

Neither may you forget rightly to inform
the people committed to your charge, that
this war, which now grows full of danger, was
not entered upon rashly and without advice,
but you are to acquaint them, that all former

treaties by a peaceable way were in the latter
end of our dear father of ever-blessed memory
dissolved as fruitless, and unfit to be longer
held on foot ; and this by the counsel of both
Houses of Parliament then sitting : so those
two great and honourable bodies of Peers and
People represented in Parliament led on this
counsel and course to a war with Spain.
To effect this, they desire our aid and
assistance, and used us to work our said dear
father to entertain this course. This upon
their persuasions, and promises of all assistance and supply, we readily undertook and
effected, and cannot now be left in that business, but with the sin and shame of all men.
Sin, because aid and supply for the defence
of the kingdom, and the like affairs of State,
especially such as are advised and assumed
by Parliamentary counsel, are due to the
King from his people, by all law both of God
and men: and shame, if they forsake the
King, while he pursues their own counsel,
just and honourable, and which could not
under God but have been as successful, if it

had been followed and supplied in time, as we
desired and laboured for. One thing there
is which proves a great hindrance of this
State, and not continued among the people,
without great offence against God, detriment
both to Church and State, and our great
disservice in this and all other business. It is
breach of unity, which is grown too great
and common amongst all sorts of men. The
danger of this goes far; for in all states it
hath made way for enemies to enter. We
have by all means endeavoured union, and
require of you to preach it, and charity, the
mother of it, frequently in the ears of the
people. We know their loyal hearts, and
therefore wonder the more what should cause
distracted affections. If you call upon them,
(which is your duty,) we doubt not but that
God will bless them with that love to Himself, to His Church, and to their own preservation, which alone will be able to bind up
the scatterings of divided affections into
strength. To this end you are to lay before
them what miseries home-divisions have

brought upon this and many other kingdoms, and to exhort all men to embrace it in time. The danger itself, besides all other Christian and prudent motives, is of force enough (where it is duly considered) to make me join in all amity against a common enemy; and to do it in time, before any secret and cunning working of his may use one part in a division to weaken the other.

And in the last place, (but first and last and all times to be insisted on,) you are to call upon God yourselves, and to incite the people to join with you in humble and hearty prayers unto God, that He would be pleased now, after long affliction of His dear people and children, to look in mercy upon them and us, and in particular for the safety of the King of Denmark, and that army which is left him, that God would bless and prosper him against his and our enemies. Thus you are to strengthen the hearts and hopes of our loyal subjects and people, in and upon God. And whereas the greatest confidence men have in God, ariseth not only from His promises, but from their experience likewise of His goodness, you must not fail often to recal to the memory of the people, with thankfulness, the late great experience we have had of His goodness towards us. For the three great and usual judgments, which He darts down upon disobedient and unthankful people, are pestilence, famine, and the sword. The pestilence did never rage more in this kingdom than of late; and God was graciously pleased in mercy to hear the prayers which were made unto Him, and the ceasing of the judgment was little less than a miracle. The famine threatened us this present year; and it must have followed, had God rained down His anger a little longer upon the fruits of the earth. But upon our prayers He stayed that judgment, and sent us a blessed season, and a most plentiful harvest. The sword is the thing which we are now to look to; and you must call the people to their prayers again against that enemy, that God will be pleased to send the like deliverance from this judgment also; that in the same mercy He will vouchsafe to strengthen the hands of His people; that He will sharpen their sword, but dull and turn the edge of that which is in our enemies' hands; that so, while some fight, others may pray for the blessing. And you are to be careful, that you fail not to direct and hearten our loving people in this and all other necessary services, both of God, His Church, and us; that we may have the comfort of our people's service; the State, safety; the Church, religion; and the people, the enjoying of all such blessings as follow these. And we end with doubling this care upon you, and all under you in their several places.

Given at our Palace at Westminster, in the second year of our Reign, September 21, 1626.

Sept. 18, Monday. My election to the Bishopric of Bath and Wells was confirmed.— Sept. 19, Tuesday. At Theobald's I swore homage to his Majesty; who there presently restored me to the temporalities, from the death of my predecessor. What passed between me and the Lord Conway, Principal Secretary to the King, in our return.—Sept. 25, Monday. About four o'clock in the morning died Lancelot Andrewes, the most worthy Bishop of Winchester, the great light of the Christian world.—Sept. 30, Saturday. The Duke of Buckingham signified to me the King's resolution, that I should succeed the Bishop of Winchester in the office of Dean of the Chapel Royal.—Oct. 2, Monday. The Duke related to me, what the King had farther resolved concerning me in case the Archbishop of Canterbury should die, &c.—Oct. 3, Tuesday. I went to Court, which was then at Hampton Court. There I returned thanks to the King for the Deanery of the Chapel, then granted to me. I returned to London.— Oct. 6. I took the oath belonging to the Dean of the Chapel, in the vestry, before the Right Honourable Philip Earl of Montgomery, Lord Chamberlain; Stephen Boughton the Sub-Dean administering it. It was Friday.— Nov. 14, or thereabout, taking occasion from the abrupt both beginning and ending of public prayer on the fifth of November, I desired his Majesty King Charles, that he would please to be present at prayers as well as Sermon every Sunday; and that at whatsoever part of the prayers he came, the Priest then officiating might proceed to the end of the prayers. The most religious King not only assented to this request; but also gave me thanks. This had not before been done from the beginning of King James's reign to this day. Now, thanks be to God, it obtaineth.

Dec. 21. I dreamed of the burial of I know not whom, and that I stood by the grave. I awaked sad.—Dec. 25, Christmas Day, Monday. I preached my first Sermon as Dean of the Chapel Royal, at Whitehall, upon St. John i. 14. pt. 1.– Jan. 5, Epiphany eve, and Friday. In the night I dreamed, that my mother, long since dead, stood by my bed, and drawing aside the clothes a little, looked pleasantly upon me; and that I was glad to see her with so merry an aspect.

She then shewed to me a certain old man,
long since deceased; whom, while alive, I both
knew and loved. He seemed to lie upon the
ground; merry enough, but with a wrinkled
countenance. His name was Grove. While
I prepared to salute him, I awoke.

Jan. 8, Monday. I went to visit the Duke
of Buckingham. He was glad to see me, and
put into my hands a paper concerning the
Invocation of Saints, which his mother had
given to him; a certain Priest, to me unknown, had given it to her.—Jan. 13, Saturday. The Bishop of Lincoln desired reconciliation with the Duke of Buckingham,
&c.—Jan. 14, Sunday. Towards morning
I dreamed that the Bishop of Lincoln came,
I know not whither, with iron chains. But
returning loosed from them, leaped on horseback, went away; neither could I overtake
him.—Jan. 16, Tuesday. I dreamed that the
King went out to hunt; and that when he
was hungry, I brought him on the sudden
into the house of my friend, Francis Windebank. While he prepareth to eat, I, in the

absence of others, presented the cup to him after the usual manner. I carried drink to him; but it pleased him not. I carried it again, but in a silver cup. Thereupon his Majesty said, You know that I always drink out of glass. I go away again; and awoke.— Jan. 17, Wednesday. I shew my reasons to the King, why the papers of the late Bishop of Winchester, concerning Bishops, that they are *jure Divino*, should be printed; contrary to what the Bishop of Lincoln had pitifully, and to the great detriment of the Church of England, signified to the King; as the King himself had before related to me.

Feb. 7, Ash Wednesday. I preached at Court, at Whitehall.—Feb. 9, Friday. The following night, I dreamed, that I was troubled with the scurvy; and that on the sudden all my teeth became loose; that one of them especially in the lower jaw, I could scarce hold in with my finger, till I called out for help, &c.—Feb. 20, Tuesday. John Fenton began the cure of a certain itch, &c. —Feb. 22, Thursday. I began my journey

towards Newmarket, where the King then
was.

March 3, Saturday. I went to Cambridge
with the Duke of Buckingham, Chancellor
of that famous University, and other Earls
and Lords. I was there incorporated; and
so I was the first who was presented to the
most illustrious, then sitting in the Congregation House. The Duke was treated by the
University in an academical manner, yet
splendidly. We returned.—March 6, Tuesday. The King returned from Newmarket,
and I with him, toward London.—March 8,
Thursday. I came to London. The night
following I dreamed that I was reconciled to
the Church of Rome. This troubled me
much; and I wondered exceedingly, how it
should happen. Nor was I aggrieved with
myself *only by reason of the errors of that
Church, but also*[1] upon account of the scandal,

[1] These words in Italics were left out by Prynne,
when he had the Diary printed and distributed at the
Archbishop's trial. Nor is this by any means a solitary
illustration of the conduct of the Puritans, to whom the

which from that my fall would be cast upon many eminent and learned men in the Church of England. So being troubled at my dream, I said with myself that I would go immediately, and, confessing my fault, would beg pardon of the Church of England. Going with this resolution, a certain priest met me, and would have stopped me. But moved with indignation, I went on my way. And while I wearied myself with these troublesome thoughts, I awoke. Herein I felt such strong impressions, that I could scarce believe it to be a dream — March 12, Monday. I went with the King to Theobald's. I returned next day, March 13. — March 17, Saturday. The eve of Palm Sunday, about midnight, I buried Charles Viscount Buckingham, the eldest and then only son of George Duke of Buckingham. He was then about a year and four months old.

epithet *conscientious* has been so strangely awarded. Even the partial and party compilations of Rushworth are full of similar instances.

1627. March 25, Easter Day. I preached at
Court, &c.—March 27, Tuesday. That night
I had the following dream. Some legacies
had been given to the Lady Dorothy Wright,
the widow of Sir George Wright, my acquaintance. The legacies amounted to above
£430, being bequeathed by a certain kinsman
named Farnham, to the widow and her children. When the executor denied or deferred
to pay the legacy, I had, at the desire of the
widow, obtained letters in her behalf from
the Duke of Buckingham, (for the Duke was
Master of the Horse, and the said Sir G. was
employed under him in the King's service.)
When I had now those letters in my hands,
and was about to deliver them to the widow,
that she might send them into Ireland, where
the executor dwelt; this night, Sir George
Wright appeared to me in my sleep, having
been dead two years before at least. He
seemed to me in very good plight, and merry
enough. I told him what I had done for his
widow and children. He, after a little thought,
answered, that the executor had satisfied him

1627

for those legacies, while he was yet alive.
And presently looking upon some papers in
his study adjoining, he added, that it was so.
He, moreover, whispering in my ear, told me,
that I was the cause why the Bishop of Lincoln
was not again admitted into favour, and to Court.

April 4, Wednesday. When his Majesty
King Charles forgave to Dr. Donne certain
slips in a Sermon preached on Sunday, April 1,
what he then most graciously said unto me,
I have wrote in my heart with indelible
characters, and great thankfulness to God
and the King.—April 7, Saturday. Going to
Court to wait upon the King at supper, in
going out of the coach, my foot stumbling, I
fell headlong. I never had a more dangerous fall; but, by God's mercy, I escaped with
a light bruise of my hip only.—April 24,
Tuesday. There were then first sent to me
the exceptions which the Archbishop of Canterbury had exhibited against Dr. Sibthorp's
Sermon[s], and what followed.—April 29, Sun-

[s] The importance and repeated publication of *single
Sermons*, has been with us an invariable symptom of

day. I was made Privy Chancellor to his Majesty King Charles. God grant it may conduce to His honour, and to the good of the kingdom and the Church!

May 13, Whit-Sunday. I preached before the King, &c.

June 7 and 8. I attended King Charles from London to Southwick by Portsmouth.— June 11. His Majesty dined aboard the Triumph; where I attended him.—June 17. The Bishopric of London was granted me at Southwick.—June 22. We came to London. —June 24. I was commanded to go all the

uneasy times in the Church. The *beginnings* of the Reformation, the times of the Puritans, the Non-Jurors and the latter days of Queen Anne's reign, may be adduced in proof of this. The pressure of circumstances in all these periods, was such as to set aside for a while the ordinary laws of literary production. The character of the English Church has for long been so eminently controversial, that our divinity is scarcely to be understood or appreciated fairly, without a considerable knowledge of history, and the connection of the various theological schools with their times.

Progress.—June 27. The Duke of Buckingham set forwards towards the Isle of Rhé.—
June 30. The Progress began to Oatlands.

July 4. The King lost a jewel in hunting of
a £1000 value. That day the message was
sent by the King for the sequestering of A. B. C.
(Archbishop of Canterbury, Dr. Abbot.)

[*Heylin's Cyp. Angl.* p. 169. The Church besides
was at that time in an heavy condition, and opportunities must be watched for keeping her from falling from bad to worse. No better her condition
now in the realm of England, than anciently in the
Eastern Churches, when Nectarius sate as supreme
Pastor in the Chair of Constantinople; of which
thus Nazianzen writes unto him: The Arians
(saith he) were grown so insolent, that they make
open profession of their heresy, as if they had been
authorized and licensed to it; the Macedonians so
presumptuous, that they were formed into a sect, and
had a titular Bishop of their own; the Apollinarians
held their conventicles with as much safety and
esteem as the orthodox Christians. And for Euno-
mius, the bosom-mischief of these times, he thought
so poorly of a general connivance, that at last
nothing would content him but a toleration. The
cause of which disorders he ascribeth to Nectarius

only. A man, as the historian (*Socrates*) saith of him, of an exceeding fair and plausible demeanour, and very gracious with the people: one that chose rather (as it seems) to give free way to all men's fancies, and suffer every man's proceedings, than draw upon himself the envy of a stubborn Clergy, and a factious multitude. Never was Church more like to Church, Bishop to Bishop, time to time, (the names of the sects and heresies being only changed,) than those of Constantinople then, and of England now. A pregnant evidence, that possibly there could not be a greater mischief in the Church of God than a popular Prelate.

This, though his Majesty might not know, yet the Bishops which were about him did; who, therefore, had but ill discharged their duty both to God and man, if they had not made his Majesty acquainted with it. He could not choose but see, by the practices and proceedings of the former Parliaments, to what a prevalency the Puritans were grown in all parts of the kingdom, and how incompatible that humour was with the regal interest. There was no need to tell him from what fountain the mischief came; how much the popularity and remiss government of Abbot did contribute towards it. Him, therefore, he sequestereth from his Metropolitical jurisdiction, confines him to his house at Ford in Kent; and by his Commission, bearing

[date the 9th day of October, 1627, transfers the
exercise of that jurisdiction to Mountaine Bishop
of London, Neile Bishop of Durham, Buckeridge
Bishop of Rochester, Houson Bishop of Oxon,
and Laud Bishop of Bath and Wells. And this
his Majesty did to this end and purpose, that the
Archiepiscopal jurisdiction, being committed to
such hands as were no favourers of that faction,
there might some stop be given to that violent current, which then began to bear all before it. Nor
did his Majesty fail of the end desired. For though
Abbot, on good reasons of State, was restored unto
his jurisdiction toward the latter end of the year
next following ; yet by this breathing time, as short
as it was, the Church recovered strength again. And
the disgrace put upon the man, did so disanimate
and deject the opposite party, that the balance
began visibly to turn on the Church's side.]

July 7, Saturday night. I dreamed that I
had lost two teeth. The Duke of Buckingham
took the Isle of Rhé.—July 26. I attended
the King and Queen at Wellingborough.—
July 29. The first news came from my
Lord Duke of his success, Sunday.

Aug. 12. The second news came from
my Lord Duke to Windsor.

L

Aug. 26. The third news came from my Lord Duke to Aldershot, Sunday.

September. News came from my Lord Duke to Theobald's. The first fear of ill success. News from my Lord Duke to Hampton Court. I went to my Lord of Rochester to consider about A. B. C. and returned to Hampton Court. The King's speech to me in the withdrawing chamber. That if any did, &c. I, &c. before any thing should sink, &c. The business of Dr. Bargrave, Dean of Canterbury, began about the Vicarage of Lidd.

October. The Commission to the Bishops of London, Durham, Rochester, Oxford, and myself, then Bath and Wells, to execute Archiepiscopal jurisdiction during the sequestration of my Lord's Grace of Canterbury. The Dean of Canterbury's speech, that the business could not go well in the Isle of Rhé. There must be a Parliament; some must be sacrificed; that I was as like as any. Spoken to Dr. W. The same speech after spoken to the same man, by Sir Dudley Diggs. I told it when I heard it doubled. "Let me desire you not to trouble yourself with any reports, till you see me forsake my other friends, &c." ITA CH. R. The retreat out of the Isle of Rhé.

November. My Lord Duke's return to Court. The Countess of Purbeck censured in the High Commission for adultery.

December 25. I preached to the King at Whitehall.

Jan. 29, Tuesday. A resolution at the Council Table for a Parliament, to begin March 17. If the Shires go on with levying money for the navy, &c.—Jan. 30, Wednesday. My Lord Duke of Buckingham's son was born, the Lord George: New Moon die 26.

Feb. 5, Tuesday. The straining of the beck sinew of my right leg, as I went with his Majesty to Hampton Court. I kept in till I preached at the opening of the Parliament, March 17, but I continued lame long after, saving that on Feb. 14, Thursday, St. Valentine's day, I made a shift to go and christen my Lord Duke's son, the Lord George, at Wallingford House.

March 17. I preached at the opening of the Parliament; but had much ado to stand. It was Monday.

[It was during the confinement from this accident, that Dr. Heylin's acquaintance with the Archbishop grew to the close intimacy which afterwards existed between them. This is noticed by Heylin with no little pride and pleasure. " These matters being in agitation, and the Parliament drawing on apace, on Tuesday, the fifth of February, he strained the back sinew of his right leg, as he went with his Majesty to Hampton Court, which kept him to his chamber till the fourteenth of the same; during which time of his keeping in, I had both the happiness of being taken into his special knowledge of me, and the opportunity of a longer conference with him than I could otherwise have expected. I went to have presented my service to him as he was preparing for this journey, and was appointed to attend him on the same day sevennight, when I might presume on his return. Coming precisely at the time, I heard of his mischance, and that he kept himself to his chamber. But order had been left amongst the servants, that if I came he should be made acquainted with it; which being done accordingly, I was brought into his chamber, where I found him sitting in a chair, with his lame leg resting on a pillow. Commanding that nobody should come to interrupt him till he called for them, he caused me to sit down by him, inquired first into the course of my studies, which he well approved of, exhorting me to hold myself in that moderate course in which he found me. He fell afterwards to discourse of some passages in Oxon. in which I was specially concerned, and told me thereupon the story of such oppositions as had been made against him in that University, by Archbishop Abbot and some others; encouraged me not to shrink, if I had already, or should hereafter, find the like. I was with him thus, remotis arbitris, almost two hours. It grew towards twelve of the clock, and then he knocked for his servants to come unto him. He dined that day in his ordinary dining-room, which was the first time he had so done since his mishap. He caused me to tarry dinner with him, and used me with no small respect, which was much noted by some gentlemen, (Elphinston, one of his Majesty's cup-bearers, being one of the company,) who dined that day with him." *Cypr. Angl.* 175.]

1628. June 1, Whitsunday. I preached at Whitehall. – June 11. My Lord Duke of Buckingham voted in the House of Commons to be the cause or causes of all grievances in the kingdom.—June 12, Thursday. I was complained of by the House of Commons for warranting Dr. Manwaring's Sermons to the press.—June 13. Dr. Manwaring answered for himself before the Lords; and the next day, June 14, being Saturday, was censured. After his censure, my cause was called to the report; and, by God's goodness towards me, I was fully cleared in the House. The same day the House of Commons were making their Remonstrance to the King. One head was " innovation of religion." Therein they named my Lord the Bishop of Winchester (Neile) and myself. One in the House stood up and said, " Now we have named these persons, let us think of some causes why we did it." Sir Edw. Coke answered, " Have we not named my Lord of Buckingham without shewing a cause, and may we not be as bold with them?"—June 17. This Remonstrance was delivered to the King on Tuesday. —June 26, Thursday. The Session of Parliament ended, and was prorogued to October 20.

July 11, Tuesday. My congé d'élire was signed by the King for the Bishopric of London.—July 15, St. Swithin, and fair with us. I was translated to the Bishopric of London. The same day the Lord Weston was made Lord Treasurer.

Aug 9, Saturday. A terrible salt rheum in my left eye had almost put me into a fever.— Aug. 12, Tuesday. My Lord Duke of Buckingham went towards Portsmouth to go for Rochelle.—Aug. 23, Saturday. St. Bartholomew's eve—the Duke of Buckingham slain at Portsmouth by one Lieutenant Felton, about nine in the morning.—Aug. 24. The news of his death came to Croydon; where it found myself and the Bishops of Winchester, Ely, and Carlisle, at the consecration of Bishop Montague for Chichester, with my Lord's Grace.—Aug. 27, Wednesday. Mr. Elphinston brought me a very gracious message from his Majesty upon my Lord Duke's death.— Aug. 30. As I was going out to meet the corpse of the Duke, which that night was brought to London, Sir W. Fleetwood brought me very gracious letters from the King's Majesty, written with his own hand.

Sept. 9, Tuesday. The first time that I went to Court after the death of the Duke of Buckingham, my dear Lord. The gracious speech, which that night the King was pleased to use to me.—Sept. 27, Saturday. I fell sick, and came sick from Hampton Court.—Tuesday, Sept. ult. I was sore plucked with this sickness, &c.

[As the Duke of Buckingham was Laud's great patron, and the language the Archbishop uses respecting him in various parts of his Diary has been objected to him, it may not be amiss to insert in this place Clarendon's character of the Duke; more especially, as he has been always a mark for party virulence, and is treated by Bishop Warburton with his usual coarseness, and indeed has been seldom judged of with any thing like historical fairness. " This great man was a person of a noble nature, and generous disposition, and of such other endowments, as made him very capable of being a great favourite to a great King. He understood the arts of a Court, and all the learning that is professed there, exactly well. By long practice in business, under a master (King James) that discoursed excellently, and surely knew all things wonderfully, and took much delight in indoctrinating his young inexperienced favourite, who, he knew, would be always looked upon as the workmanship of his own hands, he had obtained a quick conception, and apprehension of business, and had the habit of speaking very gracefully and pertinently. He was of a most flowing courtesy and affability to all men who made any address to him; and so desirous to oblige them, that he did not enough consider the value of the obligation, or the merit of the person he chose to oblige; from which much of his misfortune resulted. He was of a courage not to be daunted, which was manifested in all his actions, and in his contests with particular persons of the greatest reputation; and especially in his whole demeanour at the isle of Rhé, both at the landing and upon the retreat; in both which no man was more fearless, or more ready to expose himself to the highest dangers. His kindness and affection to his friends was so vehement, that they were as so many marriages for better and worse, and so many leagues offensive and defensive; as if he thought himself obliged to love all his friends, and to make war upon all they were angry with, let the cause be what it would. And it cannot be denied, that he was an enemy in the same excess, and prosecuted those he looked upon as his enemies with the utmost rigour and animosity, and was not easily induced to reconciliation. And yet there were some examples of his receding in that particular. And when he was in the highest passion, he was so far from stooping to any dissimulation, whereby his displeasure might be concealed and covered till he had attained his revenge, (the low method of Courts,) that he never endeavoured to do any man an ill office, before he first told him what he was to expect from him, and reproached him with the injuries he had done, with so much generosity, that the person found it in his power to receive further satisfaction, in the way he would choose for himself.

" His single misfortune was, (which indeed was productive of many greater,) that he never made a noble and a worthy friendship with a man so near his equal, that he would frankly advise him for his honour and true interest, against the current, or rather the torrent, of his impetuous passion; which was partly the vice of the time, when the Court was not replenished with great choice of excellent men; and partly the vice of the persons, who were most worthy to be applied to, and looked upon his youth, and his obscurity before his rise, as obligations upon him to gain their friendships by extraordinary application. Then his ascent was so quick, that it seemed rather a flight than a growth; and he was such a darling of fortune, that he was at the top before he was well seen at the bottom; and, as if he had been born a favourite, he was supreme the first month he came to Court; and it was want of confidence, not of credit, that he had not all at first which he obtained afterwards; never meeting with the least obstruction from his setting out, till he was as great as he could be; so that he wanted dependents before he thought he could want coadjutors. Nor was he very fortunate in the election of those dependents, very few of his servants having been ever qualified enough to assist or advise him; and they were intent only upon growing rich under him, not upon their master's growing good as well as great: insomuch, as he was throughout his fortune a much wiser man than any servant or friend he had.

"Let the fault or misfortune be what or whence it will, it may reasonably be believed, that, if he had been blessed with one faithful friend, who had been qualified with wisdom and integrity, that great person would have committed as few faults, and done as transcendent worthy actions, as any man who shined in such a sphere in that age in Europe. For he was of an excellent disposition, and of a mind very capable of advice and counsel. He was in his nature just and candid, liberal, generous, and bountiful; nor was it ever known, that the temptation of money swayed him to do an unjust or unkind thing. If he had an immoderate ambition, with which he was charged, and is a weed (if it be a weed) apt to grow in the best soils; it does not appear that it was in his nature, or that he brought it with him to the Court, but rather found it there, and was a garment necessary for that air; nor was it more in his power to be without promotion, and titles, and wealth, than for a healthy man to sit in the sun in the brightest dog-days, and remain without any warmth. He needed no ambition, who was so seated in the hearts of two such masters." *Clar*. i. p. 55, *et sqq*.]

October 20, Monday. I was forced to put on a truss for a rupture, I know not how occasioned, unless it were with swinging of a book for my exercise in private.

Nov. 29. Felton was executed at Tyburn for killing the Duke; and afterwards his body was sent to be hanged in chains at Portsmouth. It was Saturday, and St. Andrew's even; and he killed the Duke upon Saturday, St. Bartholomew's even —Dec. 25. I preached at Whitehall.—Dec. 30, Wednesday. The Statutes, which I had drawn for the reducing of the factious and tumultary election of Proctors in Oxford to several Colleges by course, and so to continue, were passed in Convocation at Oxford, no voice dissenting.

[These new Statutes, however, seem to have been the cause of no little disturbance afterwards. The election for the fresh

Proctors on the new Statutes was fixed for April 23. The Candidates were Williamson of Magdalen Coll. and More of New Coll. on the one side, and Bruch of Brasen-nose and Lloyd of Jesus on the other: Hyde of Exeter and Taylour of C. C. C. being the scrutators. Neither of the scrutators would take the oath prescribed by the new Statute. A tumult ensued; notwithstanding which, the Vice-Chancellor continued the assembly, "but was so thrust and thronged in the House, that no bedell could come to him. At length he got away, without any proceeding to election of Proctors." Of these tumults, the Chancellor was of course informed; and a letter from the King followed. "These letters, I say, (such is the narrative of Antony Wood,) being received by the Vice-Chancellor, a Convocation was celebrated May 21, at nine in the morning, wherein they being read by Mr. Hyde, the senior Procurator natus, the House proceed to an election, and went forward till about three of the clock in the afternoon with the scrutiny; but Lloyd

and Bruch, not liking their proceedings, told
the scrutators with a loud voice, ' That they
would appeal to his Majesty;' for the truth
is, there was foul play in the business.   Hereupon Taylour, the junior Procurator natus,
one of the scrutators, went away with the
scrutiny, and would proceed no further, notwithstanding he was sent for by Mr. Vice-
Chancellor.   At last about five of the clock
he came, and with a great number of Masters
with him, went into the Convocation, but
Mr. Hyde, the senior scrutator, being crowded
among them, gave a great screak as he was
sitting down in his chair, and fell down dead,
to the astonishment of all there present, and
so continuing half an hour in that condition,
the Masters got life into him again, and he
recovered well the same night."   After a
second interference on the part of the King,
the matter ended in the election of Williamson
and Lloyd.]

Jan. 26, Monday. The 240 Greek MSS.
were sent to London House.   These I got my
Lord of Pembroke to buy, and give to Oxford.

(They were bought out of the library of Franciscus Baroccius at Venice. *Ed.*)—Jan. 31, Saturday night. I lay in Court. I dreamed that I put off my rochet, all save one sleeve; and when I would have put it on again, I could not find it.

Feb. 6, Friday. Sir Thomas Roe sent to London House 28 MSS. in Greek, to have a catalogue drawn, and the books to be for Oxford.—March 2, Monday. The Parliament to be dissolved declared by proclamation, upon some disobedient passages to his Majesty that day in the House of Commons.—March 10, Tuesday. The Parliament dissolved, the King present. The Parliament, which was broken up this March 10, laboured my ruin; but, God be ever blessed for it, found nothing against me.

1629. March 29, Sunday. Two papers were found in the Dean of Paul's his yard before his house. The one was to this effect concerning myself; "Laud! look to thyself. Be assured thy life is sought. As thou art the fountain of all wickedness, repent thee of thy monstrous sins, before thou be taken out of the world, &c. And assure thyself, neither God nor the world can endure such a vile counsellor to live, or such a whisperer;"—or to this effect. The other was as bad as this against the Lord Treasurer (Weston, who we read in Clarendon succeeded to Buckingham's unpopularity.) Mr. Dean delivered both papers to the King that night. Lord! I am a grievous sinner; but I beseech Thee, deliver my soul from them that hate me without a cause!

April 2, Thursday, Maundy Thursday, as it came this year. About three of the clock in the morning, the Lady Duchess of Buckingham was delivered of her son the Lord Francis Villiers, whom I christened, Tuesday, April 21.—April 5. I preached at Whitehall.

May 13, Wednesday. This morning, about three of the clock, the Queen was delivered before her time of a son. He was christened and died within short space, his name Charles. This was Ascension eve. The next day, being May 14, Ascension Day. Paulò ante mediam noctem I buried him at Westminster. If God repair not this loss, I much fear it was Descension day to this State.

Aug. 14. Dies erat Veneris; I fell sick upon the way towards the Court at Woodstock. I took up my lodging at my ancient friend's house, Mr. Francis Windebank. There I lay in a most grievous burning fever, till Monday, Sept. 7, on which day I had my last fit.

Oct. 20. I was brought so low, that I was not able to return towards my own house at London till Tuesday, Oct. 29.—Oct. 26, Monday. I went first to present my humble duty and service to his Majesty at Denmark House. After this I had divers plunges, and was not able to put myself into the service of my place, till Palm Sunday, which was March 21.

1630. April 10. The Earl of Pembroke, Lord Steward, being Chancellor of the University of Oxford, died of an apoplexy.—April 12. The University of Oxford chose me Chancellor; and word was brought me of it the next morning, Monday.

["On Saturday, being the 10th of April, William Lord Herbert, Earl of Pembroke and Chancellor of the University of Oxford, died suddenly at his house called Baynard's Castle, in London, according to the calculations of his nativity that Mr. Thomas Allen, of Gloucester Hall, had made several years before. For which place, Dr. Laud, Bishop of London, and Philip, Earl of Montgomery, younger brother to the Earl deceased, were candidates. But the news of his death being brought to Oxford the next day betimes, Dr. Laud's friends of divers Colleges, especially of St. John's, bestirred themselves in his behalf. Those also that were not well-wishers to the Bishop, which were chiefly the Calvinian party, were active for the Earl, and so also were those of the Welsh nation, and of the four Colleges belonging to the visitation of the Bishop of Lincoln, that is to say, Balliol, Oriel, Lincoln, and Brasen-nose; to the Scholars of which, Dr Williams, (Laud's great enemy,) the Bishop of that place, had sent letters and agents in the Earl's behalf.

" The business being thus eagerly followed one day and night, a Convocation was called on the morrow, by order from the Vice-Chancellor, Dr. Frewen, (who upon news of the Chancellor's death, being then at Andover, in Hampshire, on Magdalen Coll. Progress, came presently home,) fearing lest the other party should be too strong for them. In the scrutiny for voices it is commonly reported that it passed clear for Laud; yet one (Prynne) is pleased to say, that ' by indirect means he procured himself to be elected Chancellor, and that the noble brother to the Earl of Pembroke was then really elected by most voices, though miscalculated by practice in the scrutiny by this Prelate's creatures,' &c. How true this is, I leave it to others to judge. However, this I shall say, that that party for the Earl was held to be more numerous than that for the Bishop, as divers judicious and impartial men that gave votes, lately and yet living, have attested it in my hearing. The scrutiny being finished, he was pronounced elected by the senior Proctor, and, whether lawfully or not, it is not for me to dispute it. Certain it is, it fell out very happy, not only for the encouragement of learning, but the great good of the University, as the following times made it manifest. Had he continued in his prosperity seven years longer, and not been molested by the restless faction of the Presbyterians, he would without doubt have made this University more famous for buildings, books, rarities, discipline, privileges, &c. than many, put together, in the learned world." *Ant. Wood.*]

April 28, Wednesday. The University came up to the ceremony, and gave me my oath.

May 28. To Dr. Frewen, Vice-Chancellor, about observing Formalities.

S. in Christo.

After my hearty commendations &c. your Deputy, Dr. Tolfen, hath done very well in some business in your absence, which I hope you will perfect. Now I have a little more business for you, in which I must desire you to have a special care.

I am given to understand, that Formalities (which are in a sort the outward and visible face of the University) are in a manner utterly decayed, not only abroad in the streets, but also in the very Schools, Convocation, and Congregation-Houses, and at Latin Sermons: insomuch that strangers, which come thither, have scarce any external mark, by which they may know they are in a University. If this go on, the University will lose ground every day both at home and abroad; and especially with his Majesty, who is a great lover of order and decency in all seminaries of good learning. And he hath already given me strict charge to look both to this and other particulars in their several times.

I pray, therefore, call the Heads of Colleges and Halls together with the Proctors, and read these letters to them; and with my love remembered to them all, let them know I am welcomed into my Chancellorship with many complaints from very great men. I hope, all are not true: and I hope, such as are, you and they will all in your several Houses join pains and hearty endeavours to see them rectified, as I shall in due time severally propose them.

At this time, I think it necessary, the Heads should fairly bespeak their several Companies to fit themselves with formalities fitting their Degrees, that when the Act comes, (God bless you with health, that it may hold with honour and safety,) the University may have credit by looking like itself: and then I doubt not but it will be itself too. For it will not endure but to be, as it seems. And I desire you would bespeak your Companies fairly. Both, because I presume, most men there in their generous and liberal education will be such lovers of order, that they will run to the practice: and because I heartily desire, that as I am chosen Chancellor with a great deal of unexpected love, so I may be enabled ever to govern with a like measure of it. My heart ever was, and I hope ever shall be, set to do that place all the good I can. And I shall take it for one of God's greatest temporal blessings upon me, if I may have your joint concurrence to perfect the good I wish. And I will not doubt, but that you do so love and honour that our venerable mother, that you will cheerfully afford me this assistance.

When you have made this entrance for Formalities at the Act, (for which I now give time and warning,) then the better to settle them, and all other points of government, I pray take care to go on with the Delegacy for the Statutes, that there may be a settled and a known body of them. My ever-honoured predecessor began that work with care. I know, you will give me leave to pursue it to your good and his honour. In the next long vacation it were happy, if that body of Statutes might be finished.

But whether it can or not, I heartily pray you against Michaelmas Term look the Register, and provide such Tables, as were wont to be published upon St. Mary's doors, for observance of the known Statutes, and that then you proceed to the execution of them accordingly.

I know, you and the governors there will pardon me this care, when you shall know what lies upon me here, and what begins already to be expected from me by a most gracious Prince, who is very zealous of the honour of that place. And this yet I shall promise and perform. I will not be sudden upon you, nor hasty with you in any your businesses. Neither will I proceed in any thing but that which shall promote the honour and good of yourselves and that famous University. And in this way he that gives me best assistance shall be most welcome to me. So for this time I take my leave: commending you all to God's gracious protection; and shall rest;

Your very loving friend,
GUIL. LONDON.

May 28, 1630.

May 29, Saturday. Prince Charles was born at St. James's, paulo ante horam primam post meridiem. I was in the house three hours before, and had the honour and the happiness to see the Prince before he was full one hour old.

June 27, Sunday. I had the honour, as Dean of the Chapel, my Lord's Grace of Canterbury being infirm, to christen Prince Charles at St. James's, hora fere quinta pomeridiana.

Aug. 22, Sunday. I preached at Fulham.—Aug. 24, Tuesday, St. Bartholomew. Extreme thunder, lightning, and rain: the pestilence this summer: the greatest week in London was 73, à 7 Octob. ad 14: spread in many places, miserably in Cambridge. The winter before was extreme wet; and scarce one week of frost. This harvest scarce. A great dearth in France, England, the Low Countries, &c.

Oct. 6, Wednesday. I was taken with an extreme cold and lameness, as I was waiting upon St. George's Feast at Windsor; and forced to return to Fulham, where I continued ill above a week.—Oct. 29, Friday. I removed my family from Fulham to London House.

Nov. 4, Thursday. Leighton was degraded

at the High Commission.—Nov. 9, Tuesday
Leighton broke out of the Fleet. The Warden says he got or was helped over the wall
the Warden professes he knew not this til
Wednesday noon. He told it not me til
Thursday night. He was taken again in
Bedfordshire, and brought back to the Flee
within a fortnight.—Nov. 26, Friday. Part o
his sentence was executed upon him at West
minster.

Dec. 7, Tuesday. The King sware the
Peace with Spain: Don Carlo Colonna wa
Ambassador.—Dec. 25. I preached to the
King, Christmas Day.

1631. Jan. 16, Sunday. I consecrated St
Catherine Creed Church in London.—Jan. 21
The Lord Wentworth, Lord President of the
North, and I, &c. In my little chamber a
London House, Friday.

[" Being so gained to the King, he (Went
worth) became the most devout friend of the
Church, the greatest zealot for advancing the
Monarchical interest, and the ablest Minister
of State, both for peace and war, that any o

our former histories have afforded to us. He had not long frequented the Council Table, when Laud and he, coming to a right understanding of one another, entered into a league of such inviolable friendship, that nothing but the inevitable stroke of death could part them; and joining hearts and hands together, cooperated from thenceforth for advancing the honour of the Church and his Majesty's service." *Cypr. Angl.* 194.]

Jan. 23. I consecrated the Church of St. Giles in the Fields, Sunday.

Feb. 20. This Sunday morning, Westminster Hall was found on fire, by the burning of the little shops or stalls kept there. It is thought, by some pan of coals left there overnight. It was taken in time.—Feb. 23, Ash Wednesday. I preached in Court at Whitehall.

March 20, Sunday. His Majesty put his great conscience to me, about, &c. Which I after answered. God bless him in it! The famine great this time: but in part by practice.

March 27, Coronation-day and Sunday. I preached at St. Paul's Cross.

April 10, Easter Monday. I fell ill with great pain in my throat, for a week. It was with cold taken after heat in my service, and then into an ague. A fourth part almost of my family sick this spring.

June 7, Tuesday. I consecrated the Chapel at Hammersmith.—June 21, Tuesday, and June 25, Saturday. My nearer acquaintance began to settle with Dr. S. I pray God bless us in it.—June 26 My business with L. T. (Lord Treasurer?), &c. about the trees which the King had given me in Shotover, towards my building in St. John's at Oxford. Which work I resolved on in November last. And published it to the College about the end of March. This day discovered unto me what I was sorry to find in L. T. (Lord Treasurer?) and F. C. (Francis Cottington ?)

[This is the first of a number of references to L. T. and the following passage in Clarendon leads me to suppose it relates to Weston's, afterwards Lord Portland's, jealousy of the

Archbishop.   Clarendon says of Lord Portland, that he was " a man so jealous of the
Archbishop's credit with the King, that he
always endeavoured to lessen it by all the
arts and ways he could ; which he was so far
from effecting, that, as it usually falls out,
when passion and malice make accusation, by
suggesting many particulars which the King
knew to be untrue, or believed to be no faults,
he rather confirmed his Majesty's judgment
of him, and prejudiced his own reputation."
i. p. 173.]

July 26. The first stone was laid of my
building at St. John's.

Aug. 23. In this June and July were the
great disorders in Oxford, by appealing from
Dr. Smith, then Vice-Chancellor. The chief
ringleaders were Mr. Foord of Magdalen
Hall, and Mr. Thorne of Balliol College.
The Proctors, Mr. Atherton Bruch and Mr.
John Doughty, received their appeals, as if it
had not been perturbatio pacis, &c. The
Vice-Chancellor was forced in a statutable
way to appeal to the King. The King, with

all the Lords of his Council then present,
heard the cause at Woodstock, Aug. 23, 1631,
being Tuesday in the afternoon.   The sentence upon the hearing was: That Foord,
Thorne, and Hodges of Exeter College, should
be banished the University: and both the
Proctors were commanded to come into the
Convocation House, and there resign their
office; that two others might be named out
of the same Colleges.   Dr. Prideaux Rector
of Exeter College, and Dr. Wilkinson Principal of Magdalen Hall, received a sharp admonition for their misbehaviour in this business.
—Aug. 29, Monday. I went to Brentwood,
and the next day began my visitation there,
and so went on, and finished it.

Nov. 4, Friday.   The Lady Mary, Princess,
born at St. James's, inter horas quintam et
sextam matutinas.   It was thought she was
born three weeks before her time.—Dec. 25.
I preached at Court.

1632. Jan. 1. The extremest wet and warm
January that ever was known in memory.—
Feb. 15. I preached at Court: Ash-Wednes-

day.—Feb. 19. D. S. came to my chamber, troubled about going quite from Court at spring: First Sunday in Lent, after Sermon.—April 1. I preached at Court. Easter Day.—May 26, Saturday. Trinity Sunday Eve. I consecrated the Lord Treasurer's Chapel at Roehampton.—May 29, Tuesday. My meeting and settling upon express terms with K. B. in the Gallery at Greenwich. In which business God bless me.

June 15. Mr. Francis Windebank, my old friend, was sworn Secretary of State; which place I obtained for him of my gracious master King Charles.—June 18, Monday. I married my Lord Treasurer Weston's eldest son to the Lady Frances, daughter to the Duke of Lennox, at Roehampton.—June 25, Monday. D. S. with me at Fulham, cum Ma. &c.— *Junius.* This was the coldest June clean through, that was ever felt in my memory.

July 10, Tuesday. Dr. Juxon, then Dean of Worcester, at my suit sworn Clerk of his Majesty's Closet. That I might have one that I might trust near his Majesty, if I grow

weak or infirm; as I must have a time.—
July 17, Tuesday. I consecrated the Church
at Stanmore Magna in Middlesex, built by
Sir John Wolstenham. The cold summer;
harvest not in within forty miles of London
after Michaelmas, &c.

Dec. 2, Sunday. The small pox appeared
upon his Majesty; but, God be thanked, he
had a very gentle disease of it.—Dec. 27,
Thursday. The Earl of Arundel set forward
towards the Low Countries, to fetch the Queen
of Bohemia and her children.—Dec. 25. I
preached to the King. Christmas Day.

1633. Jan. 1. My being with K. B. this day
in the afternoon .... troubled me much; God
send me a good issue out of it. The warm
open Christmas.—Jan. 15, Tuesday. K. B.
and I unexpectedly came to some clearer
declaration of ourselves, which God bless.

Feb. 11, Monday night, till Tuesday morning, the great fire upon London Bridge.....
houses burnt down.—Feb. 13, Wednesday.
The Feoffees, that pretended to buy in Impropriations, were dissolved in the Chequer-

Chamber. They were the main instruments of the Puritan faction to undo the Church. The criminal part reserved. — Feb. 28, Thursday. Mr. Chancellor of London, Dr. Duck, brought me word how miserably I was slandered by some Separatists. I pray God give me patience, and forgive them.

March 6, Ash-Wednesday. I preached at Whitehall.

1633. April 13. The great business at the Council Table, &c. when the Earl of Holland made his submission to the King. ["We shall say no more of the Earl of Holland now, than that he neither loved the Marquis of Hamilton ..... nor Wentworth ....; nor the Archbishop of Canterbury; nor almost any thing that was then done in Church or State..... He was a very well bred man, and a fine gentleman in good times; but too much desired to enjoy ease and plenty, when the King could have neither; and did think poverty the most insupportable evil that could befal any man in this world." *Clarend. i.*

216. vi. 262.] This April was most extreme
wet, and cold, and windy.

May 10. A passage of my letters to the
Vice-Chancellor touching Formalities.

"This ensuing passage of my letters I desire
may be read to the Heads at the next meeting,
the rather because I know, and am sorry for
it, that divers things concerning Form, especially in the younger sort, are not in so good
order, as some men would make me believe
they are; and though you complain not much
yourself, yet I can hear by strangers, how the
market goes. For I am told by divers, that
though the Masters come very duly in caps,
which I am right glad to hear of; yet the
younger sort, which should be most in awe,
are least in order, and came not (divers of
them) to St. Mary's in that form, which they
ought to do. Which disorder of theirs cannot possibly be remedied by the care of the
Vice-Chancellor only, be it never so great.
But it must be done by the Heads in their
several Colleges, who must either punish such
as they find faulty, or put up their names to

the Vice-Chancellor, that he may. I thought
fit therefore, now before my entrance upon
this my long and tedious journey, to desire
you for the public, and every Head of
College and Hall in their several Houses
respectively, to see that the youth conform
themselves to the public discipline of the
University, that his Majesty, who is graciously
sensible of all the defects of that place, may at
his return hear a good and true report of
things amended there ; which, as it will much
advantage the place itself, so will it also much
advance the reputation of the several Governors in his Majesty's good opinion. And
particularly I pray see, that none, youth or
other, be suffered to go in boots and spurs,
or to wear their hair indecently long, or with
a lock in the present fashion, or with slashed
doublets, or in any light or garish colours.
And if Noblemen will have their sons court
it too soon, and be more in, that is, out of
fashion, than the rest, the fault shall be their
own, not mine ; but under that degree, I will
have no dispensation for any thing in this

kind. And it were very well, if they to whose trust they are committed, would fairly and seasonably take some occasion (especially hereafter at their first coming) to acquaint the Lords, their fathers, with the course of discipline in the University, that their sons may conform in every thing, as others do, during the time of their abode there, which will teach them to know differences of places and orders betimes; and when they grow up to be men, it will make them look back upon that place with honour to it, and reputation to you. And of this, and all other particulars of like nature, I shall look for an account from you, if God bless me with a safe return. In the mean time I commend my love heartily both to yourself, and to all the Heads, and desire mutual return of your prayers, as you have mine daily.

GUIL. LONDON.

May 10, 1633.

May 13, Monday. I set out of London to attend King Charles into Scotland.—May 24.

The King was to enter into York in state. The day was extreme windy and rainy, that he could not all day long. I called it *York Friday.*

June 6. I came to Berwick. That night I dreamed that K. B. sent to me in Westminster church, that he was now as desirous to see me, as I him, and that he was then entering into the church. I went with joy; but met another in the middle of the church, who seemed to know the business, and laughed. But K. B. was not there.—June 8, Saturday, Whitsun eve. I received letters from K. B. unalterable, &c. <u>By this, if I return, I shall see how true or false my dream is, &c.</u>— June 15, Saturday. I was sworn Counsellor of Scotland.—June 18, Tuesday after Trinity Sunday. King Charles crowned at Holyrood-Church in Edinburgh. I never saw more expressions of joy than were after it, &c.— June 19, Wednesday. I received second letters from K. B. no changeling, &c. Within three hours after, other letters from K. B. Believe all that I say, &c.—June 29, Friday.

Letters from K. B. no D. true, if not to my contentment, &c.—June 30. I preached to his Majesty in the Chapel in Holyrood-House in Edinburgh.

July 1, Monday. I went over Forth, to Brunt Island.—July 2, Tuesday. To St. Andrews.—July 3, Wednesday. Over Taye, to Dundee.—July 4, Thursday. To Faukland.

At the Vespers upon the 6th of July, Dr. Heylin, one of the Proceders, had these questions following out of the 20th Article of the Church of England.

"Ecclesia authoritatem habet in fidei controversiis determinandis.

"Ecclesia authoritatem habet interpretandi Sacras Scripturas.

"Ecclesia potestatem habet decernendi Ritus et Ceremonias."

Upon these questions Dr. Prideaux, then Professor, had these passages following, and were then offered to be avowed against him upon oath, if need were; and it happened that the Queen's Almoner was present. The passages were these:

" Ecclesia est mera chimæra.

" Ecclesia nihil docet nec determinat.

" Controversiæ omnes melius ad Academiam
" referri possunt, quam ad Ecclesiam.

" Docti homines in Academiis possunt de-
" terminare omnes controversias etiam seposi-
" tis Episcopis."

Upon an occasion of mentioning the absolute decree, he brake into a great and long
discourse, that his mouth was shut by authority, else he would maintain that truth contra
omnes qui sunt in vivis, which fetched a great
hum from the country Ministers, that were
there, &c.

These particulars by the command of his
Majesty I sent to Dr. Prideaux, and received
from him this answer following, and his
Protestation under his hand.

" Ecclesia authoritatem habet in fidei con-
" troversiis determinandis.

" Ecclesia authoritatem habet interpretandi
" Sacras Scripturas.

" Ecclesia potestatem habet decernendi
" Ritus et Ceremonias."

These questions I approved, when they were brought unto me, and wished the bedell, that brought them, to convey them to the Congregation to be allowed according to custom; conceiving them to be especially bent (according to the meaning of the Article cited) against Papal usurpations and Puritanical innovations, which I detest as much as any man; whereby it appears, what I positively hold concerning the authority of the Church in all the proposed particulars, namely, that which that 20th Article prescribeth, and not otherwise.

Certain passages that came from Dr. Prideaux in the discussing the questions at Oxford.

" Ecclesia est mera chimæra.

" Ecclesia nihil docet nec determinat.

" Controversiæ omnes melius ad Academ-" iam referri possunt, quam ad Ecclesiam.

" Docti homines in Academiis possunt de-" terminare omnes controversias, etiam sepo-" sitis Episcopis."

The passages, therefore, imperfectly catched

at by the informer, were no positions of mine. For I detest them, as they are laid, for impious and ridiculous. But oppositions according to my place, proposed for the further clearing of the truth, to which the Respondent was to give satisfaction; and the General Protestation I hope takes off all that can be laid against me in the particulars.

Notwithstanding, to touch on each of them, as they are laid.

To the first, I never said the Church was " Mera chimæra," as it is, or hath a being, and ought to be believed; but as the Respondent by his answer made it. In which I conceived him to swerve from the Article, whence his questions were taken.

To the second, my argument was to this purpose; " Omnis actio est suppositorum vel singularium; ergo Ecclesia in abstracto nil docet aut determinat, sed per hos aut illos Episcopos, Pastores, Doctores:" as, " Homo non disputat, sed Petrus et Johannes," &c.

The third and fourth may be well put together. My prosecution was, That the

Universities are eminent parts and seminaries of the Church, and had fitter opportunity to discuss controversies, than divers other assemblies. Not by any means to determine them, but to prepare them for the determination of ecclesiastical assemblies, of Synods, Councils, Bishops, that have superior authority, wherein they might do service to the Church and those superiors; not prescribing any thing unto them. As the debating of a thing by a learned counsellor makes the easier passage for the Bench's sentence. And this was urged only " commodum," not as " necessarium."

The QUEEN's ALMONER present.

I am told no. For he departed, as they say that were in the seat with him, being tired as it should seem by the tedious preface of the Respondent, before the disputations began: but be it so or otherwise, to what purpose this is interposed, I know not.

Upon an occasion of mentioning the absolute decree, he brake into a great and long discourse, that his mouth was shut by authority, else he would maintain the truth "contra omnes, qui sunt in vivis;" which fetched a great hum from the country Ministers that were there, &c.

This argument was unexpectedly cast in by Mr. Smith of St. John's, but bent, as I took it, against somewhat I have written in that behalf; which the Respondent not endeavouring to clear, I was put upon it to shew, in what sense I took "absolutum decretum;" which indeed I said I was ready to maintain against any, as my predecessors in that place had done. This was not in a long discourse, as it is suggested; but in as short a solution, as is usually brought in schools to a doubt on the bye. And from this I took off the opponent's farther proceeding in obedience to authority. Whereupon, if a hum succeeded, it was more than I used to take notice of. It might be as well of dislike as approbation, and of other auditors, as soon as country Ministers. A hiss I am sure was given before, when the Respondent excluded the King and

Parliament from being parts of the Church. But I remember whose practice it is to be κατήγορος τῶν ἀδελφῶν. I had rather bear and forbear, and end with this.

PROTESTATION.

THAT as I believe the Catholic Church in my Creed, so I reverence this Church of England, wherein I have had my baptism and whole breeding, as a most eminent member of it. To the doctrine and discipline of this Church have I hitherto often subscribed, and by God's grace constantly adhered; and resolve by the same assistance, according to my ability, (under his Majesty's protection,) faithfully to maintain against Papists, Puritans, or any other that shall oppose it. The Prelacy of our Reverend Bishops in it I have ever defended in my place to be "jure Divino," which I dare say has been more often, and with greater pains-taking, than most of those have done, who have received greater encouragement from their Lordships. I desire nothing but the continuance of my vocation in a peaceable course, that after all my pains in the place of his Majesty's Professor almost for these eighteen years together, my sons especially be not countenanced in my declining age to vilify and vex me. So shall I spend the remainder of my time in hearty prayer for his Majesty, my only master and patron, for the Reverend Bishops, the State, and all his Majesty's subjects and affairs, and continue my utmost endeavours to do all faithful service to the Church, wherein I live. To whose authority I ever have, and do hereby submit myself and studies to be according to God's word directed or corrected.

J. PRIDEAUX.

July 7, Sunday. To St. Johnston.—July 8, Monday. To Dunblaine, and Sterling. My dangerous and cruel journey, crossing part of the Highlands by coach, which was a wonder there.—July 9, Tuesday. To Lithgow, and so to Edinburgh.—July 10, Wednesday. His Majesty's dangerous passage from Brunt Island to Edinburgh.—July

11, Thursday. I began my journey from Edinburgh towards London. — July 12, Friday. That night at Anderweek, I dreamed that L. L. came and offered to sit above me at the Co. Ta. and that L. H. came in, and placed him there.—July 20, Saturday. The King came from Scotland to Greenwich; having come post from Berwick in four days.—July 26, Friday. I came to my house at Fulham from Scotland. —July 28, Sunday. K. B. and I met. All the strange discourses mistaken. And that which was a very high tide at ———, was then the lowest ebb at Greenwich that ever I saw. I went away much troubled. But all settled again well, August 3, Saturday following.

August 4, Sunday. News came to Court of the Lord Archbishop of Canterbury's death, and the King resolved presently to give it me. 'Which he did, August 6.—August 4. That very morning, at Greenwich, there came one to me, seriously, and that avowed ability to perform it, and offered me to be a

Cardinal. I went presently to the King, and acquainted him both with the thing and the person.—August 7, Wednesday. An absolute settlement between me and K. B. after I had made known my cause at large. God bless me in it.—August 14, Wednesday. A report brought to me, that I was poisoned. —August 17, Saturday. I had a serious offer made to me again to be a Cardinal: I was then from Court, but so soon as I came thither, (which was Wednesday, August 21,) I acquainted his Majesty with it. But my answer again was, that somewhat dwelt within me, which would not suffer that, till Rome were other than it is.—August 25, Sunday. My election to the Archbishopric was returned to the King, then being at Woodstock.

Sept. 19, Thursday. I was translated to the Archbishopric of Canterbury. The Lord made me able, &c. The day before, viz. Sept. 18, when I first went to Lambeth, my coach, horses, and men sunk to the bottom of the Thames in the ferry-boat, which

was overladen; but I praise God for it, I
lost neither man nor horse. A wet summer, and by it a casual harvest. The rainy
weather continuing till Nov. 14, which made
a marvellous ill seed-time. There was barley
about this year, within thirty miles of London,
at the end of October.

Nov. 13, Wednesday. Richard Boyer, who
had formerly named himself Lodowick, was
brought into the Star-Chamber, for most
grossly misusing me, and accusing me of no
less than treason, &c. He had broke prison
for felony, when he did this. His censure
is upon record; and God forgive him. About
the beginning of this month, the Lady Davis
prophesied against me, that I should very
few days outlive the fifth of November.
And a little after that, one Green came into
the Court at St. James's, with a great sword
by his side, swearing, the King should do
him justice against me, or he would take
another course with me. All the wrong I
ever did this man was, that being a poor
printer, I procured him of the Company of

the Stationers, £5 a year during his life. God preserve me, and forgive him. He was committed to Newgate.—Nov. 24, Sunday in the afternoon I christened King Charles's second son, James Duke of York, at St. James's.

Dec. 10 and 29. Twice or thrice in the interim, I advertised his Majesty of the falsehood and practice that was against me, by L. T. &c. This brake out then.

1634. Jan. 1. The way to do the town of Reading good for their poor; which may be compassed by God's blessing upon me, though my wealth be small. And I hope God will bless me in it, because it was His own motion in me. For this way never came into my thoughts (though I had much beaten them about it) till this night, as I was at my prayers. Amen, Lord.

March 30, Palm Sunday. I preached to the King at Whitehall.

May 13. I received the seals of my being chose Chancellor of the University of Dublin in Ireland. To which office I was chosen Sept. 14, 1633. There were now, and some-

what before, great factions in Court; and
I doubt many private ends followed to the
prejudice of public service.   Good Lord,
preserve me!

June 11.   Mr. Prynne sent me a very
libellous letter, about his censure in the Star-
Chamber for his Histriomastix, and what I
said at that censure; in which he hath many
ways mistaken me, and spoken untruth of me.
—June 16. I shewed this letter to the King;
and by his command sent it to Mr. Attorney
Noye.—June 17. Mr. Attorney sent for Mr.
Prynne to his chamber; shewed him the
letter, asked him whether it were his hand.
Mr. Prynne said, he could not tell, unless
he might read it. The letter being given
into his hand, he tore it into small pieces,
threw it out at the window, and said, that
should never rise in judgment against him:
fearing, it seems an ore tenus for this.—June
18. Mr. Attorney brought him, for this, into
the Star-Chamber; where all this appeared
with shame enough to Mr. Prynne.   I there
forgave him, &c.

To my very loving friends, the Vice-Chancellor, the Doctors, the Proctors, and the rest of the Convocation of the University of Oxford.

After my hearty commendations, &c.

The Statutes of the University, so often and by so many undertaken and left again, are now by God's blessing, and the great pains of them, to whom that care was committed, brought to perfection. This work, I hope, God will so bless, as that it may much improve the honour and good government of that place; a thing very necessary in this age both for Church and Commonwealth, since so many young gentlemen, and others of all ranks and conditions, have their first breeding for the public in that seminary. To save the purse of the University, and to gain time, it was thought fit rather to print, than to transcribe so many copies as might serve for the present necessary use of the University and the several Colleges and Halls respectively. And, for my part, I thought it expedient, that in every House they might have the rule of the public government by them, and so see the way to their duty: which being as much for their particular good, as the advance of the public service, every man, I hope, will be most willing and ready to conform himself to that, which is required of him. There is to be a great ledger book written out fair, which is to be the authentic copy under seal, and to rest in Archivis, to be the future judge of all Statutes, which may hereafter be corruptly either printed or transcribed. But before this be written, I hold it very expedient to put these Statutes (as they are now corrected and set in order) into practice and execution for the space of one whole year, to the end it may better appear, if any necessary thing have slipped the care of myself, and those whom the University trusted with me. For then if any such thing was discovered, it may easily be amended in the margin, or otherwise, of these printed books. And after this experience made, the authentic copy may be written fair, without any interlining or other blemish, and so be a rule to posterity of greater credit. These are therefore according to the power given unto me by an Act, with full consent in Convocation, bearing date in August, 1683, to declare and publish to the University, and every Member thereof, that the Statutes now printed are and shall be the Statutes, by which that University shall be governed for this year ensuing, that is, until the Feast of St. Michael the Archangel, which shall be in the year of our Lord God 1635, reserving to myself power, according to the decree before mentioned, to add or alter that, which shall be fit, and take away from these Statutes, or any of them, that, which shall be found by this intervening practice to be either unnecessary or incommodious for that government. And then, (God willing,) at or before that time I will discharge the trust, which the University hath commended to me, and absolutely make a settlement of the Statutes for future times, even as long as it shall please God to bless them with use and continuance. And I account it not the least of God's blessings upon myself, that He hath given me strength and ability to do this service for my ancient mother, the University, whom I have ever so much honoured, and am still ready to serve. And thus much comfort I can already give you, that his Majesty being made acquainted by me, that the work was finished, expressed extraordinary contentment in it, and commanded me to let you know so much, and withal that he doubts not of your ready obedience to them: than which nothing can from thence be more acceptable to him. Thus assuring myself, that you will all strive to yield full obedience to these your Statutes, which will be your own honour as well as the University's, I leave you to God's blessed protection and rest.

Your very loving friend and Chancellor,

W. CANT.

July 18, 1634.

July 26. I received word from Oxford, that the Statutes were accepted, and published, according to my letters, in the Convocation House that week.

Aug. 9, Saturday. Mr. William Noye, his Majesty's Attorney-General, died at Brentford, circa horam noctis decimam. And Sunday morning, Aug. 19, his servant brought me word of it to Croydon, before I was out of my bed. I have lost a dear friend of him, and the Church the greatest she had of his condition, since she needed any such.—Aug. 11. One Rob. Seal of St. Alban's came to me to Croydon; told me somewhat wildly about a vision he had at Shrovetide last, about not preaching the word sincerely to the people. And a hand appeared unto him, and death; and a voice bid him go tell it the Metropolitan of Lambeth, and made him swear he would do so; and I believe the poor man was overgrown with phantasy. So I troubled not myself further with him or it.—Aug. 30, Saturday. At Oatlands the Queen sent for me, and gave me thanks for a business, with which she trusted me; her promise then, that she would be my friend, and that I should have immediate address to her, when I had occasion.

Sept. 30. I had almost fallen into a fever with a cold I took; and it held me above three weeks.

Oct. 20. The extreme hot and faint October and November, save three days frost, the dryest and fairest time. The leaves not all off the trees at the beginning of December. The waters so low, that the barges could not pass. God bless us in the Spring, after this green Winter.

December 1, Monday. My ancient friend, E. R. came to me, and performed great kindness, which I may not forget.—Dec. 4. I visited the Arches, it was Thursday.—Dec. 10, Wednesday. That night the frost began, the Thames almost frozen; and it continued until the Sunday sevennight after.—Dec. 15, X. E. R.

1635. January 8, Thursday. I married the Lord Charles Herbert and the Lady Mary, daughter to the Duke of Buckingham, in the Closet at Whitehall.—Jan. 5, Monday night, being Twelfth Eve, the frost began again; the Thames was frozen over, and continued so till Feb. 3. A mighty flood at the thaw.

Feb. 5, Thursday. I was put into the great Committee of Trade and the King's Revenue, &c.

March 1, Sunday. The great business, which the King commanded me to think on, and gave him account, and L. T.—March 14, Saturday. I was named one of the Commissioners for the Exchequer, upon the death of Richard Lord Weston, Lord High Treasurer of England. That evening K. B. sent to speak with me at Whitehall; a great deal of free and clear expressions, if it will continue.—March 16, Monday. I was called against the next day into the foreign Committee, by the King. — March 22, Palm Sunday. I preached to the King at Whitehall.

April 9, Wednesday, and from thenceforward, all in firm kindness between K. B. and me.

May 18, Whitsun Monday. At Greenwich, my account to the Queen put off till

Trinity Sunday, May 24, then given her by myself. And assurance of all that was desired by me, &c.—May, June, and July. In these months, the troubles at the Commission for the Treasury, and the difference, which happened between the Lord Cottington and myself, &c.

Vestris mihi amicissimis Dri. Pinck, Vice-Cancellario, aliisque Doctoribus, Procuratoribus, necnon singulis in Domo Convocationis intra Almam Universitatem Oxon. congregatis.

S. in Christo.

Salus vestra mihi in primis votis, et (ut ita dicam) suprema semper lex fuit; post salutem honos. Hinc a Cancellariatu meo dicam, an vestro (nam non petenti, imo contra nitenti, summa et singulari vestrâ benevolentiâ collatus est) omnem navavi operam, ut vestra sive Statuta, sive Privilegia, sive alia cujuscunque generis negotia, quæ, meam manum exposcerent, ad optatum finem facile et plenis velis perducerentur. Siquæ restant adhuc non indulta, aut non satis confirmata, potestis

(nil dubito) a Rege Serenissimo, Ecclesiæ et
Academiis addictissimo, non frustra expectare.
Vos saltem prudenter circumspicite, quid ulte-
rius in vestram gratiam possim, antequam fato
fungi et ad Deum meum redire detur.

Et quia annis jam ingravescentibus, melius
videtur sarcinam deponere, quam mole ejus
opprimi, exuvias quasdam meas vobis præ-
misi; ipse, quum Deus vocaverit, sequuturus.
Exuere autem primo placuit libros manu-
scriptos. Quid enim mihi cum illis, cui nec
otium datur vel inspicere? Et si daretur, nec
oculi ad perlegendum satis firmi, nec memoria
ad retinendum satis fida reperitur. Nostris
enim inter exteriores sensus oculos, et inter
interiores facultates memoriam primo senec-
tutem et prodere et fallere. Libros igitur
hosce malui vivus dare vobis clarissimis filiis,
quam testamento legare mortuus, tum ob
alias causas, tum etiam ob hanc, ne manus
aliqua media furtiva forte selectiores præ-
riperet.

Mitto autem nec tot, nec tales, ut vestris
studiis dignos existimem, sed quales amor

meus, et erga communem matrem pietas parare potuerunt; mitto tamen (ut per catalogum, quem una misi, constabit) Hebraica volumina manuscripta quatuordecim, Arabica quinquaginta quinque, Persica septemdecim, Turcica quatuor, Russica sex, Armenica duo, Chinensia duodecim, Græca quadraginta quatuor, Italica tria, Gallica totidem, Anglicana quadraginta sex, Latina supra bis centum, præter alia quadraginta sex, sed recentiora, et e Collegio Herbipolensi in Germania tempore belli suecici desumpta.

Hos libros, amoris mei testes, vestra fidei committo, in Bibliothecâ reponendos, hâc conditione, ut nunquam inde extrahantur, vel mutuo cuipiam dentur sub quocunque prætextu, *nisi solum, ut typis mandentur*, et sic publici et juris, et utilitatis fiant, nec tamen illum in finem, nisi data prius cautione a Vice-Cancellario, et Procuratoribus approbanda, et ut statim a prælo locis suis in Bibliothecâ prædicta restituantur, ut cautio istæc libros hosce a furibus, et conditio ista eosdem a Blattis Tineisque tutos conservare possit; quibus aliter præda futuri sunt, dum suo pulvere situque sepulti jaceant. Siqui alii libri similes, aut meliores ad meas forte manus pervenerint, eos etiam ad vos mittendos curabo, sub eadem conditione, et eodem loco figendos.

Nolo alia negotia libris immiscere; sed omnia nobis prospera corde, quo decet, pio exoptans, Academiam illam et vosmetipsos omnes et singulos, speciali Dei gratiæ commendo.

Cancellarius vester et amicus,

W. Cant.

Datum ex ædibus meis Lambethanis, Maii 22, 1635.

July 11, Saturday, and July 22, Wednesday. Two sad meetings with K. B. and how occasioned. — July 12, Sunday. At Theobalds, the soap business was ended, and settled again upon the new Corporation, against my offer for the old soap boilers; yet my offer made the King's profit double; and to that, after two years, the new Corporation was raised; how it is performed,

let them look to it, whom his Majesty shall
be pleased to trust with his Treasurer's staff.
In this business and some other of great consequence, during the Commission for the
Treasury, my old friend Sir F. W. forsook
me, and joined with the Lord Cottington;
which put me to the exercise of a great deal
of patience, &c.

Aug. 16, Sunday night. Most extreme
thunder and lightning. The lightning so
thick, bright, and frequent, I do not remember that I ever saw.

Sept. 2, Wednesday. I was in attendance
upon the King at Woodstock, and went thence
to Cuddesden, to see the house which Dr. John
Bancrof, then Lord Bishop of Oxford, had
there built, to be a house for the Bishops of
that See for ever. He having built that
house at my persuasion.—Sept. 3, Thursday.
I went privately from the Bishop of Oxford's
house at Cuddesden, to St. John's in Oxford,
to see my building there, and give some
directions for the last finishing of it; and
returned the same night, staying there not

two hours.—Sept. 23, Wednesday. I went to St. Paul's to view the building, and returned that night to Croydon.—Sept. 24. Scalding Thursday.—Sept. 29. The Earl of Arundel brought an old man out of Shropshire. He was this present Michaelmas-day shewed to the King and the Lords, for a man of 152 or 153 years of age.

Oct. 26, Monday. This morning, between four and five of the clock, lying at Hampton Court, I dreamed, that I was going out in haste, and that when I came into my outer chamber, there was my servant Will. Pennell, in the same riding-suit which he had on that day sevennight at Hampton-Court with me. Methought I wondered to see him, (for I left him sick at home,) and asked him how he did, and what he made there. And that he answered me, he came to receive my blessing; and with that fell on his knees. That hereupon I laid my hand on his head, and prayed over him, and therewith awaked. When I was up, I told this to them of my chamber; and added, that I should find Pennell dead or dying. My coach came; and when I came home, I found him past sense, and giving up the ghost. So my prayers (as they have frequently before) commended him to God.

Nov. 15, Sunday, at afternoon, the greatest tide that had been seen. It came within my gates, walks, cloisters, and stables, at Lambeth. — Nov. 21, Saturday. Charles Count Elector Palatine came to Whitehall to the King. This month the plague, which was hot in some parts of France and in the Low Countries, and Flanders, began at Greenwich. God be merciful unto us!—Nov. 30, Saint Andrew's day, Monday. Charles Prince Elector Palatine, the King's nephew, was with me at Lambeth, and at solemn evening prayer.

Dec. 1. Many elm-leaves yet upon the trees; which few men have seen.—Dec. 14, Monday. Charles Prince Elector came suddenly upon me, and dined with me at Lambeth. — Dec. 25, Christmas-Day. Charles Prince Elector received the Communion with the King at Whitehall. He kneeled a little beside on his left hand. He sate before the Communion upon a stool by the wall, before the traverse; and had another stool and a cushion before him to kneel at.—Dec. 28, Monday, Innocents'-day, about ten at night, the Queen was delivered at St. James's of a daughter, Princess Elizabeth. I christened her on Saturday following, Jan. 2.

Feb. 2, Tuesday, Candlemas-day. My nearer care of J. S. was professed, and his promise to be guided by me, and absolutely settled on Friday after, Feb. 5.

To My Lord of Winchester, concerning New College, Oxford.

" Another business there is, which I think may be very well worthy your consideration; and if you do not give it remedy, (as I think it abundantly deserves,) I do not know who either can or will. I have often wondered, why so many good scholars came from Winchester to New College, and yet so few of them afterwards prove eminent men: and while I lived in Oxford, I thought upon

divers things, that might be causes of it, and
I believe true ones; but I have lately heard
of another, which I think hath done and
doth the College a great deal of harm, in
the breeding of their young men. When
they come from Winchester they are to be
Probationers two years, and then Fellows.
A man would think those two years, and
some years after, should be allowed to Logic,
Philosophy, Mathematics, and the like
grounds of learning, the better to enable
them to study Divinity with judgment. But
I am of late accidentally come to know, that
when the Probationers stand for their Fellowships, and are to be examined how they
have profited; one chief thing in which they
are examined is, how diligently they have
read Calvin's Institutions; and are more
strictly held to it, how they have profited in
that, than almost in any kind of learning
besides. I do not deny but that Calvin's
Institutions may profitably be read, and as
one of their first books for Divinity, when
they are well grounded in other learning;

resolve
Latin

but to begin with it so soon, I am afraid doth
not only hinder them from all grounds of
judicious learning, but also too much possess
their judgments before they are able to judge,
and makes many of them humorous in, if not
against, the Church. For so many of them
have proved in this latter age, since my own
memory in that University. Your Lordship
is Visitor there, and I think you cannot do a
better deed, than to advise on a way, how to
break this business with the Warden, who is
a learned and discreet man, and then think
upon some remedy for it For I am verily
persuaded, it doth that College a great deal
of harm. I do not hold it fit that your Lordship should fall upon this business too suddenly. When the Warden comes next to
the election, may be a fit time; nor would
I have you let it be known, that you have
received this information from me; but sure
I am 'tis true, and needs a remedy.

W. CANT."

Feb. 2, 1635.

Feb. 14, Sunday night. My honest old

servant, Richard Robinson, died of an apoplexy. — Feb. 28. 1 consecrated Dr. Roger
Manwaring, Bishop of St. David's.

March 6, Sunday. William Juxon, Lord
Bishop of London, made Lord High Treasurer of England. No Churchman had it
since Henry VII.'s time. I pray God bless
him to carry it so, that the Church may have
honour, and the King and the State service
and contentment by it. And now if the
Church will not hold up themselves under
God; I can do no more.

Archbishop Laud's Letter to Sir Kenelm Digby.

Salutem in Christo.

Worthy Sir,

I am sorry for all the contents of your
Letter, save that which expresses your love
to me. And I was not a little troubled at
the very first words of it. For you begin,
that my Lord Ambassador told you, I was
not pleased to hear you had made a defection
from the Church of England. It is most
true, I was informed so; and thereupon I

writ to my Lord Ambassador, to know what
he heard of it there.   But it is true likewise,
that I writ to yourself; and Mr. Secretary
Cooke sent my Letters very carefully.   Now
seeing your Letters mentioned my Lord
Ambassador's speech with you, without any
notice taken of my writing; I could not but
fear these Letters of mine came not to your
hands.   Out of this fear, your second Letters
took me; for they acknowledged the receipt
of mine, and your kind acceptance of them.
Had they miscarried, I should have held it
a great misfortune.   For you must needs have
condemned me deeply in your own thoughts,
if in such a near and tender business, I should
have solicited my Lord Ambassador, and not
written to yourself.

In the next place I thank you, and take it
for a great testimony of your love to me,
that you have been pleased to give me so
open and clear account of your proceedings
with yourself in this matter of religion.   In
which as I cannot but commend the strict
reckoning, to which you have called yourself;

so I could have wished, before you had absolutely settled the foot of that account, you would have called in some friend, and made use of his eye as a bye-stander, who oftentimes sees more than he that plays the game. You write, I confess, that after you had fallen upon these troublesome thoughts, you were nigh two years in the diligent discussion of this matter; and that you omitted no industry, either of conversing with learned men, or of reading the best authors, to beget in you a right intelligence of this subject. I believe all this, and you did wisely to do it. But I have some questions, out of the freedom of a friend, to ask about it. Were not all the learned men, you conversed with for this particular, of the Roman party? Were not the best authors, you mention, of the same side? If both men and authors were the same way; can they beget any righter intelligence in you, than is in themselves? If they were men and authors on both sides, with whom you conversed; why was I (whom you are pleased to style one of your best friends) omitted? True, it may be, you could not reckon me among those learned men and able for direction, with whom you conversed: suppose that; yet yourself accounts me among your friends. And is it not many times as useful, when thoughts are distracted, to make use of the freedom and openness of a friend not altogether ignorant, as of those which are thought more learned; but not so free, nor perhaps so indifferent?

But the result, you say, that first began to settle you, was, that you discerned by this your diligent conversation, and studious reading, that there were great mistakings on both sides, and that passion and affection to a party, transported too many of those that entered into the lists in this quarrel. Suppose this also to be true, I am heartily sorry, and have been ever since I was of any understanding in matters of religion, to hear of sides in the Church. And I make no doubt, but it will one day fall heavy upon all, that wilfully make, or purposely continue, sidings in that body. But when sides are

made and continued, remember you confess
there are great mistakings on both sides.
And how then can you go from one side to
the other, but you must go from one great
mistaking to another? And if so, then by
changing the side, you do but change the
mistaking, not quit yourself from mistakes.
And if you do quit yourself from them, by
God's goodness, and your own strength; yet
why might not that have been done without
changing the side; since mistakes are on
both sides? As for the passion and transport-
ation of many that enter the lists of this
quarrel; I am sure you mean not to make
their passion your guide; for that would
make you mistake indeed. And why then
should their passion work upon your judgment? especially, since the passion as well as
the mistakes are confessed to be on both sides.

After this follows the main part of your
Letters, and that which principally resolved
you to enter again the communion of the
Church of Rome, in which you had been
born and bred, against that semblance of

good reason, which formerly had made you adhere to the Church of England.

And first you say, you now perceive that you may preserve yourself in that Church, without having your belief bound up in several particulars, the dislike whereof had been a motive to you to free yourself from the jurisdiction which you conceived did impose them. It is true all Churches have some particulars free. But doth that Church leave you free to believe, or not believe, any thing determined in it? And did not your former dislike arise from some things determined in and by that Church? And if so, what freedom see you now, that you saw not then? And you cannot well say, that your dislike arose from any thing not determined; for in those, the jurisdiction of that Church imposes not.

You add, that your greatest difficulties were solved, when you could distinguish between the opinions of some new men raised upon wrested inferences, and the plain and solid articles of faith delivered at the first.

Why, but I cannot but be confident you could distinguish these long since, and long before you joined yourself to the Church of England. And that therefore your greatest difficulties (if these were they) were as fully and fairly solved then, as now they are, or can be. Besides, if by these plain and solid Articles you mean none but the Creed, (and certainly no other were delivered at the first,) you seem to intimate by comparing this and the former passage, that so you believe these plain and first Articles, you may preserve yourself in that Church, from having your belief bound up to other particulars; which I think few will believe, besides yourself, if you can believe it. And the opinions of new men, and the wrested inferences upon these, are some of those great mistakes which you say are on both sides, and therefore needed not to have caused your change.

To these first Articles you say, The Church in no succeeding age hath power to add (as such) the least tittle of new doctrine. Be it so; and I believe it heartily, (not as such,) especially if you mean the Articles of the Creed. But yet if that Church do maintain, that all her decisions in a General Council, are Articles Fidei Catholicæ, and that all Christians are bound to believe all and every one of them, eâdem Fide, quâ Fidei Articulos; and that he is an heretic which believes them not all; where is then your freedom, or your not being bound up in several particulars? And if you reply, you dislike no determination which that Church hath made; then why did you formerly leave it, to free yourself from that jurisdiction that you conceived imposed them? For if the things which troubled you were particulars not determined, they were not imposed upon your belief. And if they were determined, and so imposed; how are you now set free more than then?

You say again, You see now, that to be a Catholic, doth not deprive them of the fore-named liberty, who have abilities to examine the things you formerly stuck at, and drive them up to their first principles. But first then; what shall become of their liberty,

who are not able to examine? shall they
enthral their consciences? Next; what shall
secure them, who think themselves, and are
perhaps thought by others, able to examine,
yet indeed are not? Thirdly; what assurance is there in cases not demonstrable, (as
few things in religion are,) that they which
are able to examine, have either no affection
to blind their judgment, or may not mistake
themselves and their way in driving a doubtful point to its first principles? Lastly; how
much doth this differ from leaning upon a
private spirit, so much cried out against by
that side, when men, under pretence of their
ability, shall examine the tenets of the Church,
and assume a liberty to themselves under
colour of not being bound?

But, you say, this is not the breaking of
any obligation that the Church lays upon
you; but only an exact understanding of the
just and utmost obligations that side ties men
to. I must here question again. For, first,
what shall become of their freedom, that
cannot reach to this exact understanding?

And next, do not you make yourself, as a private man, judge of the Church's obligations upon you? And is it not as great an usurpation upon the Church's power and right, to be judge of her obligations, as of her tenets? For if the points be left free, there is no obligation; nor can you, or need any other, have any scruple. But if the points be binding by the predetermination of the Church, can you any way be judge of her obligation, but you must be judge also of the point to which she obliges? Now, I think, that the Church will hardly give liberty to any private man to be so far her judge, since she scarce allows so much to any, as judicium discretionis, in things determined by her.

These utmost obligations, to which that side ties men, you believe many men (and not of the meanest note) pass over in gross, without ever throughly entering into the due consideration thereof. And truly I believe so too, that among too many men on both sides, neither the points nor the obligations to them are weighed as they ought. But that is no warrant (pardon my freedom) that yourself hath considered them in all circumstances, or that you have considered them better now than you did before, when the dislike of that imposing jurisdiction was your first motive to free yourself from it. by joining to the Church of England.

And whereas you say, that you have returned into that Communion, who from your birth had right of possession in you, and therefore ought to continue it, unless clear and evident proof (which you say surely cannot be found) should have evicted you from it: truly, Sir, I think this had been spoken with more advantage to you and your cause, before your adhering to the Church of England, than now; for then right of possession could not have been thought little. But now, since you deserted that Communion, either you did it upon clear and evident proof, or upon apparent only. If you did it then upon clear and evident proof, why say you now no such can be found? If you did it but upon apparent and seeming proof, (a semblance of very good reason as yourself calls it,) why did you then come off from that Communion, till your proof were clear and evident? And why may not that, which now seems clear and evident, be but apparent, as well as that, which then seemed clear unto you, be but semblance now? Nor would I have you say, that clear and evident proof cannot be found for a man, in this case of religion, to forego the Communion which had right of possession in him from his birth; for the proposition is an universal negative, and of hard proof. And therefore, though I think I know you and your judgment so well, that I may not without manifest wrong charge you, that you did in this great action, and so nearly concerning you, ad pauca respicere, which our great master tells us breeds facile and easy, rather than safe and warrantable determinations, yet it will be upon you not only in honour without, but also in conscience within, to be able to assure yourself that you did ad plurima, if not ad omnia respicere.

The thing being so weighty in itself, and

the miserable division of Christendom (never
sufficiently to be lamented) making the doubt
so great, that you who have been on both
sides, must needs be under the dispute of
both sides, whether this last act of yours, be
not in you rather a relapse into a former
sickness, than a recovery from a former fall.

But against this, the temper of your mind
(you say) arms you against all censures, no
slight air of reputation being able to move
you.   In this, I must needs say, you are
happy : for he that can be moved from himself by the changeable breath of men, lives
more out of than in himself; and (which
is a misery beyond all expression) must in
all doubts go to other men for resolution ;
not to himself; as if he had no soul within
him.   But yet post conscientiam fama.   And
though I would not desire to live by reputation ; yet would I leave no good means
untried, rather than live without it.   And
how far you have brought yourself in question,
tion, which of these two, conscience or reputation, you have shaken by this double

change, I leave yourself to judge; because you say your first was with a semblance of very good reason. And though you say again, that it now appears you were then misled; yet you will have much ado to make the world think so.

The way you took in concealing this your resolution of returning into that Communion, and the reasons which you give why you so privately carried it here, I cannot but approve. They are full of all ingenuity, tender and civil respects, fitted to avoid discontent in your friends, and scandal that might be taken by others, or contumely that might be returned upon yourself. And as are these reasons, so is the whole frame of your Letter (setting aside that I cannot concur in judgment) full of discretion and temper, and so like yourself, that I cannot but love even that which I dislike in it. And though I shall never be other than I have been to the worth of Sir Kenelm Digby; yet most heartily sorry I am, that a man whose discourse did so much content me, should thus slide away from me, before I had so much as suspicion to awaken me, and suggest that he was going. Had you put me into a dispensation, and communicated your thoughts to me before they had grown up into resolutions, I am a priest, and would have put on what secresy you should have commanded. A little knowledge I have, (God knows a little,) I would have ventured it with you in that serious debate you have had with yourself. I have ever honoured you, since I knew your worth, and I would have done all offices of a friend to keep you nearer than now you are. But since you are gone, and settled another way, before you would let me know it, I know not now what to say to a man of judgment; and so resolved: for to what end should I treat, when a resolution is set already? So set, as that you say no clear and evident proof can be found against it: nor can I tell how to press such a man as you to ring the changes in religion. In your power it was not to change; in mine it is not to make you change again. Therefore to the moderation of your own heart, under the grace of God, I must and do now leave you for matter of religion; but retaining still with me, and entirely, all the love and friendliness which your worth won from me; well knowing, that all differences in opinion shake not the foundations of religion.

Now to your Postscript, and then I have done. That I am the first, and the only person to whom you have written thus freely: I thank you heartily for it. For I cannot conceive any thing thereby, but your great respect to me, which hath abundantly spread itself all over your Letter. And had you written this to me, with a restraint of making it further known, I should have performed that trust: but since you have submitted it to me, what further knowledge of it I shall think fit to give to any other person; I have, as I took myself bound, acquainted his Majesty with it, who gave a great deal of very good expression concerning you, and is not a little sorry to lose

the service of so able a subject. I have likewise made it known in private to Mr. Secretary Cook, who was as confident of you as
myself. I could hardly believe your own
Letters, and he as hardly my relation. To
my Secretary I must needs trust it, having
not time to write it again out of my scribbled
copy; but I dare trust the secresy in which
I have bound him. To others I am silent,
and shall so continue, till the thing open
itself; and I shall do it out of reasons, very
like to those which you give, why yourself
would not divulge it here. In the last place,
you promise yourself, that the condition you
are in will not hinder me from continuing
to be the best friend you have. To this
I can say no more, than that I could never
arrogate to myself to be your best friend;
but a poor, yet respective friend of yours
I have been, ever since I knew you: and it
is not your change, that can change me, who
never yet left, but where I was first forsaken;
and not always there. So praying for
God's blessing upon you, and in that way

which He knows most necessary for you,
I rest,

Your very loving friend,

To serve you in Domino.

Lambeth, March 27, 1636.

I have writ this Letter freely; I shall look
upon all the trust that ever you mean to carry
with me, that you shew it not, nor deliver
any copy to any man. Nor will I look for
any answer to the Queries I have herein
made. If they do you any good, I am glad;
if not, yet I have satisfied myself. But
leisure I have none, to write such Letters;
nor will I entertain a quarrel in this wrangling age; and now my strength is past. For
all things of moment in this Letter, I have
pregnant places in the Council of Trent,
Thomas, Bellarmin, Stapleton, Valentia, &c.
But I did not mean to make a volume of
a Letter.

Endorsed this with the Archbishop's own
hand. March 27, 1636.

April 7, Thursday. The Bill came in this day, that two died of the plague in Whitechapel. God bless us through the year! An extreme dry and hot April and May, till the middle of June.

May 16, Monday. The settlement between L. M. St. and me. God bless me, &c.—May 17, Tuesday. I visited the Dean and Chapter of St. Paul's, London, &c.—May 19, Thursday. The agreement between me and L. K. Ch. which began very strangely, and ended just as I thought it would.

June 21, Tuesday. My hearing before the King about my right to visit both the Universities Jure Metropolitico. It was ordered with me: the hearing was at Hampton-Court. —June 22, Wednesday. The Statutes of Oxford finished, and published in Convocation.

These Letters were read in Convocation upon the 22d of June, 1636, wherein Mr. Secretary Cook made a weighty speech fitting the occasion, and so likewise did the Vice-Chancellor. Mr. Secretary's speech follows in hæc verba.

Reverend Vice-Chancellor, Doctors, and
   Masters,

You have heard with due respect and attention the Letters brought by us from his sacred
Majesty; you have also heard in conformity
thereunto other Letters, sent from your most
Reverend Chancellor, signifying his Majesty's
grace and goodness in recommending unto
you this volume of Statutes, which we now
deliver, and you are to receive, as the rules,
by which you must be governed hereafter.
You have also seen and heard the confirmation and establishment of these Statutes.
First by his Majesty's royal signature, and
under the great seal of his kingdom: and
respectively under the hand and seal of the
Lord Archbishop, both as Primate and Metropolitan of England, and as most worthy
Chancellor of this University, whereby it is
manifest, that these laws and ordinances are
so established and ratified both by sovereign
and subalternal authority, temporal and spiritual, that nothing further can be required,

but your ready acceptance and obedience,
whereof I make no doubt. For (to do you
right) you have already shewed so effectual
conformity ; and at this present express such
alacrity and forwardness, that I rather see
cause to commend and encourage you, than
to exhort and stir you up, or any way to im-
portune you by any further speech ; yet
because there is generally in man's nature a
secret curiosity and prejudice against all
things, that appear extraordinary and new,
especially when they impose any duty, and
require obedience at their hands; I must
crave leave in discharge of my own duty to
satisfy those, which hereafter may be in-
quisitive into these proceedings, to insist a
little upon those principal respects which
demonstrate the full authorization and absolute necessity of submission to these laws.

That which commands in chief, and which
no reason can withstand, is his Majesty's
sovereign power, by which these Statutes (as
you see) are both enacted and confirmed.
Him we all acknowledge to be our supreme

overnor both of Church and Commonwealth,
ver all causes and persons; and to his suprem-
y and allegiance, we are all obliged by oath.
his then we must build upon, as an axiom
d fundamental rule of government, that all
r Laws and Statutes are the King's Laws,
d that none can be enacted, changed, or
rogated without him; so all Courts of
w or Equity are properly the King's
urts; all justice therein administered, be
civil or martial, is the King's justice; and no
rdon or grace proceeds from any, but from
e King. And as of justice, so is he the source
honour; all dignities, all degrees, all titles,
ms, and orders come originally from the
ing, as branches from the root. And not
ly particular men and families, but all
rporations, societies, nay counties, pro-
nces, and depending kingdoms, have all their
risdictions and governments established by
m; and by him (for public good) to be
anged or dissolved. So his power reacheth
foreign plantations, where he may erect
incipalities, and make laws for their good

government, which no man may disobey.
And as in the temporal, so in the State
ecclesiastical, his regal power by ancient
right extendeth to the erection of Bishoprics,
Deaneries, and Cathedral Churches, and to
settle orders for government in all Churches,
by the advice of his own Clergy, without
any concurrence of foreign usurping power.

But for Universities and Colleges, they
are the rights of Kings in a most peculiar
manner. For all their establishments, endowments, privileges, and orders by which they
subsist and are maintained, are derived from
regal power.   And as it is your greatest
honour, so it is your greatest safety, that
now this body of your laws, as well as your
privileges and immunities, are established,
ratified, and confirmed by the King.   And
more I shall not need to say in this point.

In the next place you may consider for
your encouragement to receive this great
favour and benefit from his Majesty with
ready and thankful minds, that your Chancellor's worthy care had a chief operation in

advancing this great work; whose nearness
to his Majesty in a place of that eminency
and sincere conformity to his orders and
commands, and most watchful care over that
part of the government which is committed
to his trust, enableth him to support, and
may give you confidence to obey that which
his Majesty recommendeth by so good a
hand, specially in matters concerning the
good government of the Church or of the
Schools.

In the Church, (whereof he is Primate and
Metropolitan,) his power is very large, and
his extraordinary endeavours in it deserve at
least to be well understood. In former times,
when Churchmen bore rule, the greatest Prelates gave the first way to alienate Church
Livings: whereas this worthy Prelate maketh
it his chief work to recover to the Church for
the furtherance of God's service what may
be now restored. And what therein he hath
effected under his Majesty's gracious and
powerful order, not England alone, but Scotland and Ireland can abundantly witness.

Again, what help and relief he procureth
daily for Ministers oppressed by rich en-
croaching neighbours or patrons; what col-
lections and contributions he obtaineth to
re-edify, to repair and adorn churches; and
what great structures are now in hand, and
much advanced by his judgment, care and
zeal in our most famous monuments dedicated
to God's service, we may behold with joy,
and future ages will commemorate to his
Majesty's eternal glory, by whose power and
order all is performed, and to the honour of
our country, and for encouragement and example of those that shall succeed; who will
acknowledge with us, that this man is indeed,
as he is by his just style, a most reverend
and beneficial Father of the Church: and for
this University what better evidence can be
desired of his singular love and beneficence,
than first that stately building, whereby he
hath made himself another founder of that
College, which bred him to this height of
worth? And secondly, those many rare and
exquisite Manuscripts and Authors, wherewith

he hath replenished your renowned public Library? And if you add hereunto his constant care to maintain you in all your rights and privileges, and to assist you in your preferments; and finally in collecting this great volume of ordinances for the present and future government of this famous University. You have monuments sufficient to eternise among you and all men his memory and desert. And this work is that, which now remaineth in the third place to be further stood upon. For it is not (as some may think) either a rhapsody of overworn and unuseful ordinances, nor yet an imposition of novel constitutions to serve the present times; but our royal Justinian by the labour and direction of this prudent person hath collected into a Pandect or Corpus Juris Academici all the ancient approved Statutes, which in former times were scattered and so neglected. And though many great Prelates have heretofore undertaken this work, yet it ever miscarried, till the piercing judgment and indefatigable industry of this man took it in hand, and happily, as now you see, hath put you into possession of it, whereof the use can hardly be valued. For by these rules, you, that are governors, may know what to command, and those, that are under you may know how to obey, and all may understand how to order their behaviour, and their studies, whereby they may become most profitable members in the Church and Commonwealth, which is the main cause, why his Majesty requireth them so strictly to be obeyed. For let me speak freely out of that true affection which I bear to you all: deceive not yourselves with a vain opinion, that Kings and Princes give great donations, privileges, and honours, to their Schools and Universities for a popular applause, or out of mere bounty, or for honour, or for opinion of merit, by which the art of Clergymen transported them heretofore: but the very truth is, that all wise Princes respect the welfare of their estates, and consider, that Schools and Universities are (as in the body) the noble and vital parts, which being vigorous and sound, send good blood

and active spirits into the veins and arteries,
which cause health and strength: or if feeble
or ill affected, corrupt all the vital powers;
whereupon grow diseases, and in the end
death itself.   What inconveniences have
grown in all ages by the ill government and
disorders of schools, your books can inform
you.   And to come home to yourselves, have
not our late Parliaments complained? Nay
hath not the land exclaimed, that our great
schools of virtue were become schools of vice?
This I mention unwillingly, but withal do most
willingly tell you to your eternal praise, that
since it pleased his Majesty to take to heart
a reformation, and by advice of your never
too often named Chancellor, sent you down
some temporary orders, whereby to reduce
you to some reasonable moderation, thereupon
by the wisdom and resolution of you the worthy governors, and by the inclinable conformity of all the students in general, it is now come
to pass, that scholars are no more found in
taverns or houses of disorder, nor seen loitering
in the streets, or other places of idleness or

ill example, but all contain themselves within
the walls of their Colleges, and in the Schools
or public Libraries: wherein, I must confess, you have at length gotten the start, and
by your virtue and merit have made this
University, which before had no paragon in
any foreign country, now to go beyond itself,
and give a glorious example to others not to
stay behind.

And if those temporary and imperfect
orders produced so good effect, what may now
be expected from this body of Laws and Statutes, so complete and so digested, that no
former age did ever enjoy the like?

Thus you have understood how the goodness of our great King, how the care and
respect of your Chancellor, and how the
worth and substance of the work itself, may
forcibly induce you to congratulate your own
happiness.   And therefore I might here forbear to trouble you any longer with a harsh
interrupted speech; but that I cannot omit
to put you in mind of one thing, which I
know you will hear with willingness and

attention, because it tendeth chiefly to the honour of our God, and then by His power to the honour of our King; and thence to the comfort of every true-hearted subject, who will readily acknowledge, with reverence and thankfulness, the great blessings we now enjoy above all other nations. I will tell you but what I know, (for I speak within my element;) I have seen our neighbouring countries in great prosperity and renown, their cities stately built and strongly fortified, with walls raised up to heaven, full of people, full of trade, so full of peace and plenty, that they surfeited in all excess; but from hence they are since fallen, partly by the boundless ambition of great Princes, partly by the factions and divisions in religion; and generally by their disorders, into such condition, that men of great honour sent in remote employment, found whole provinces so sacked and depopulated, that in divers journeys they encountered scarce a man, and of those they found dead, some had grass in their mouths and stomachs, and some were torn in pieces

by beasts and ravenous fowls; and those that
were alive, had no other care or study than
how to save themselves from fire and sword.
In general there is such desolation, that, without a kind of horror, the horror thereof cannot
be expressed.

Now we, by God's blessing, are in a better
case; we sit here in God's house, thankful in
true devotion for this wonderful favour towards us.   We enjoy peace and plenty; we
are like to those who, resting in a calm haven,
behold the shipwreck of others, wherein we
have no part, save only in compassion to help
them with our prayers; which we all ought
to do, as interested in their sufferings, lest the
like may fall on us.   What then remaineth,
but seriously to consider, how all these great
blessings are conferred upon us, not for our
merits, or for our more virtuous and holy
lives, but only by God's favour to his true
religion, and under him by the happy government of our gracious King; which should
confirm us all to a constancy in our obedience,
and to a ready subjection to all those rules

and orders, which his Majesty shall prescribe for the public good. Wherein this general admonition may fruitfully be applied to the business now in hand, whereof I make no doubt. So I crave your pardon and your good acceptance of that, which I have rudely spoken, but with a true affection to this whole body, whereof, (though I had my education from another nurse,) yet I had the honour to be an adopted son, and (as I suppose) one of the ancientest that lives amongst you at this day.

It remaineth, that Mr. Vice-Chancellor perform his part; and proceed to the subscriptions and depositions of you the Heads.

JOHN COOK.

Letter to the Vice-Chancellor, concerning the entertainment of the King at Oxford.

S. in Christo.

Sir,

Since I writ last to you, the Dean of Christ Church came to me, and acquainted me with two things, which are very necessary you should both know and remedy.

The one is, that the University seems to be unwilling to contribute to the charge of the Plays, which are to be at Christ Church. Now this charge, as by reason of their building, they are not able to bear alone; so I must needs acknowledge, there is no reason that they should, whatever their ability be: for the King is to be entertained by Oxford, not by Christ Church. And that he lies there, is but for the conveniency of the place, where there are so many fair lodgings for the great men to be about him. Indeed, if Christ Church men will say, they will have no actors but of their own House, let them bear the charge of their own Plays, in God's name: but if they will take any good actors from any other College or Hall, upon trial of their sufficiency to be as good, or better than their own; then I see no reason in the world, but that the whole University should contribute to the charge. And I pray see it ordered, and let your successor follow you accordingly.

The other is, that since the University must

contribute to this charge, (for so it was done when King James came, and at the last coming of Queen Elizabeth, both within my own memory,) I hold it very fit, that all the materials of that stage, which are now to be made new, and the proscenium, and such apparel, whatever it be, as is wholly made new, shall be laid up in some place fit for it; to which the Vice-Chancellor for the time being shall have one key, and the Dean of Christ Church the other, that it may not be lost, as things of like nature and use have formerly been. And if any College or Hall shall at any time, for any play or show that they are willing to set forth, need the use of any or all of these things, it shall be as lawful and free for them to have and to use them, as for Christ Church; provided that after the use, they do carefully restore them to the place whence they were taken. And to the end these things may be kept with the more safety and indifferency to the University, I think it very fit that an inventory be made of them, and that one copy thereof remain with them. at Christ

Church, and the other in such fit and convenient place, as the Vice-Chancellor and the Heads shall agree on. For my part, I think it fittest, that an inventory should be kept in the University registry, that so you may not only have access to it, so often as you shall have cause, but also leave it ready for direction in future times in like cases of expense. And I think it not amiss, that these my Letters which concern the ordering of these businesses, should be registered also.

And further, that the University may see how the money, which they allow towards these charges, is expended, I think it very requisite, that yourself and the Heads should name three or four men of good experience in those things, that may see at what rates all things are bought or paid for; and an account delivered in to the Vice-Chancellor and the Heads, at such time as the Vice-Chancellor shall call for them. And also, that their hands be set to both copies of the above-named inventories. I have thought upon Dr. Fell, Dr. Sanders, and the Warden of Wadham, as very fit men for this purpose; and if you and the Heads shall think it requisite to join any more to them, you may name whom you please.

For the Play, which I intend shall be at St. John's, I will neither put the University nor the College to any charge, but take it wholly upon myself. And in regard of the great trouble and inconvenience I shall thereby put upon that House, as also in regard it shall set out one of the Plays by itself, I think there is great reason in it, and do therefore expect it, that no contribution should be required from St. John's towards the Plays at Christ Church. And I pray let me have an account from you of the settlement of these things. So I leave you to the grace of God, and rest,

Your loving friend,
W. CANT.

Croydon, July 15, 1630.

Aug. 3. Wednesday night. Towards the morning, I dreamed that L. M. St. came to

me the next day, Aug. 4, and shewed me all
the kindness I could ask. And that Thursday
he did come, and was very kind towards me.
Somniis tamen haud multum fido.—Aug. 19,
Friday. I was in great danger of breaking
my right leg. But God be blessed! for His
providence only delivered me. — Aug. 29,
Monday. King Charles and Queen Mary
entered Oxford, being to be there entertained
by me as Chancellor of the University.

Concerning the King's entertainment at Oxford.

This year his Majesty and the Queen
invited themselves to me to Oxford, and
brought with them Charles, Prince Elector
Palatine, and his brother Prince Rupert,
being both then in England. They came
into Oxford at the end of this summer's progress, on Monday, August 29. The Vice-
Chancellor made a very good speech unto
them, where myself and the University met
them, which was a mile, before they entered
the town. That speech ended, they passed
along by St. John's, where Mr. Tho. Atkinson

made another speech unto them very brief, and very much approved of by his Majesty afterwards to me. Within Christ Church gate, Mr. William Strode, the University Orator, entertained them with another speech, which was well approved. Thence the King accompanied his Queen to her lodging, and instantly returned, and went with all the Lords to the Cathedral. There after his private devotions ended, at the west door, Dr. Morris, one of the Probendaries, entertained him with another short speech, which was well liked. And thence his Majesty proceeded into the quire, and heard service. After supper, they were entertained with a Play at Christ Church, which was very well penned, but yet did not take the Court so well. The next day being Tuesday, the King came to service soon after eight in the morning. It was at Christ Church, and Mr. Thomas Brown, being then Proctor, made an excellent Sermon, which gave great content. The Sermon ended, the Prince Elector, and his brother Prince Rupert, attended by

many of the Lords, came to the Convocation-
House, where the place was full of University
men, all in their forms and habits very orderly. And the two Princes, with divers
Lords, were pleased to be made Masters of
Arts; and the two Princes' names were, by
his Majesty's leave, entered in St. John's College, to do that house that honour for my sake.
In Convocation, the Vice-Chancellor having
first placed the Princes, and briefly expressed
the cause of that Convocation, I made a short
speech, which here follows in hæc verba.

Florentes Academici, et hoc tempore flo-
rentissimi quibus Caroli Regis et pientissimi et
prudentissimi: simulque Mariæ illustrissimæ
heroinæ, consortis suæ charissimæ, præsentiâ
frui datur nec eâ solum, sed et præsentiâ exi-
miæ spei Principum, nepotum M. Jacobi
sacratissimæ memoriæ Monarchæ, et de Academia literatisque omnibus optime meriti;
Principes hi sunt, et hoc titulo, et suo, omni
honoris genere dignissimi. Vos eos omni,
quo potestis, prosequimini.

Quid expectatis ultra, Academici? An ut
ego oratorio in hoc senatu fungar munere?
At illud et memoria, curis simul et annis
fracta, et lingua per se inculta, et desuetudine
loquendi hæsitans; et præsens negotium, quod
ad alia festinat, omnino prohibent. Nec Principes hi proceresve illud a me expectant, cui
aliud satis jam incumbit negotium : et qui
illis brevitatem in omnibus sum pollicitus.

Breviter itaque quod ad vos attinet, Principes, non ortu magis quam virtutibus illus-
tres. Non expectat a vobis Academia, ut
possitis totam entis profunditatem exhaurire,
ut sic sitis Artium Magistri, sed liceat dicere :
freta ætatis vestræ nondum transiistis. Æstus
jam urgent juveniles. Hos discite superare
fluctus, procellas has in auras redigere, et
omnium insimul Artium Magistri eritis, et
quid ni fortunæ? Atque utinam nostræ
potestatis esset, cæcæ illi Deæ oculos dare,
quibus virtutes vestras cerneret, et agnosceret
jura.

Et vos etiam proceres, Principum horum
cultores, convocata hac Academia exultat vi-

dere, et non solum conferre gradus suos in voe
gestit, quos omni honoris cultu veneratur:
sed potius eos conferendo, honorem summum
gradibus suis quærit; quod placeat Princi-
pibus hisce vobisque pannis suis (nam et
pannus in purpura est) inaugurari. Floreat
sic sæpius Academia, et nativis simul et adop-
tivis filiis gaudeat. Egregie Vice-Cancellarie,
ad creationem et admissionem simul pro officio
tuo descende.

After this the Vice-Chancellor proceeded,
made another short speech, and after creation
and admission of the Princes and other honourable persons, ended the Convocation. That
finished, they all returned to Christ Church
to attend upon the King, (the Princes having
formerly in the morning seen some of the
fair Colleges.) Then the Queen being not
ready, the King, with the Princes and the
Nobles, myself also waiting upon him, went
to the Library, where the King viewed the
new buildings and the books, and was entertained with a very neat speech by the son of

the Earl of Pembroke and Montgomery, then Lord Chamberlain.

Then word was brought up, that the Queen was come. So the King went into the coach to her, and they went away to St. John's to dinner, the Princes and Nobles attending them.

When they were come to St. John's, they first viewed the new building; and that done, I attended them up the Library stairs; where, so soon as they began to ascend, the music began, and they had a fine short song fitted for them, as they ascended the stairs. In the Library they were welcomed to the College with a short speech made by ———, one of the Fellows.

And dinner being ready, they passed from the old into the new Library, built by myself, where the King, the Queen, and the Prince Elector dined at one table, which stood cross at the upper end. And Prince Rupert, with all the Lords and Ladies present, which were very many, dined at a long table in the same room. All other several tables, to the num-

ber of thirteen besides these two, were disposed in several chambers of the College,
and had several men appointed to attend
them; and I thank God I had that happiness,
that all things were in very good order, and
that no man went out at the gates, courtier
or other, but content; which was a happiness quite beyond expectation.

When dinner was ended, I attended the
King and the Queen together with the Nobles
into several withdrawing chambers, where
they entertained themselves for the space of
an hour. And in the mean time I caused the
windows of the Hall to be shut, the candles
lighted, and all things made ready for the
Play to begin. When these things were
fitted, I gave notice to the King and the
Queen, and attended them into the Hall,
whither I had the happiness to bring them
by a way prepared from the President's lodging to the Hall, without any the least disturbance; and had the Hall kept as fresh
and cool, that there was not any one person
when the King and Queen came into it.

The Princes, Nobles, and Ladies entered the same way with the King, and then presently another door was opened below to fill the Hall with the better sort of company; which being done, the Play was begun and acted. The plot was very good, and the action. It was merry, and without offence, and so gave a great deal of content. In the middle of the Play, I ordered a short banquet for the King, the Queen, and the Lords. And the College was at that time so well furnished, as that they did not borrow any one actor from any College in town. The Play ended, the King and the Queen went to Christ Church, retired and supped privately, and about eight o'clock, went into the Hall to see another Play, which was upon a piece of a Persian story. It was very well penned and acted, and the strangeness of the Persian habits gave great content; so that all men came forth from it very well satisfied. And the Queen liked it so well, that she afterwards sent to me to have the apparel sent to Hampton Court, that she might see her own players

act it over again, and see whether they could
do it as well, as it was done in the University.
I caused the University to send both the
clothes, and the perspectives of the stage;
and the Play was acted at Hampton Court in
November following.   And by all men's confession, the players came short of the University actors.   Then I humbly desired of
the King and the Queen, that neither the
Play, nor clothes, nor stage, might come into
the hands and use of the common players
abroad, which was graciously granted.

But to return to Oxford.   This Play being
ended, all men betook themselves to their
rest: and upon Wednesday morning, August
31, about eight of the clock, myself with the
Vice-Chancellor and the Doctors attended
the coming forth of the King and Queen;
and when they came, did our duties to them.
They were graciously pleased to give the University a great deal of thanks; and I for myself,
and in the name of the University, gave their
Majesties all possible thanks for their great
and gracious patience and acceptance of our

poor and mean entertainment. So the King and Queen went away very well pleased together.

That Wednesday night, I entertained at St. John's, in the same room where the King dined the day before, at the long table, which was for the Lords, all the Heads of Colleges and Halls in the town; and all the other Doctors, both the Proctors, and some few friends more, which I had employed in this time of service; which gave the University a great deal of content, being that which had never been done by any Chancellor before. I sat with them at table, we were merry, and very glad that all things had so passed to the great satisfaction of the King, and the honour of that place.

Upon Thursday, September 1, I dined privately with some few of my friends: and after dinner went to Cuddesden to my ancient friend, my Lord, the Bishop of Oxford's house; there I left my steward, and some few of my servants with him at Oxford, to look to my plate, linen, and other things, and to pay all reckonings, that no man might ask a penny after we had left the town; which was carefully done accordingly. Upon Friday, September 2, I lay at a house of Mr. Justice Jones's, of Henley-upon-Thames, upon his earnest invitation. And upon Saturday, September 3, (God be thanked,) I returned safe home to my house at Croydon. The week after, my steward and other servants, which stayed with him, came from Oxford to me; where the care of my servants, with God's blessing upon it, was such, as that having borrowed all the King's plate, which was in the progress, and all my Lord Chamberlain's, and made use of all mine own, and hired some of my goldsmith, I lost none, but only two spoons which were of mine own plate, and but little of my linen.

My retinue (being all of my own, when I went to this entertainment) were between forty and fifty horse; though I came privately into Oxford, in regard of the nearness of the King and Queen, then at Woodstock. There was great store of provision in all

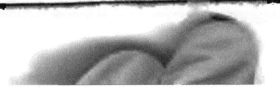

kinds sent me in towards this entertainment; and yet (for I bare all the charge of that Play, which was at St. John's, and suffered not that poor College to be· at a penny loss or charge in any thing) besides all these sendings in, the entertainment cost me . . . . . .

Aug. 30. On Tuesday, I entertained them at St. John's College. It was St. Felix's day; and all passed happily. Charles Prince Elector Palatine, and his brother Prince Rupert, were there. These two were present in Convocation; and, with other Nobles, were made Masters of Arts.—Aug. 31, Wednesday. They left Oxford, and I returned homewards the day after, having first entertained all the Heads of Houses together.

Oct. 14, Friday night. I dreamed marvellously, that the King was offended with me, and would cast me off, and tell me no cause why. Avertat Deus! for cause I have given none.

November 4, Friday night. The most extreme wind that ever I heard; and much hurt done by sea and by land. Twice or thrice since, thunder, and lightning, and hail. —Nov. 20, Sunday night. My fearful dream. Mr. Cobb brought me word, &c.

Letter to the Vice-Chancellor, concerning the Service at St. Mary's.

Salutem in Christo.

Sir,

The sickness of these times, and my many other occasions, made me forget to write to you before the beginning of Michaelmas Term last, concerning the Sermon and Prayers usually had at St. Mary's at the beginning of Terms, which were wont to be not so orderly as they should, nor with so good example to other places at large in the kingdom, as such a University should give.

For, first, the Communion was celebrated in the body of the church, and not in the chancel; which, though it be permitted in the Church of England in some cases of necessity, where there is a multitude of people; yet very indecent it is, and unfitting in that place, where so few (the more the pity) use to communicate at these solemn times. But this abuse I caused to be rectified in Dr. Duppa's time, and I hope neither you nor your successors will suffer it to return again into the former indecency.

Secondly, though none do come to those solemn Prayers and Sermons but scholars, and those too of the best rank, yet to no small dishonour of that place, the Sermon is in Latin, and the Prayers in English; as if Latin prayers were more unfit for a learned congregation than a Latin Sermon. And the truth is, the thing is very absurd in itself, and contrary to the directions given at the beginning of the reformation of this Church; for in the Latin Service Books, which were first printed in the beginning of Queen Elizabeth, there is an express both direction and charge, that notwithstanding the altering of the ordinary Form of Prayers throughout the whole body of the kingdom from Latin into English; yet in the Universities such Prayers, unto which none but they which were learned did resort, should be in Latin. And for my part, I do much wonder, considering how public that direction was, that the University at the beginning of Terms should fall from this ordinance, and so divide the Service and Sermon between Latin and English.

Upon consideration of this I acquainted his Majesty both with that printed direction of Queen Elizabeth, and with the breach of it by the University at the beginning of Terms; whereupon his Majesty was pleased to give me in charge to see this ordered, and to take a course for a remedy in the future, and that hereafter Service, Sermon, and Communion, should be at all beginnings of Terms uniformly in Latin, since none resort to either, but such as well understand it. These are therefore to pray and require you, at some convenient Meeting of the Heads, to acquaint them with this direction of his Majesty, and to take care, that both at the beginning of the next Term, and of all Terms following, the Service and Communion be in Latin, as well as the Sermon. And that such, as are not furnished, may the better provide themselves of Service Books in Latin, so soon as conveniently they can, you shall do well to make it so much the sooner known to the Heads. And this I must not forget to tell you, that when I took this first into consideration, it was thought fitting to put it into the University Statutes. But afterwards I considered, that since the Statutes were to remain to posterity, it would lay no small scandal upon these times, when they should see by the very Statute itself, what a stranger the University was to the prayers of the Church in a learned language. And hereupon having first acquainted his Majesty with this also, I thought it better to leave it out of the Statutes, and to reduce it to this privater way, which opinion of mine his Majesty was pleased graciously to approve.

Two things there are, which you and the Heads must take present care for: the one is, that the Vice-Chancellor, and he that helps him to execute, (whosoever he be,) be in surplices; but whether the Vice-Chancellor will put on his surplice, when he goes to the

Communion, or put it on at the first, and so read Service, and sit at the Sermon in it, I leave to his own judgment; but I like the latter better, and the surplice must be under both the habit and the hood. The second is, that there must be care taken with the Singing Men, that they may answer the Litany, and all other places of the Service, where they interpose, in Latin, which they may easily practise, and be ready to perform at the beginning of the next Term; but if they cannot, the Litany must be sung, or answered by the Masters without the organ, till they can: for the main business to have all things in Latin must go on. So wishing you all health and happiness, and the University that honour, that belongs unto her entire, I leave to the grace of God, and rest

Your very loving friend,

W. CANT.

Croydon, Nov. 26, 1636.

December 24, Saturday, Christmas-eve. That night I dreamed I went to seek Mr. St.

and found him with his mother sitting in the room. It was a fair chamber. He went away, and I went after, but missed him, and after tired myself extremely; but neither could I find him, nor so much as the house again.

1637.

To Dr. Prideaux, concerning his review of Mr. Chillingworth's answer, &c.

Sir,

I had almost forgotten a business to you of greater consequence than this, and I cannot well tell whether Mr. Vice-Chancellor hath acquainted you with it or no; for I writ not unto him very expressly in the business, but now recalling it, I thought fit to write thus much to yourself. You know, that Mr. Chillingworth is answering of a book, that much concerns the Church of England; and I am very sorry, that the young man hath given cause, why a more watchful eye should be held over him and his writings. But since it is so, I would willingly desire this favour from you in the Church's name, that you

would be at the pains to read over this Tract,
and see that it be put home in all points
against the Church of Rome, as the cause
requires.   And I am confident Mr. Chillingworth will not be against your altering
of any thing that shall be found reasonable.   And to the end that all things may
go on to the honour of the Church of England, I have desired Dr. Potter, (who is particularly concerned in this business,) so soon
as ever he is returned from London, to speak
with you about it.   And when all these trials
are over, I would be content, that both this
book, and all others that shall be hereafter
licensed in the University, have such an Im-
primatur of the licenser before it, as we use
here above, which I shall leave to the wisdom
of the Vice-Chancellor and the Heads.

W. CANT.

Lambeth, March 3, 1634.

March 30, Thursday. I christened the
Lady Princess Ann, King Charles's third
daughter. She was born on Friday, March 17.

Concerning the calling in of Bishop Sale's Book of Devotion.

Mr. Vice-Chancellor,

There was an English translation of a Book of Devotion, written by Sales Bishop of Geneva, and entitled, " Praxis Spiritualis sive Introductio ad Vitam Devotam," licensed by Dr. Haywood, then my Chaplain, about the latter end of November last; but before it passed his hands, he first struck out divers things, wherein it varied from the doctrine of our Church, and so passed it. But by the practice of one Burrowes, (who is now found to be a Roman Catholic,) those passages struck out by Dr. Haywood were interlined afterwards, (as appears upon examination before Mr. Attorney-General, and by the Manuscript copy,) and were printed according to Burrowes's falsifications. The book being thus printed, gave great and just offence, especially to myself, who, upon the first hearing of it, gave present orders to seize upon all the copies, and to burn them publicly in Smithfield. Eleven or twelve hundred copies were seized and burnt accordingly; but it seems two or three hundred of the impression were dispersed before the seizure. Now my desire is, that if any copies of this translation be, or shall be sent to Oxford, you would call them in, and take such order for the suppressing of them there, as is here already taken. And so I commend you to God's grace, and rest

Your loving friend,

W. CANT.

Lambeth, May 4, 1637.

June 10. My book of the Records in the Tower, which concerned the Clergy, and which I caused to be collected, and written in vellum, was brought me finished. It is ab Ann. 20 Edw. I. ad Ann. 14 Edw. IV.—June 14. This day, Jo. Bastwick, Doctor of Physic; Henry Burton, Bachelor of Divinity, and William Prynne, Barrister at Law, were censured for their libels against the hierarchy of the Church, &c.

*Extract from a Letter to the Vice-Chancellor,
concerning Mr. Crofts.*

Sir,

For Mr. Crofts and his great horses, he
may carry them back if he please, as he
brought them.   For certainly it cannot be fit
for the University, though the exercise in
itself be exceeding commendable: for the
gentlemen there are most part too young,
and not strong enough; besides, you cannot
put that charge upon their parents, without
their particular leave and directions; but
this especially is considerable, that where-
ever this place of riding shall be, where one
scholar learns, you shall have twenty or forty
to look on, and there lose their time, so that
upon the whole matter, that place shall be
fuller of scholars, than either Schools or Library.   Therefore I pray give Mr. Crofts
thanks fairly for his good intentions; but as
thus advised, I cannot give way to his staying there to the purpose he intends; nor is
it altogether inconsiderable, that you shall

suffer scholars to fall into the old humour of going up and down in boots and spurs, and then have their excuse ready, that they are going to the riding-house; and I doubt not, but other inconveniences may be thought on, therefore I pray no admittance of him.

W. CANT.

Lambeth, June 23, 1637.

In this year the Porch of St. Mary's was finished at the cost of my Chaplain, Dr. Morgan Owen, which was £230.

June 16. The speech I then spake in the Star-Chamber, was commanded by the King to be printed. And it came out June the 25th.—June 26. This day, Monday, the Prince Elector and his brother Prince Rupert began their journey toward the sea side, to return for Holland.—June 30, Friday, the above-named three libellers left their ears.

July 7, Friday. A note was brought to me, of a short libel pasted on the cross in Cheapside: that the Arch-Wolf of Cant. had his hand in persecuting the saints, and shedding the blood of the Martyrs. Memento, for the last of June.

July 11, Tuesday. Dr. Williams Lord Bishop of Lincoln was censured in the Star-Chamber for tampering, and corrupting of — Wit, in the King's cause.—July 24, being Monday, he was suspended by the High Commission, &c.

Aug. 3, Thursday. I married James Duke of Lennox, to the Lady Mary Villiers, sole daughter of the Lord Duke of Buckingham: the marriage was in my Chapel at Lambeth; the day very rainy; the King present.—Aug. 23, Wednesday. My Lord Mayor sent me a libel found by the watch at the south gate of St. Paul's. That the devil had left that house to me, &c.—Aug. 25, Friday. Another libel brought me by an officer of the High Commission, fastened to the north gate of St. Paul's. That the government of the Church of England is a candle in the snuff going out in a stench.—Aug. 25. The same day at night, my Lord Mayor sent me another libel, hanged upon the standard in Cheap-

side. My speech in the Star-Chamber, set
in a kind of pillory, &c.—Aug. 29, Tuesday.
Another short libel against me, in verse.

Letter to the Vice-Chancellor.
Salutem in Christo.
Sir,

I have yet received no Letter from you
this week ; if I do, you shall have an answer
on Friday, if I have so much leisure.   In the
mean time I send you this inclosed, which
came to my hands this present afternoon.
I pray examine the business with all the care
and industry you possibly can, as well for the
discharge of your own duty and credit, as
mine, in the government of that place.   And
if there be such a man as Pully here mentioned, be sure to make him fast, and examine
him throughly touching all particulars, that
you shall think material for the discovery of
these unworthy practices for the seducing of
youths in that University, or elsewhere, especially concerning the author of this Letter,
and what youths have been dealt withal after

this sort, either in that House or any other of the town. And whether any Jesuits, or others, have lain hankering up and down thereabouts, or be there at this present to that purpose, or any other as bad. In all which, I desire you to use the utmost diligence and discretion that you can, and let me have an account with all convenient speed. So I leave you to God's grace, and rest

Your very loving friend,

W. CANT.

Croydon, August 29, 1637.

P.S. This falls out very unhappily, not only for the thing itself, which ought by all means to be prevented; but also for the clamours, which the late libellers have made, that there are great endeavours for reintroducing of Popery.

Extract from a Letter to the Vice-Chancellor.

Sir,

I am glad you found all in health, and all things else so well at your return; and yet I cannot but see, that both factions would be

busy there. Concerning the Popish fac
tion, I writ hastily to you to prevent
danger, which I thought was imminent, an
God grant you may secure it! but in an
case name not Fish, if you can possibly avoi
it ;· but carry it as if the letter were inter
cepted, and be as careful as possibly you car
And concerning the Puritan, I see plainly
that Brazen-nose hath some as bad, or wors
than Cook was about four years since. An
that Greenwood, who preached on Sunda
last, is like to prove a peevish man, which
am the more sorry for; because you write h
is a good master of his pen, and therefor
like to do the more harm. But since h
hath so cunningly carried it, (for the fashio
is now to turn the libellous part into a prayer,
I think the best way is to take no notice of i
at all: but the more carefully to observe
what the man doth in the University: for
would have no man publicly called in ques
tion, where a fair answer may be given an
taken, that the peace both of the Churcl
and of that place may be preserved, as mucl

as may be. And yet to confess my thoughts to you, I think Mr. Greenwood had in this business a very factious and a rancorous meaning.

W. CANT.

September 1, 1637.

Letter to the Vice-Chancellor.

Sir,

You cannot carry too careful an eye, either over Pullin or the rest; for certainly some are about that place to seduce as many as they can. And particularly Dr. Potter writes me word, that Knott is now in Oxford, (I would you could lay hold of him,) and hath the sheets from the press as they are done; and that he pays five shillings for every sheet, and that you are acquainted with this rumour. I pray be very careful in this also, for I know the Jesuits are very cunning at these tricks; but if you have no more hold of your printers, than that the press must lie thus open to their corruption, I shall take a sourer course, than perhaps is expected. For though perhaps they go so cunningly to

work, as that I shall not be able to make
legal proof of this foul misdemeanour: yet
find that Knott makes a more speedy answer
than is otherwise possible, without such
seeing of the sheets; I shall take that for
proof enough, and proceed to discommission
your printer, and suppress his press. And
pray fail not to let him know so much from me

W. Cant.

Croydon, Sept. 15, 1637.

Oct. 22, Sunday. A great noise about the
perverting of the Lady Newport: speech of
it at the Council: my free speech there to
the King, concerning the increasing of the
Roman party, the freedom at Denmark-house,
the carriage of Mr. Wal. Montague and Sir
Toby Matthews. The Queen acquainted
with all I said that very night, and highly
displeased with me; and so continues.

Letter to Dr. Sheldon.

Sir,

Dr. Fell is now with me, and returns to Oxford in the beginning of the next week. At his

return, I would have you or Mr. Vice-Chancellor speak with him about his resignation, which he hath promised me to make, both of his Lecture and Prebend of Worcester; and that so soon as their Worcester audit is over, (which I take is this November,) he having this year an office in that church to be accountable for. And when you have once spoken with him about it, you may then go on, and make the business as sure as you can.

When all is done, you must deal with Dr. Lawrence to be very mindful of the waspishness of these times, and to be sure to read upon no argument, that may make any the least trouble in Church or University, which I shall in part lay upon your care to look to for so much as concerns Dr. Lawrence; so wishing you all health, &c.

Your very loving friend,

W. CANT.

Lambeth, Nov. 8, 1637.

Letter to the Vice-Chancellor, concerning
Prayers before Sermon.

Sir,

I sent to the Vice-Chancellor to speak to
the Heads at the Monday meeting, that they
follow the Canon in their prayers before
Sermons, both in the University and out, and
to require them to give notice of it to their
several Companies.

W. CANT.

Nov. 22, Wednesday.   The extreme and
unnatural hot winter weather began, and
continued till Dec. 8.

Dec. 12, Tuesday.   I had speech with the
Queen a good space, and all about the business of Mr. Montague, but we parted fair.

1638. April 29.   The tumults in Scotland,
about the Service Book offered to be brought
in, began July 23, 1637, and continued increasing by fits, and have now brought that
kingdom in danger.   No question, but there
is a great concurrence between them, and the

Puritan party in England. A great aim there to destroy me in the King's opinion, &c.

May 26, Saturday. James Lord Marquess Hamilton set forth, as the King's Commissioner, to appease the tumults in Scotland. God prosper him, for God and the King. It was a very rainy day.

June. My Visitation then began of Merton College in Oxford by my Visitors; was adjourned to my own hearing, against and upon Oct. 2.

Oct. 2, 3, 4. I sate upon this business these three days, and adjourned it to July 1, inter horas primam et tertiam, Lambeth. The Warden appeared very foul.—Oct. 19, Friday. News was brought to us, as we sate in the Star-Chamber, that the Queen Mother of France was landed at Harwich: many and great apprehensions upon this business; extreme windy and wet weather a week before, and after; the watermen called it, 'Queen Mother weather.—Oct. 26, Friday. A most extreme tempest upon the Thames. I was in it, going from the Star-

Chamber home, between six and seven night. I was never upon the water in th like storm: and was in great danger at m landing at Lambeth bridge.—Oct. 31, Wed nesday. The Queen Mother came to Londor and so to St. James's.

Nov. 13, Tuesday. The agreement be tween me and Ab. S. &c.—Nov. 21, Wed nesday. The General Assembly in Scotlan began to sit.—Nov. 29, Thursday. Th Proclamation issued out, for dissolving th General Assembly in Scotland, under pai of treason.

Dec. 20. They sate notwithstanding; an made very strange acts, till Dec. 20, whicl was Thursday, and then they rose. Bu have indicted another Assembly against Jul next.

The King's Letter to Christ Church, Oxford for suppressing their Westminster Supper.

Trusty and well-beloved, &c.

We are informed that you have for som years suffered a very ill custom to continue i that our Collegiate Church; for whereas there are divers Scholars chosen to be Students of that House, and divers others that live there as Commoners, but the greatest part of the Scholars are chosen from our School at Westminster; there is a supper maintained yearly, commonly called a Westminster supper, at which all and only Westminster scholars do meet. This supper we hold to be a very ill custom, and no way fit to be continued. For first, it is a thing not allowable in government, that any party of men should have a several meeting, which is a direct way to faction and combination, and it teacheth the rest of the Students in such a Society to bandy themselves together against the other, that they may not be thought to be neglected. Secondly, such a meeting must needs cause more expenses than many Students are able to bear, especially in such chargeable times as these are. Thirdly, it gives an occasion of much drinking and riot, and consequently of all the bad effects which follow such excesses; besides no small disorder in leaving or keeping open the gates of the College for ingress and egress, for resort to that disorderly meeting, at later hours than are fit. And most usually to add to all this disorder, this supper must be kept upon a Friday night, against both the Canons of the Church and laws of the Realm, and to the great scandal of all sober men that hear of it.

These are therefore to will and require you, the Dean and Chapter, to suppress that supper or meeting, by what name soever it be called; and to call the Students together, and to command them in our name, that they presume not at any time hereafter to resort together to any such meeting, either in the College or out of it; and to register these our Letters among the Orders and Decrees for the government of that Church, as you and every of you will answer it at your utmost perils; and these our Letters we will shall be binding, not only upon yourselves, but upon your successors, that this ill and dangerous custom may never rise up into practice again. Given, &c.

1689. Jan. 14, Monday. About five at
ght, a most grievous tempest of wind,
nder, lightning, and rain.

Feb. 10. My Book against Fisher the
suit was printed; and this day, being
nday, I delivered a copy to his Majesty.—
b. 12, Tuesday night. I dreamed that
. C. was to be married to a Minister's
dow, and that I was called upon to do
. No Service Book could be found; and
my own Book, which I had, I could not
nd the Order for Marriage.

Letter to the Vice-Chancellor.

Sir,

I pray take care of Lent, and the disputa-
ions in their beginnings, and speak to the
Jeads of Houses at your next meeting, that
hey warn their several Companies, that they
eep disputations at the Schools diligently,
ut very orderly and peaceably. And since
have now by many years' experience ob-
erved, that coursing between one College

and another is the great mother of all disorder, and that it is almost impossible to
have decent and orderly disputations, if that
be permitted; these are to require you, that
you suffer no such coursing at all under any
pretence. And farther, I would have you
speak with the Principal of Brazen-nose, that
he would command their cellar to be better
looked to, that no strong and unruly argument be drawn from that topic-place. And
I pray desire the Heads to be very careful,
that the disputations may be school-like and
peaceable.

W. CANT.

Lambeth, Feb. ult. 163⅞.

March 27, Wednesday, Coronation day.
King Charles took his journey northward,
against the Scottish covenanting rebels. God
of His infinite mercy bless him with health
and success!—March 29, Friday. An extreme fire in St. Olave's parish, Southwark:
forty houses burnt down.

April 3, Wednesday. Before the King's going, I settled with him a great business for the Queen; which I understood she would never move for herself. The Queen gave me great thanks. And this day I waited purposely on her, to give her thanks for her gracious acceptance. She was pleased to be very free with me, and to promise me freedom.

April 29, Monday. This day the King went from York towards Newcastle; but stayed at Durham for a week at least.

May 28. His Majesty encamped two miles west from Berwick by Tweed.

June 4, Whitsun Tuesday. As I was going to do my duty to the Queen, an officer of the Lord Mayor met me, and delivered to me two very seditious papers, the one to the Lord Mayor and Aldermen, the other to excite the apprentices, &c. Both subscribed by John Lilburn, a prisoner in the Fleet, sentenced in the Star-Chamber, &c. June 5, Wednesday. I delivered both these to the Lords of the Council. — June 15 and 17,

Saturday and Monday.   The peace concluded between the King and the Scottish rebels. God make it safe and honourable to the King and kingdom.—June 28, Friday.   I sent the remainder of my manuscripts to Oxford, being in number 576; and about an hundred of them were Hebrew, Arabic, and Persian. I had formerly sent them above 700 volumes.

Aug. 1, Thursday.   His Majesty came back from his northern journey to Theobalds, and to Whitehall on Saturday, Aug. 3.   Many varieties since the Assembly held and ended in Scotland.   The Bishops thrust out... The Parliament there yet sitting.

Oct. 11 and 12, Friday and Saturday. The Spanish navy was set upon by the Hollanders in the Downs.   The fight began to be hot, when they were past Dover.   They were in all near 60 sail.   The Spaniards suffered much in that fight, not without our dishonour, that they should dare to begin the fight there.   But this is one of the effects of the Scottish daring.

Extract of a Letter to Dr. Fell, Dean of Ch. Ch.

Concerning the hour of your Vespers, I would have you to weigh well one main thing; which is, that as the Morning Service is every where to end by twelve at farthest, so the Vespers never begin before three, and end by five. And this I take it is universal. And the reason of it (as I conceive) is, that the prayers of the Church, howsoever different in place, might be jointly put up to God in all places at the same time. How fit it will be upon particular respects to vary such an universal tradition, would be well thought on. As for the hour which they say they shall gain to their studies by this change, that works little upon me. For if men be so studiously minded, that hour may be taken, as well after prayers as before. And prayers coming between, will rather be a relaxation to them than a hindrance. Besides, I cannot foresee what example this may produce in other Cathedrals. And I would be very loth they should learn an ill example from the University. Therefore I pray think well of these and other circumstances, before you make any change.

W. CANT.

Lambeth, Oct. 18, 1639.

Extract from Dr. Frewen's Letters to the Archbishop.

Whilst I was at the examinations on Saturday, Nov. 16, there came into the School a stranger, who seemed to be of very good quality; for he had three or four servants attending him. There he sat a diligent auditor for the space of an hour. Then went forth, and taking horse at the gate, vanished, without leaving any possibility of a discovery what he was; for there was not any scholar seen in his company; nor can I find that he did so much as stop at any inn. Whatever the ends of his coming were, he cannot but speak well of the exercise; for it was at that very time singularly well performed.

A. FREWEN.

November 18, 1639.

My judgment upon this was as follows:

Sir,

'Tis a pretty accident of the gentleman's coming to hear the examinations upon Saturday last: and I am heartily glad the exercise was so good, and worthy his audience. But as his coming was unexpected, and his departure sudden, so we must be contented to leave his person unknown, unless some accident discover it. But what say you to this? May it be some Jesuit attended with three or four novices, that came to see what this new business is in the University? For why any gentleman in the kingdom should come and go in that fashion, without so much as saluting the Vice-Chancellor, being present upon the place, I for my part cannot tell, nor do I believe any would so do.

W. Cant.

Lambeth, Dec. 20, 1639.

Dec. 2, Monday. A. Sh. my chirurgeon in trust, gave me great and unexpected ease in my great infirmity. But after, the weakness continued. — Dec. 6, Thursday. The King declared his resolution for a Parliament, in case of the Scottish rebellion. The first movers to it were my Lord Deputy of Ireland, my Lord Marquess Hamilton, and myself. And a resolution voted at the Board, to assist the King in extraordinary ways; if the Parliament should prove peevish, and refuse, &c. —Dec. 27, Friday. Being St. John's day, at night, between 12 and 2 of the clock next morning, the greatest wind that ever I heard blow. Many of the poor watermen at Lambeth had their boats tumbled up and down, as they lay on the land, and broken to pieces. One of my servants went into London, and durst not come home, the evening was so foul. And it was God's great blessing both on him and me. For that night the shafts of two chimneys were blown down upon the roof of his chamber, and beat down both the lead and the rafters upon his bed; where had he been that night, he must have perished. At Croydon, one of the pinnacles fell from the steeple; and beat down the lead

and the roof of the church, near 200 feet
square.

Jan. 24, Friday. At night I dreamed that
my father (who died 46 years since) came to
me; and, to my thinking, he was as well and
as cheerful as ever I saw him. He asked
me, what I did here? And after some speech,
I asked him, how long he would stay with
me? He answered, he would stay, till he
had me away with him. I am not moved
with dreams, yet I thought fit to remember
this.—Jan. 25, Saturday. St. Paul's, a very
blustering and a tempestuous day. – Jan. 26,
Sunday. I received the Queen's gracious
assurance of her favour in the business,
which his Majesty had committed to me
with others, &c.

*To the Vice-Chancellor, concerning Disputations
in Lent, &c.*

At this time I writ to the Vice-Chancellor
to speak to the Heads before Lent begin, and
to desire them, that they would be very careful of their several Companies, that the public

disputations then may be quick and scholar-like, and yet without tumult. And this I left principally upon his care to look to, calling the Proctors to his assistance.

I received a letter this last week from a Reverend Bishop in this kingdom, in which he complains that Amesius and Festus Hommius (though I think before your time) have been reprinted in the University. They are professed friends to the Presbyterial government. And though they may speak and print what they please at Leyden or Amsterdam, yet methinks it is a great oversight to make them speak by ourselves and our presses, especially in the Universities. For too many men, in these broken times, will be apt enough to say, that we allow and approve of that doctrine, which we print by licence. I pray speak with the printers; and let them know from me, that I will not allow them to print any book, though it hath been printed before, without new leave from the Vice-Chancellor for the time being. And that if they do print any thing without such leave, I will utterly suppress them. And I pray send me word in what year of our Lord these two books were printed there.

W. CANT.

Lambeth, Feb. 7, 1628.

Feb. 9. Sunday. [A large passage inserted, and afterwards blotted out.]

Letter from Oxford to the Archbishop, concern-ing Tavern-haunting, &c.

Right Honourable and my singular good
    Lord,

It was objected unto me at my late being in London, by persons of good quality, that our Universities of England were grown to that corruption, especially of excessive drink-ing, that many did miscarry by the liberty and ill example which was given them there. Insomuch, that many, to avoid the danger, did send their sons beyond seas for their education. Whereunto I made answer, that the humours of men are such in this age, that innocence and perfection itself, being in au-thority, could hardly avoid calumny. That the times are much better than heretofore they were; and that the fault (if there were any) did much proceed from the parents themselves, who think it a great disparagement to their sons, that they should be kept within the limits of discipline.

Notwithstanding all which, and what else may justly be replied, the serious consideration of what was objected, hath caused me so much to forget mine own unworthiness, as by my own pen to intimate unto your Grace, (what I have long wished that some other would have done,) that the liberty of resorting to taverns, and other drinking-houses, and the excess committed there, is such, as may give some occasion of scandal, being dangerous to youth, and shameful in others, who ought to be examples of sobriety and virtue. Having upon this occasion enquired into times past, since the happy reformation of this University, I understand by credible information, that Dr. Pinck, by his personal visiting of suspected places, left the University, in this respect, in better state than it is

at this present. For me to write how dangerous the relapse into so loathsome and general
a disease may prove, were to forget myself,
and my principal intention, which was only
to make known unto you this defect, and
thereby to do service to this place, and in
part to express my thankfulness to yourself
for the much favour vouchsafed unto me.

Oxford, Feb. 24, 1644.

This information I had from a Master of
Arts in Oxford, whom I dare trust, but will
not name. Whereupon, I wrote to the Vice-
Chancellor as follows:

I received a Letter this week from Oxford,
from an ordinary plain man, but a good
scholar, and very honest. And it troubles
me more than any Letter I have received
many a day. It is true, I have heard of late
from some men of quality here above, that
the University was relapsing into a drinking
humour, to its great dishonour. But, I confess, I believed it not, because I had no inti-
mation of it from you. But this Letter comes

from a man that can have no ends but
honesty, and the good of that place.   And
because you shall see what he writes, I send
you here a copy of his Letter, and do earnestly beg of you, that you will forthwith set
yourself to punish all haunting of taverns and
ale-houses with all the strictness that may
be, that the University, now advancing in
learning, may not sink in manners, which
will shame and destroy all.

I am informed too from a very good, but
another, hand, that there is extreme liberty
given and taken by young noblemen and
gentlemen of the better sort in the University: that Tutors in most Colleges do only
bestow a little pains in reading to them, if
they will come at them, but use no power of
government over them, or any restraint; as
if they had nothing to do but only to read to
them. Besides, almost all of them are suffered to keep horses. And by that means,
when they are restrained from taverns, and
ill company within the University, they ride
forth to the neighbouring places, both to

drink and perhaps to do worse. I know you cannot be blamed for the neglect of Tutors in private Colleges: but, I pray, at your next meeting with the Heads, let them know what I have here written, and desire their care for amendment, if this report be true. But true or false, I took it my duty to let you know what is come to my ears from some, who are perhaps too nearly interested in it.

W. CANT.

Lambeth, Feb. 28, 1644.

From the Archbishop to Dr. Bailey, concerning the above Letter.

In the business of the Examinations, you write thus: " The Vice-Chancellor's successors cannot be so wanting to themselves, and the common good, as not to pursue so fair an example." It is true, it is a very fair example: but can it not therefore choose but be pursued by the successors? I pray tell me! Was not Dr. Pinck's care for suppressing the Scholars haunting of taverns and ale-houses a very fair example? Were not you and Dr. Frewen

his successors? And have you two pursued
his fair example? I have this reason to
believe you have not.   I have at this present
received a Letter from Oxford, from a very
private, but a very honest hand; and with
an expression full of grief, that the University is fallen again into that drunken relapse,
in which it swam before Dr. Pinck's Vice-
Chancellorship.   And I assure you, it troubles me very much, because this very week I
have heard also, that some persons of honour
and credit have lately spoken very much
concerning this relapse: which yet I confess
I did not believe till I received this Letter,
which I cannot distrust, knowing the man
which writ to be without spleen or ends.
And I pray God send you governors there to
take better care, or else all my care will be
lost.

                              W. CANT.

Lambeth, Feb. 28, 164⅜.

Reply of the Vice-Chancellor.

The information given up to your Grace
against me, hath been long expected; yet

never less than at this time. For strange it
is to me, that an increase of drunkards should
follow upon a decrease of ale-houses. Had
the informer (who ever he be) been with me
in my dirty night walks this winter, and
sped as ill as I have done, his eyes would not
serve him so well to espy faults where none
are boldly; I dare say it, there seldom passes
one night in a whole week, in which one of
the Proctors, or myself, do not walk the
round. And divers times I have gone (as
my servants can witness) from one end of
the town to the other, after Christ Church
bell hath tolled, and not found one Scholar,
either in the streets, or in any of the four
taverns. Few hours before the receipt of
your Grace's Letters, I committed one of
Trinity College to prison for disorder in the
night; but beside him, I have not, I protest, of late met with any.—Yet, not to justify
ourselves too far, there is, I confess, too much
good fellowship amongst us; but the informer mislays it: it is driven out of town
(as others besides myself observe) into our

private Colleges and Halls. There they can
and do debauch themselves more securely,
being out of the reach of the public Magis-
trate: yea, and of their own governors too
in some houses, the more the pity.   There
have indeed (for which I am heartily sorry)
one or two disasters lately happened here,
(for seldom they come single ;) but that the
actors were in their drink I cannot say, much
less that they fetched it out of the town ; for
as yet I cannot trace them in any ale-house.
Hull is in the castle ; for (as I told the Dean)
I know him to be a very disorderly man.
Others suspected to have had a hand in that
barbarous assault are upon bail, and so shall
continue a while ; though a messenger from
my Lord of Oxon yesterday brought me
word, that the party hurt is in the judgment
of his chirurgeons now past danger.

A. FREWEN.

Oxford, March 2, 1648.

April 13, Monday.   The Parliament sat
down, called about the rebellion of Scotland.

-April 14, Tuesday. The Convocation egan at St. Paul's.—April 24, Friday. The ot contestation in the Lords' House, which hould have precedence, the King's supply, r the subjects' grievance. Voted in the Jpper House for the King.

May 5, Tuesday. The Parliament ended, ind nothing done. The Convocation coninued.—May 9, Saturday. A paper posted ipon the Old Exchange, animating prentices o sack my house upon the Monday following, May 11, early.

[H. W. From this place, four pages together in the original are in part burned, in the form of a crescent. This damage was done to the book, while it was in Mr. Prynne's hands, before it was produced as evidence against the Archbishop at his trial. For in the following history, at March 13, 1643, the Archbishop saith, I know into whose hands my book is fallen; but what hath been done with it, I know not. This is to be seen; some passages in that book are half burnt out; whether purposely, or by chance,

God knoweth.   And the like words of the
Archbishop occur afterwards, at July 29, 1644.
That passage (of Feb. 11, 1640, urged against
the Archbishop out of his Diary) is more
than half burnt out; as is to be seen; whether of purpose by Mr. Prynne, or casually,
I cannot tell; yet the passage as confidently
made up, and read to your Lordships, as if
nothing were wanting.   It is indeed un-
deniably evident to any one, who compareth
the original with Prynne's printed copy,
that this accident had befallen the book,
before Prynne had caused it to be transcribed for the press.   Yet he taketh no notice
of it; but filleth up the places with such
words, as himself pleaseth; and published
the whole without any distinction of his own
additions.   I have partly from Prynne,
partly from my own conjecture, supplied
the mutilated places, as well as I could; but
have included all such suppletory words in
crotchets; that so the reader may easily distinguish those words, which are yet to be
read in the original, from those which are

not; and may judge, whether the several places be aptly filled up.]

May 11, Monday night. At midnight my house at Lambeth was beset with 500 of these rascel routers. I had notice, and strengthened the house as well as I could; and, God be thanked, I had no harm: they continued there full two hours. Since, I have fortified my house as well as I can; and hope all may be safe. But yet libels are continually set up in all places of note in the city. My deliverance was great, God make me thankful for it.—May 21, Thursday. One of the chief being taken, was condemned at Southwark, and hanged and quartered on Saturday morning following, May 23. But before this, May 15, some of these mutinous people came in the day time, and brake the White-Lion prison; and let loose their fellows, both out of that prison, and the King's Bench, and the other prisoners also out of the White-Lion.—May 29, Friday. The Convocation sate after the ending of the Parliament till May 29, and then ended; having made in that time 17

Canons; which, 1 hope, will be useful to the Church.—May 29. The Bishop of Gloucester, Godfrey Goodman, suspended for notorious scandal to the Church, in refusing first to subscribe the Canons, and after to profess a reservation. He had long before been suspected as inclining to popery. The Canons were all voted nemine dissentiente, save this Bishop, who had in general consented before.

July 10, Friday. I took my oath to the new Canons at the Council table; and so did my Lord Bishop of London; and after him the Bishop of Gloucester submit himself, and took the oath; and was released out of prison by the King's command.—July 22, Tuesday. I christened the King's young son Henry, at Oatlands. The Queen was there happily delivered of him, July 8, on Wednesday, being the day of the Solemn Fast, about six of the clock in the evening.—Aug. 20, Thursday. His Majesty took his journey towards the north in haste, upon information that the Scots were entered the

Monday before into England, and meant to be at Newcastle by Saturday. The Scots entered Aug. 20.

Aug. 22, Saturday. A vile libel brought me, found in Covent Garden; animating the apprentices and soldiers to fall upon me in the King's absence.

Sept. 21. I received a letter from John Rockel, a man both by name and person unknown to me. He was among the Scots, as he travelled through the Bishopric of Durham; he heard them inveigh and rail at me exceedingly, and that they hoped shortly to see me, as the Duke was, slain by one least suspected. His letter was to advise me to look to myself.

Sept. 24, Thursday. A great Council of the Lords was called by the King to York, to consider what way was best to be taken to get out the Scots; and this day the meeting began at York, and continued till Oct. 28.

Oct. 22, Thursday. The High Commission sitting at St. Paul's, because of the troubles of the times. Very near 2000 Brownists made a tumult at the end of the Court, tore down all the benches in the Consistory, and cried out, They would have no Bishop, nor no High Commission.—Oct. 27, Tuesday, Simon and Jude's eve. I went into my upper study to see some Manuscripts, which I was sending to Oxford. In that study hung my picture taken by the life; and coming in, I found it fallen down upon the face, and lying on the floor, the string being broken by which it was hanged against the wall. I am almost every day threatened with my ruin in Parliament. God grant this be no omen!

Nov. 3, Tuesday. The Parliament began: the King did not ride, but went by water to King's Stairs, and through Westminster Hall to the Church, and so to the House.—Nov. 4, Wednesday. The Convocation began at St. Paul's.—Nov. 11, Wednesday. Thomas Viscount Wentworth, Earl of Strafford, accused to the Lords by the House of Commons for high treason, and restrained to the Usher of the House.—Nov. 25, Wednesday. He was sent to the Tower.

Dec. 2, Wednesday. A great debate in the House, that no Bishop should be so much as of the Committee for preparatory examinations in this cause, as accounted causa sanguinis; put off till the next day.—Dec. 3, Thursday. The debate declined.—Dec. 4, Friday. The King gave way, that his Council should be examined upon oath in the Earl of Strafford's case. I was examined this day.

Letter to the Vice-Chancellor.

I thank you for your pains in your search for arms among recusants, and am glad you find all so safe, and them so unfurnished. As for Mr. Hunt, if he be a stranger, the sooner the town is rid of him, the better.

For the confirmation of your endowments upon your Professors and Orators, you shall do well when the great businesses are more over, (for till then it will not be intended,) to move for confirmation in Parliament. And in the mean time it may be very fit for you to prepare a Bill by some good Counsel, which may contain them all in one, if it may be.

It is true, you write that most Colleges have upon Christmas-day a Sermon and a Communion in their private Chapels, and by that means cannot come to the public Sermon of the University at Christ Church. And whereas you write farther, that some have wished, that in regard of this, the morning Sermon for the University might be put off to the afternoon, (as it is upon Easter-day for the like occasion;) I for my part think the motion very good, it being a day of solemn observation. Yet I would have it proposed to the Heads, and then that which you shall do by public consent shall very well satisfy me.

W. CANT.

Lambeth, Dec. 4, 1640.

Letter from the Archbishop concerning Mr. Wilkinson's Sermon.

Mr. Wilkinson complained in Parliament against the Vice-Chancellor, for censuring of his Sermon. The Vice-Chancellor, according to the command of the Committee for Religion in the House of Commons, sent up the copy of Wilkinson's Sermon, and his exceptions against it, upon Tuesday, December 8th, the time appointed for the Committee. But the carrier's late coming in hindered the delivery for that time; but it was delivered the next morning by Dr. Baylie.

W. Cant.

Letter from the Vice-Chancellor and Heads of Houses.

Whereas upon enquiry made by Dr. Frewen, late Vice-Chancellor of Oxford, in two several assemblies of the Heads of Houses there, none of them could inform him of any University-man, whom he knew or probably suspected to be a Papist, or popishly affected: notwithstanding which care of the governors, and clearness of the University, it could not be avoided but some persons' suggestions should be put up to the High Court of Parliament, as if Mass were ordinarily said in the University, and frequented by University-men, without any control of the governors there.

We therefore the present Vice-Chancellor and the Heads of Houses, for the better clearing of our University from such foul imputations, have thought fit under our hands to testify, that we are so far from conniving at the celebration of Mass here, or knowing of any such matter, that we neither know, nor can probably suspect, any Member of our University to be a Papist, or popishly addicted.

Dec. 4, 1640.

In witness whereof we have subscribed,

    Christo. Potter, Vice-Chanc. Oxon.
    Nat. Brent, Præfect. Coll. Mert.
    Ro. Kettle, President of Trin. Coll.
    Jo. Prideaux, Rector Coll. Exon. and S. T. P. Reg.
    Jo. Wilkinson, Aul. Magd. Princ.
    Samuel Radclif, Coll. Æn. Nas. Princ.
    Jo. Tolson, Coll. Oriel. Præpos.
    Paul Hood, Rector Coll. Lincoln.
    A. Frewen, Pres. Coll. Magd.
    Rich. Baylie, Præsid. S. John.
    Tho. Clayton, Coll. Pemb. Mag. Med. Prof. Reg.
    Tho. Lawrence, Magis. Coll. Bal.
    Fran. Mansel, Coll. Jesu Princ.
    Tho. Walker, Universit. Mr.
    Gilbert Sheldon, Ward. of All Souls Coll.
    Daniel Escott, Ward. of Wadh. Coll.
    Guil. Strode, Eccl. Christ. Subdec.
    Adam Airay, Princip. of Edmund Hall.

Ro. Newlin, Præs. Coll. Corp. Christ.
Rich. Zouch, Aul. All. Princip.
Philip Parsons, Aul. Cervin. Princip.
John Saunders, Aul. Mar. Princ.
Degory Wheare, Princ. Glou. Hall.
P. Alliboad, Proc. Sen.
N. Greaves, Proc. Jun.

The other Heads of Houses were not in town when this was subscribed.

Dec. 16, Wednesday. The Canons condemned in the House of Commons, as being against the King's prerogative, the fundamental laws of the Realm, the liberty and propriety of the subject, and containing divers other things tending to sedition, and of dangerous consequence. Upon this I was made the author of them, and a Committee put upon me to enquire into all my actions, and to prepare a charge. The same morning, in the Upper House, I was named as an incendiary by the Scottish Commissioners, and a complaint promised to be drawn up tomorrow.—Dec. 18, Friday. I was accused by the House of Commons for high treason, without any particular charge laid against me; which, they said, should be prepared in convenient time. Mr. Densill Hollis was the man that brought up the message to the Lords. Soon after, the charge was brought into the Upper House by the Scottish Commissioners, tending to prove me an incendiary. I was presently committed to the Gentleman Usher; but was permitted to go in his company to my house at Lambeth, for a book or two to read in, and such papers as pertained to my defence against the Scots. I stayed at Lambeth till the evening to avoid the gazing of the people. I went to evening prayer in my chapel. The Psalms of the day, Ps. xciii. and xciv. and chap. l. of Isaiah, gave me great comfort. God make me worthy of it, and fit to receive it! As I went to my barge, hundreds of my poor neighbours stood there, and prayed for my safety, and return to my house. For which I bless God and them. —Dec. 21, Monday. I was fined £500 in the Parliament House, and Sir John Lambe and Sir Henry Martin £250 a-piece, for keeping Sir Robert Howard close prisoner in the case

of the escape of the Lady Viscountess Pur-
becke out of the Gate-House; which lady he
kept avowedly, and had children by her. In
such a case, say the imprisonment were more
than the law allow; what may be done for
honour and religion sake? This was not a
a fine to the King, but damage to the party.—
Dec. 23, Wednesday. The Lords ordered me
to pay the money presently; which was
done.

Jan. 21, Thursday. A Parliament-man
of good note, and interested with divers
Lords, sent me word, that by reason of my
patient and moderate carriage since my
commitment, four Earls of great power
in the Upper House of the Lords were
not now so sharp against me as at first.
And that now they were resolved only to
sequester me from the King's Council, and to
put me from my Archbishopric. So I see,
what justice I may expect; since here is a
resolution taken, not only before my answer,
but before my charge was brought up against
me.

Feb. 14, Sunday. A. R. And this, if I live, and continue Archbishop of Canterbury till after Michaelmas-day come twelve-month, anno 1642, God bless me in this!—Feb. 26, Friday. This day I had been full ten weeks in restraint at Mr. Maxwell's house. And this day, being St. Augustin's day[a], my charge was brought up from the House of Commons to the Lords, by Sir Henry Vane the younger. It consisted of fourteen articles. These generals they craved time to prove in particular. The copy of this general charge is among my papers. I spake something to it. And the copy of that also is among my papers.—I had favour from the Lords not to go to the Tower till the Monday following.

March 1, Monday. I went in Mr. Maxwell's coach to the Tower. No noise, till I came into Cheapside. But from thence to the

[a] In the English Calendar, as well as the Roman, the memory of St. Augustine of Canterbury is celebrated May 26; and of St. Augustin of Hippo, August 28. In the Paris Breviary, the Feast of S. Aug. Cantuar. is put back one day. Ed.

Tower, I was followed and railed at by the apprentices and rabble, in great numbers, to the very Tower gates, where I left them; and I thank God, He made me patient.—March 9, Shrove-Tuesday. —— was with me in the Tower; and gave great engagements of his faith to me.—March 13, Saturday. Divers Lords dined with the Lord Herbert at his new house by Fox-Hall in Lambeth. Three of these Lords in the boat together, when one of them saying he was sorry for my commitment, because the building of St. Paul's went slow on there-while; the Lord Brooke replied, I hope some of us shall live to see no one stone left upon another of that building.— March 15, Monday. A Committee for Religion settled in the Upper House of Parliament. Ten Earls, ten Bishops, ten Barons. So the Lay-votes shall be double to the Clergy. This Committee will meddle with Doctrine as well as Ceremonies; and will call some Divines to them to consider of the business. As appears by a Letter hereto annexed, sent by the Lord Bishop of Lincoln, to some

Divines to attend this service. Upon the whole matter, I believe this Committee will prove the national Synod of England, to the great dishonour of this Church. And what else may follow upon it, God knoweth.— March 22, Monday. The Earl of Strafford's trial began in Westminster Hall ; and it continued till the end of April, taking in the variation of the House of Commons, who after a long hearing drew a Bill of Attainder against him.

1641. March 25, Thursday. A. Sh. performed his promise to the uttermost.

May 1, Saturday. The King came into the Upper House ; and there declared before both Houses, how diligently he had hearkened to all the proceedings with the Earl of Strafford ; and found that his fault, whatever it was, could not amount to high treason : that if it went by Bill it must pass by him ; and that he could not with his conscience find him guilty, nor would wrong his conscience so far. But advised them to proceed by way of misdemeanour ; and he would concur with them. The same day, after the

King was gone, a Letter was read in the Upper House from the Scots; in which they did earnestly desire to be gone. It was moved for a present conference with the House of Commons about it. The debate about it was very short; yet the Commons were risen beforehand.

May 9. That night late, Sir Dudly Carlton, one of the Clerks of the Council, was sent to the Tower, to give the Earl warning that he must prepare to die the Wednesday morning following. The Earl of Strafford received the message of death with great courage, yet sweetness; (as Sir Dudly himself after told me.) On Monday morning the Earl sent for the Lord Primate of Armagh to come to him. He came; and the same day visited me, and gave me very high testimony of the Earl's sufficiency and resolution: and among the rest this; that he never knew any layman in all his life that so well and fully under-stood matters of divinity, as the Earl did; and that his resolutions were as firm and as good. In the mean time an offer was made to him. It was this; that, if he would employ his power and credit with the King for the taking of Episcopacy out of the Church, he should yet have his life. His Christian answer was very heroical; that he would not buy his life at so dear a rate. The man that sent him this message was his brother in law, Mr. Densill Hollis, one of the great leading men in the House of Commons; and my Lord Primate of Armagh avowed this from the Earl of Strafford's own mouth. And, as he was of too generous a spirit to lie basely, so, being in preparing of himself to leave the world, it cannot be thought he would with a dying mouth belie his brother. From the " Troubles, &c." p. 177.

May 12, Wednesday. The Earl of Strafford beheaded upon Tower Hill.

The Earl prepared himself: and upon Wednesday morning, about ten of the clock, being May the 12th, he was beheaded on the Tower Hill, many thousands beholding him. The speech which he made at his end was a great testimony of his religion and piety, and

was then printed. And in their judgment
who were men of worth, and some upon,
some near the scaffold, and saw him die, he
made a patient and pious and courageous end.
Inasmuch that some doubted whether his
death had more of the Roman or the Christian in it, it was so full of both. And, notwithstanding this hard fate which fell upon
him, he is dead with more honour, than any
of them will gain who hunted after his
life. Thus ended the wisest, the stoutest,
and every way the ablest subject, that this
nation hath bred these many years. The
only imperfections which he had, that were
known to me, were his want of bodily health,
and a carelessness or rather roughness not to
oblige any. And his mishaps in this last
action were, that he groaned under the
public envy of the nobles; served a mild
and a gracious Prince, *who knew not how to be,
or be made great*[b]; and trusted false, perfi-

[b] These grave and sad, yet surely gentle words,
furnish the only instance I know of, in which the loyal
Primate has ventured to reflect upon his King; and it

dious, and cowardly men in the northe
employment; though he had many doub

would be a wrong to his high name and memory, ev
more than to the memory of Charles, to let them sta
now, except in company with the bitter and earne
words of penitence, which the King has written
against himself for his great sin in Strafford's dea
"I am so far from excusing or denying that complian
on my part (for plenary consent it was not) to 1
destruction, whom in my judgment I thought not,
any clear law, guilty of death, that I never bare a
touch of conscience with greater regret; which, as
sign of my repentance, I have often with sorrow co
fessed both to God and men, as an act of so sin!
frailty, that it discovered more a fear of man than
God, Whose Name and Place on earth no man
worthy to bear, who will avoid inconveniences of Sta
by acts of so high injustice, as no public convenien
can expiate or compensate. I see it a bad exchan
to wound a man's own conscience, thereby to sal
State sores; to calm the storms of popular discontent
by stirring up a tempest in a man's own bosom. B
Thou, O God of infinite mercies, forgive me that act
sinful compliance, which hath greater aggravatio
upon me than any man. O Lord, I acknowledge n
transgression, and my sin is ever before me." Ki
Charles's Works, folio, 648.

put to him about it. This day was after called by divers, Homicidium Comitis Straffordiæ, The day of the murder of Strafford: because, when malice itself could find no law to put him to death, they made a law of purpose for it. God forgive all, and be merciful!

The Earl being thus laid low, and his great services done in Ireland made part of his accusation, I cannot but observe two things. The one, that upon Sunday morning before, Francis Earl of Bedford (having about a month before lost his second son, in whom he most joyed) died, the small pox striking up into his brain. This Lord was one of the main plotters of Strafford's death: and I know where he, with other Lords, before the Parliament sat down, resolved to have his blood. But God would not let him live to take joy therein, but cut him off in the morning, whereas the Bill for the Earl of Strafford's death was not signed till night. The other is, that at this time the Parliament tendered two, and but two, Bills to the King

to sign.   This to cut off Strafford's head was
one; and the other was, that this Parliament
should neither be dissolved, nor adjourned,
but by the consent of both Houses: in
which, what he cut off from himself[b], time
will better shew than I can.   God bless the
King and his royal issue!

Among divers others they spread one
(untruth), in which they delivered to the
world, that the Earl of Strafford drawing
near to his end, when he saw no remedy but
he must die, fell into great and passionate
expressions against me: that I and my counsels had been the ruin of him and his house;
and that he cursed me bitterly.   Now
as this is most false in itself, so am I
most able to make it appear so.   For his
Lordship, being to suffer on the Wednesday
morning, did upon Tuesday in the afternoon desire the Lord Primate of Armagh,
then with him, to come to me, and desire me
that I would not fail to be in my chamber
window at the open casement the next

[b] Moribundi solent vaticinari.

morning, when he was to pass by it, as he went to execution; that, though he might not speak with me, yet he might see me, and take his last leave of me. I sent him word I would, and did so. And the next morning as he passed by, he turned towards me, and took the solemnest leave, that I think was ever by any at distance taken one of another; and this in the sight of the Earl of Newport, then Lord Constable of the Tower, the Lord Primate of Armagh, the Earl of Cleveland, the Lieutenant of the Tower, and divers other knights and gentlemen of worth. *Troubles*, p. 178.

[Heylin (*Cypr. Angl.* p. 480.) thus relates it:—The Lord Strafford, the night before the execution, sent for the Lieutenant of the Tower, and asked him whether it were possible he might speak with the Archbishop. The Lieutenant told him he might not do it, without order from the Parliament. Whereupon the Earl replied, " You shall hear what passeth between us; for it is not a time now either for him to plot heresy, or me to plot

treason." The Lieutenant answered, that he
was limited; and therefore desired his
Lordship would petition the Parliament for
that favour. " No," said he, " I have gotten
my dispatch from them, and will trouble
them no more. I am now petitioning an
higher Court, where neither partiality can
be expected, nor error feared. But, my Lord,"
said he, turning to the Primate of Ireland,
whose company he had procured of the
Houses in that fatal exigent, " I will tell
you what I would have spoken to my Lord's
Grace of Canterbury. You shall desire the
Archbishop to lend me his prayers this night,
and to give me his blessing when I do. go
abroad to-morrow; and to be in his window,
that by my last farewell I may give him
thanks for this, and all other his former
favours." The Primate, having delivered the
message without delay, the Archbishop replied, that in conscience he was bound to
the first, and in duty and obligation to the
second: but he feared his weakness and
passion would not lend him eyes to behold

his last departure. The next morning at his coming forth he drew near to the Archbishop's lodging, and said to the Lieutenant, " Though I do not see the Archbishop, yet give me leave, I pray you, to do my last observance towards his rooms." In the mean time the Archbishop, advertised of his approach, came out to the window. Then the Earl bowing himself to the ground, " My Lord," said he, " your prayers and your blessing." The Archbishop lift up his hands, and bestowed both: but overcome with grief, fell to the ground in animi deliquio. The Earl, bowing the second time, said, " Farewell, my Lord; God protect your innocency." And because he (the Archbishop) feared that it might perhaps be thought an effeminacy or unbecoming weakness in him to sink down in the manner, he added, that he hoped by God's assistance, and his own innocency, that when he came to his own execution, which he daily longed for, the world should perceive he had been more sensible of the Lord Strafford's loss than

of his own; "and good reason it should be
so," said he, "for the gentleman was more
serviceable to the Church (he would not
mention the State) than either himself, or
any of all the Churchmen had ever been."
A gallant farewell to so eminent and beloved
a friend.]

June 23, Wednesday. I acquainted the
King by my Lord of London, that I would
resign my Chancellorship of Oxford, and
why.

And the truth is, I suffered much by the
Earl of Pembroke, who thought it long till
he had that place, which he had long gaped
for; and after the cloud was once spread
over me, spared me in no company: though
I had in all the time of my prosperity observed him in Court more than ever he had
deserved of me. And I had reason, notwithstanding all this causeless heat, to keep the
place, till I had justified myself against the
townsmen's petition (about the markets. Ed.).
So this great, and most malicious complaint
of the City of Oxford vanished, when they,

and somebody else for them, had shewed their teeth, but could not bite. *Troubles.*

June 25, Friday. I sent down my resignation of the Chancellorship of Oxford, to be published in Convocation.

God bless the University therewhile, and grant they may never have need of me, now unable to help them! *Troubles.* [In this year, 1647, they (the rebels) had begun a visitation of the University of Oxford, which they finished not till the next year; in which the Earl of Pembroke had been contented to be employed as Chancellor of the University: who had taken an oath to defend the rights and privileges of the University. Notwithstanding which, out of the extreme weakness of his understanding and the miserable compliance of his nature, he suffered himself to be made a property in joining with Brent, Prynne, and some Committee-men, and Presbyterian Ministers, as Commissioners for the Parliament to reform the discipline and erroneous doctrine of that famous University, by the rule of the Covenant; which was the

standard of all men's learning, and ability to
govern; all persons of what quality soever
being required to subscribe that test; which
the whole body of the University was so far
from submitting to, that they met in their Convocation, and, to their eternal renown, (being
at the same time under a strict and strong
garrison, put over them by the Parliament;
the King in prison; and all their hopes desperate,) passed a public Act (mainly from the
pen of Bishop Sanderson. Ed.), and declaration against the Covenant, with such invincible
arguments of the illegality, wickedness, and
perjury contained in it, that no man of the
contrary opinion, nor the Assembly of Divines,
(which then sat at Westminster, forming a
new Catechism, and scheme of religion,) ever
ventured to make any answer to it; nor
is it indeed to be answered, but must remain
to the world's end, as a monument of the
learning, courage, and loyalty of that excellent
place, against the highest malice and tyranny
that was ever exercised in or over any nation;
and which those famous Commissioners only

answered by expelling all those who refused
to submit to their jurisdiction, or to take the
Covenant; which was, upon the matter, the
whole University; scarce one Governor and
Master of College or Hall, and an incredible
small number of the Fellows, or Scholars,
submitting to either: whereupon that desolation being made, they placed in their rooms
the most notorious factious Presbyterians,
in the government of the several Colleges
or Halls; and such other of the same leaven
in the Fellowships, and Scholars' places, of
those whom they had expelled, without any
regard to the Statutes of the several Found-
ers, and the incapacities of the persons that
were put in. The omnipotence of an ordinance of Parliament confirmed all that was
this way done; and there was no farther
contending against it.

It might reasonably be concluded, that this
wild and barbarous depopulation would even
extirpate all that learning, religion, and loyalty, which had so eminently flourished there;
and that the succeeding ill-husbandry, and un-

skilful cultivation. would have made it fruitful
only in ignorance, profanation, atheism, and
rebellion. But, by God's wonderful blessing,
the goodness and richness of that soil could
not be made barren by all that stupidity and
negligence. It choked the weeds, and would
not suffer the poisonous seeds, which were
sown with industry enough, to spring up.
But after several tyrannical governments,
mutually succeeding each other, and with the
same malice and perverseness endeavouring
to extinguish all good literature and allegiance, it yielded a harvest of extraordinary
good and sound knowledge in all parts of
learning. And many, who were wickedly
introduced, applied themselves to the study
of good learning, and the practice of virtue,
and had inclination to that duty and obedience they had never been taught. So that,
when it pleased God to bring King Charles
the Second back to his throne, he found that
University (not to undervalue the other',

* There is a passage in the Strafford Papers, quoted
by Mr. Forster, (*Life of Straff.* p. 290.) which exhibits

which had nobly likewise rejected the ill in-
fusions which had been industriously poured
into it) abounding in excellent learning, and
devoted to duty and obedience, little inferior
to what it was before its desolation; which
was a lively instance of God's mercy and
purpose, for ever so to provide for His

very amusingly the college feeling of Laud and Strafford,
both Johnians, though of different Universities. " I am
sorry to speak it, but truth will out," writes Strafford to
Laud concerning an Episcopal delinquent, " this Bishop
is a St. John's man—of Oxford, I mean, not Cambridge; our Cambridge panniers never brought such
a fairing to the market." Laud makes merry upon
this, and retorts; " Yes, my good Lord, but it hath;
for what say you of Dean Palmer? who, besides his
other virtues, sold all the lead from off the church at Peterborough; yet he was brought in your Cambridge panniers: and so was Bishop Howland too, who used that
Bishopric as well as he did the Deanery. I pray examine your Cambridge panniers again, for some say such
may be found there. But I, for my part, will not
believe it unless your Lordship make me." Wentworth
appears to have contested this point in Laud's own
humour. The Bishop retorts, by asking him what his
" Jesuism" means.

Church, that the gates of hell shall never prevail against it; which were never opened wider, nor with more malice, than in that time. *Clarendon*, v. 481.]

Resignation of the Chancellorship, in a Letter to the University.

My present condition is not unknown to the whole world, yet by few pitied or deplored; the righteous God best knows the justice of my sufferings, on whom both in life and death I will ever depend: the last of which shall be unto me most welcome, in that my life is now burdensome unto me, my mind attended with variety of sad and grievous thoughts, my soul continually vexed with anxieties and troubles, groaning under the burden of a displeased Parliament, my name aspersed and grossly abused by the multiplicity of libellous pamphlets, and myself debarred from wonted access to the best of Princes, and it is vox populi that I am Popishly affected. How earnest I have been

in my disputations, exhortations, and otherwise, to quench such sparks, lest they should
become coals, I hope after my death you will
all acknowledge; yet in the midst of all my
afflictions, there is nothing more hath so
nearly touched me, as the remembrance of
your free and joyful acceptance of me to be
your Chancellor, and that I am now shut up
from being able to do you that service which
you might justly expect from me. When I
first received this honour, I intended to have
carried it with me to the grave; neither were
my hopes any less, since the Parliament
(called by his Majesty's royal command)
committed me to this royal prison. But since
(by reason of matters of greater consequence
yet in hand) the Parliament is pleased to
procrastinate my trial, I do hereby as thank-
fully resign my office of being Chancellor, as
ever I received that dignity, entreating you
to elect some honourable person, who upon
all occasions may be ready to serve you; and
I beseech God send you such an one as may
do all things for His glory, and the further-

ance of your most famous University. Thi
is the continual prayer of,

    Your dejected Friend and Chancellor,

        Being the last time I shall write so,

                    W. CAN1

Tower, June 28, 1641.

July 1, Thursday. This was done; an
the Earl of Pembroke chosen Chancellor b
joint consent.

Aug. 10, Tuesday. The King went po
into Scotland, the Parliament sitting, and th
armies not yet dissolved.

Sept. 23, Thursday. Mr. Adam Torle
my ancient, loving, and faithful servant, the
my steward, after he had served me ful
forty-two years, died, to my great loss an
grief.

Oct. 23. The Lords in Parliament se
questered my jurisdiction to my inferior offi
cers; and ordered, that I should give n
benefice, without acquainting them first t
whom I would give it; that so they migh
approve. This order was sent me on Tues
day, Nov. 2, in the afternoon.

Nov. 1. News came to the Parliament of the troubles in Ireland, the King being then in Scotland, where there were troubles enough also —Nov. 25, Thursday. The King, at his return from Scotland, was sumptuously entertained in London; and great joy on all hands. God prosper it!

On Thursday, Nov. 25, the King returning from Scotland, entered into London, was received with great state and joy, and sumptuously entertained. This made divers men think there would have been a turn in the present business. And what it might have proved, if the King would have presently and vigorously set himself to vindicate his own just power, and leave them their ancient and just privileges, is not, I think, hard to judge. But he let it cool; and gave that which is truly the *malignant faction* (but call others so) time to underwork him, and bring the City round, and all ran then stronger in the same current than ever it did. So God of His mercy bless all! *Troubles.*

Dec. 30, Thursday. The Archbishop of

York, and eleven Bishops more, sent to t
Tower for High Treason, for delivering
petition and a protestation into the Hou
that this was not a free Parliament, sin
they could not come to vote there, as th
are bound, without danger of their lives.

Jan. 4, Tuesday. His Majesty went in
the House of Commons, and demanded t
persons of Mr. Denzill Hollis, Sir Arth
Haslering, Mr. John Pym, Mr. John Ham
den, and Mr. William Stroude; whom h
Attorney had the day before, together wi
the Lord Kimbolton, accused of High Tre
son, upon seven articles. They had inforn
ation, and were not then in the Hous
they came in after, and great stir was ma
about this breach of the privileges of Pa
liament.

Feb. 6, Saturday. Voted in the Lord
House, that the Bishops shall have no vot
there in Parliament. The Commons ha
passed that Bill before. Great ringing f
joy, and bonfires in some parishes.—Feb. 1
Friday. The Queen went from Greenwic

toward Dover, to go into Holland with her
daughter the Princess Mary, who was lately
married to the Prince of Orange's son.
But the true cause was, the present dis-
contents here. The King accompanied her
to the sea.—Feb. 14. His Majesty's message
to both Houses printed, by which he puts
all into their hands; so God bless us!—Feb. 14.
An order came, that the twelve Bishops
might put in bail, if they would; and that
they should have their hearing upon Friday,
Feb. 25. They went out of the Tower on
Wednesday, Feb. 16, and were sent in again
Feb. 17, the House of Commons, on Wednesday night, protesting against their coming
forth, because they were not in a Parliamentary way made acquainted with it.—Feb.
20, Sunday. There came a tall man to me,
under the name of Mr. Hunt. He professed,
he was unknown to me; but came, he said, to
do me service in a great particular; and
prefaced it, that he was not set on by any
Statesman, or any of the Parliament. So he
drew a paper out of his pocket, and shewed

me four Articles drawn against me to the
Parliament, all touching my near conversation with Priests, and my endeavours by
them to subvert Religion in England. He
told me, the Articles were not yet put into
the House: they were subscribed by one
Willoughby, who, he said, was a Priest, but
now come from them. I asked him, what
service it was he could do me: He said, he
looked for no advantage to himself. I conceived hereupon, this was a piece of villany;
and had him tell Willoughby, he was a villain; and bid him put his Articles into the
Parliament when he will. So I went presently into my inner chamber, and told
Mr. Edward Hyde, and Mr. Richard Cobb,
what had befallen me. But after I was sorry
at my heart, that my indignation at this base
villany made me so hasty, to send Hunt
away; and that I had not desired Mr. Lieutenant to seise on him, till he brought forth
this Willoughby.—Feb. 25, Friday. The
Queen went to sea for Holland, and her
eldest daughter the Princess Mary with her.

March 6, Sunday. After Sermon, as I was walking up and down my chamber before dinner, without any slip or treading awry, the sinew of my right leg gave a great crack, and broke asunder in the same place where I had broken it before, Feb. 5, 162¾. Orders about Stisted.

It was two months before I could go out of my chamber. On Sunday, (May 15,) I made shift between my man and my staff to go to church. There one Mr. Joslin preached, with vehemency becoming Bedlam, with treason sufficient to hang him in any other State, and with such particular abuse to me, that women and boys stood up in the church, to see how I could bear it. I humbly thank God for my patience. All along things grew higher between the King and the Parliament. God send a good issue!

May 29. Four ships came into the river, with part of the ammunition from Hull.

Aug. 22, Monday, the King set up his standard at Nottingham.—Aug. 24. The Parliament having committed three officers of the ordinance, and sent two new ones in the room; this day they brake open all the doors, and possessed themselves of the stores. —Aug. 27, Saturday. Earl of Southampton and Sir John Culpepper sent from the King to have a treaty for peace, refused; unless the King would take down his standard, and recal his Proclamation, which made them traitors.

Sept. 1, Thursday. Bishops voted down, and Deans and Chapters, in the Lower House. That night bonfires and ringing all over the city: ordered cunningly by Pennington, the new Lord Mayor. About this time (ante ult. Aug.) the Cathedral of Canterbury grossly profaned.—Sept. 9, Friday. An order from the House, about the giving of Allhallows, Bread Street. The Earl of Essex set forward towards the King.—Sept. 10. Voted down in the Upper House (dubitatur.)

Oct. 15, Saturday. Resolved upon the question, that the fines, rents, and profits of Archbishops, Bishops, Deans, and Chapters, and of such notorious delinquents who have taken up arms against the Parliament, or have been active in the commission of array, shall be sequestered for the use and service of the Commonwealth.—Oct. 23, Sunday. Keinton field.—Oct. 24, Monday. An order from the House to keep but two servants, speak with no prisoner or other person, but in the presence of my Warder; (this common to other prisoners.)—Oct. 26, Wednesday, Mr. Cook's relation to me of some resolutions taken in the city, &c.—Oct. 27. The order of Oct. 24, not shewn me till Oct, 26, and I sent a petition to the House, for a cook and a butcher, Thursday.—Oct. 28. This order revoked, Friday: and this granted me.

Nov. 2, Wednesday night, I dreamed the Parliament was removed to Oxford; the Church undone: some old courtiers came in to see me, and jeered: I went to St. John's, and there I found the roof off from some parts of the College, and the walls cleft, and ready to fall down. God be merciful!—Nov. 8. Seventy-eight pounds of my rents taken from my comptroller, by Mr. Holland and Mr.

Ashhurst; which they said was for maintenance of the King's children.—Nov. 9, Wednesday morning, five of the clock, Captain
Brown and his company entered my house at
Lambeth, to keep it for public service; and
they made of it.   The Lords, upon my
petition to them, denied they knew of any
such order; and so did the Committee; yet
such an order there was, and divers Lords'
hands to it; but upon my petition, they
made an order, that my books should be
secured, and my goods.—Nov. 10. Some
Lords went to the King about an accommodation.—Nov. 12, Saturday. A fight about
Brentford: many slain of the Parliament
forces, and some taken prisoners; such as
would not serve the King, were sent back
with an oath given them.   The fight is said
to begin casually about billetting.   Since this,
voted in the House for no accommodation, but
to go on, and take all advantages.—Nov. 16,
Wednesday. An order to barr all prisoners'
men from speaking one with another, or any
other, but in presence of the Warder; nor

go out without the Lieutenant's leave; and to
barr them the liberty of the Tower.—Nov. 22,
Tuesday. Ordered, that any one of them
may go out to buy provision.—Nov. 24,
Thursday. The soldiers at Lambeth House
brake open the Chapel door; and offered
violence to the organ; but before much hurt
was done, the Captains heard of it, and
stayed them.

Dec. 2, Friday. Some of the King's forces
taken at Farnham; about an hundred of them
brought in carts to London; ten carts full,
their legs bound. They were sufficiently
railed upon in the streets.—Dec. 19, Monday.
My petition for Mr. Coniers to have the
Vicarage of Horsham. Before it came to be
delivered, the House had made an order
against him, upon complaint from Horsham
of his disorderly life. So, Dec. 21, St.
Thomas's day, I petitioned for my Chaplain,
Mr. William Brackstone. Refused, yet no
exception taken. That day, in the morning,
my young dun horses were taken away, by
warrant under the hands of Sir John Evelyn,

Mr Pim, and Mr. Martin.—Dec. 23, Thursday. Dr. Layton came with a warrant from the House of Commons, for the keys of my house to be delivered to him, and more prisoners to be brought thither, &c.—Jan. 5. A final order from both Houses, for selling of Lambeth prison, &c. Thursday. All my wood and coals spent, or to be spent there, not reserving in the order, that I shall have any for my own use; nor would that motion be hearkened to.

Jan. 6, Friday, Epiphany. Earl of Manchester's letter from the House, to give All-Hallows, Bread Street, to Mr. Seaman.—Jan. 26, Thursday. The Bill passed the Lords' House for abolishing Episcopacy, &c.

Feb. 3, Friday. Dr. Heath came to persuade me to give Chartham to Mr. Corbet, &c. —Feb. 14, Tuesday. I received a letter from his Majesty, dated January 17, to give Chartham to Mr. Reddinge, or lapse it to him. That afternoon, the Earl of Warwick came to me, and brought me an order of the House, to give it to one Mr. Culmer. This order bare date, Feb. 4.—Feb. 25, Saturday. Mr. Culmer came to me about it. I told him, I had given my Lord an answer.—March 2, Thursday, St. Chad's day. The Lord Brooke shot in the left eye, and killed in the place, at Litchfield, going to give the onset upon the Close of the Church; he having ever been fierce against Bishops and Cathedrals: his beaver up, and armed to the knees; so that a musquet at that distance could have done him but little harm. Thus was his eye put out, who about two years since said, he hoped to live to see at St. Paul's not one stone left upon another.

[The Lord Brook was now in action. A bitter enemy he was to the Church, and her government by Bishops. On March 2, he was going to give onset upon the Close of the Cathedral at Litchfield: and, he was taking view of the place from a window in a house opposite to the Close, and his beaver up, so that a musket at such a distance could have done him but little harm; yet was he shot in the left eye, and killed dead in the place without speaking one word. Whence I shall observe three things. First, that this great and known enemy to Cathedral Churches died thus fearfully in the assault of a Cathedral. A fearful manner of death in such a quarrel! Secondly, that this happened upon St. Chad's day, of which Saint the Cathedral bears the name. Thirdly, that this Lord coming from dinner about two years since, from the Lord Herbert's house in Lambeth, upon some discourse of St. Paul's Church, than in their eye upon the water, said to some young Lords that were with him, *that he hoped to live to see that one stone of that building should not be left upon another.* But that Church stands yet, and that eye is put out that hoped to see the ruins of it. Many heavy accidents have already fallen out in these unnatural wars; and God alone knows how many more shall, before they end. But I intend no history but of my own sad misfortunes; nor would I have mentioned this, but that it relates to the Church, which, for my calling sake, I take as a part, and a near one, of myself. *Troubles.*]

March 10, Friday. This night preceding, I dreamed a warrant was come to free me; and that I spake with the Lieutenant, that my Warder might keep the keys of my lodging, till I had got some place for myself and my stuff, since I could not go to Lambeth. I waked, and slept again; and had the very same dream a second time.—March 20, Monday. The Lord of Northumberland, Mr. Pierrepoint, Sir John Holland, Sir William Ermin, and Mr. Whitlock, went from both Houses to treat of peace with his Majesty. God of His mercy bless it and us!—March 24, Friday. One Mr. Foord told me, (he is a Suffolk man,) that there was a plot to send me and Bishop Wrenn[d], as delinquents, to New England, within fourteen days. And that Wells, a Minister that came thence, offered wagers of it. The meeting was at Mr. Burks, a merchant's house in Friday Street, being this Foord's son in law. I never saw Mr. Foord before.

[d] "A man of a severe, sour nature, but very learned, and particularly versed in the old Liturgies of the Greek and Latin Churches." *Clarend.* i. 184.

1643. March 28, Tuesday. Another order from the Lords, to give Chartham to one Mr. Edward Hudson. My answer as before.

April 11, Tuesday. Another order for the same, and very peremptory. This came to me April 12, whereupon I petitioned the House, Thursday, April 13. My former answer being wilfully mistaken by Hudson. That present day another order, very quick; which was brought to me Friday, April 14. I petitioned the House again the same day with great submission; but could not disobey the King.—April 21. Another peremptory order, to collate Chartham on Mr. Edw. Corbet, brought to me Saturday, April 22.— April 24, Monday. I gave my answer as before, but in as soft terms as I could.— April 25, Tuesday. It was moved in the House of Commons to send me to New England. But it was rejected. The plot was laid by Peters, Wells, and others.

May 1, Monday. My Chapel windows at Lambeth defaced, and the steps torn up.— May 2, Tuesday. The Cross in Cheapside taken down.—May 9, Tuesday. All my goods seized upon, books and all.—The seizers were Captain Guest, Layton, and Dickins. The same day an order for further restraint of me, not to go out of it without my keeper. This order was brought to me May 10.—May 16, Tuesday. An order of both Houses for the disposing of my benefices, &c. void, or to be void. This order was brought to me Wednesday.—May 17, at night. Methinks, I see a cloud rising over me, about Chartham business: there having been a rumour twice, that I shall be removed to a prison lodging.—May 23. Tuesday. I sent my petition for maintenance. This day the Queen was voted a traitor in the Commons' House.—May 20, Saturday. Another order to collate Edward Corbet to Chartham. It was brought to me Friday, May 26. I answered it Saturday, May 27, as before.

[H. W. Thus far the Archbishop had proceeded in his Diary; when it was violently seized, and taken out of his pockets by Wil-

liam Prynne, on the last day of May, 1643.
The seizure of it is related by Prynne himself, (Breviat of the Archbishop's Life, p. 28.)
and gloried in, as a most worthy action.
But the barbarous manner of it is more largely
described by the Archbishop himself in the
following history.   After the book came into
his enemies' hands, it was frequently urged
against him as evidence at his trial; and
when the trial was near finished, Prynne
caused it to be printed, and published it in
the beginning of September, 1644, but cor-
rupted, and in part only. The Archbishop had
almost filled up his paper book (wherein he
wrote his Diary) when it was taken from him.
But in the last leaf of it, are found certain
projects wrote with his own hand, (at what
time or in what year is uncertain,) which I
have subjoined.]   See Appendix.

[The remainder of the autobiography is
made up from the Archbishop's history of
his " Troubles and Trial."]

May 20. And soon after came another
Ordinance, requiring me, by virtue of the

said Ordinance, to give Chartham to Mr.
Corbet. This order was not brought me
till Friday, May 26. Then it was brought
unto me by Mr. Corbet himself, and Sir John
Corbet, a Parliament man, came with him.
Now upon the Tuesday before I had sent an
humble petition to the Lords for maintenance. The prayer of which petition was
as follows: "Humbly prayeth that your
Lordships will take his sad condition into
your honourable consideration, that somewhat may be allowed him out of his estate
to supply the necessities of life; assuring
himself that in honour and justice you will
not suffer him either to beg or starve. And
your petitioner shall ever pray, &c." The
answer which this petition had in the Lords'
House was, *Let him give Chartham as is
ordered, and then we will consider of maintenance.* So my petition was sent down to
the House of Commons. To the last fore-
named order, I gave my former answer, and
humbly petitioned the Lords accordingly,
May 27 following. So they departed, and

as they went down the hill together, Sir Joh
was overheard to say to Mr. Corbet thus
" The Archbishop hath petitioned the Lord
for maintenance, and they have sent hi
petition to the Commons; and since he wi
not give you the benefice, I'll warrant yo
he shall have no maintenance." And s
accordingly my petition was rejected in th
House of Commons.

[Mr. Corbet, of Merton Coll. was one wh
had opposed the Archbishop at Oxford; an
Mr. Culmer, the other man for whom Pax
liament at the instigation of Lord Warwicl
demanded Chartham, was known to th
Archbishop to be " ignorant, and with hi
ignorance one of the most daring schismatic
in that country." Besides which, he ha
already promised King Charles that he woul
give it to Mr. Reddinge. Ed.]

May 31. This was Wednesday, the last o
May. It was the fast day. A search cam
betimes in the morning into the Tower upoi
all the prisoners, for letters and other papers
But I have some reasons to think the searcl

had a special aim at me. First; because following me thus close about Chartham as they did, I conceive they were desirous to see whether I had any such letter from the King as I pretended. If I had not, they had advantage against me for my falsehood. If I had, they meant to see what secret passed from his Majesty to me. Secondly; because I had lately petitioned for maintenance, and by this search they might see what I had by me. And he that searched my chamber told me upon occasion, that he was to take all papers which might discover delinquents' estates. Thirdly; because all other prisoners had their papers re-delivered them before the searchers went from the Tower, except some few verses of Sir Edward Hern's. But mine were carried to the Committee; yet with promise, that I should have them again within two or three days. Fourthly; because as Leighton was put into Lambeth House, so my implacable enemy Mr. Prynne was picked out (as a man whose malice might be trusted) to make the search upon me. And he did it exactly.

The manner of the search upon me was thus. Mr. Prynne came into the Tower, with other searchers, so soon as the gates were open. Other men went to other prisoners. He made haste to my lodging, commanded the Warder to open my doors, left two musqueteers sentinels below, that no man might go in or out, and one at the stairhead: with three other, which had their musquets ready cocked, he came into my chamber, and found me in bed, as were also my servants in theirs. I presently thought upon my blessed Saviour, when Judas led in the swords and staves about Him. Mr. Prynne, seeing me safe in bed, falls first to my pockets to rifle them; and by that time my two servants came running in, half ready. I demanded the sight of his warrant. He shewed it me, and therein was expressed that he should search my *pockets*. The warrant came from the Close Committee, and the hands that were to it were these: E. Manchester, W. Saye and Seale, Wharton, H. Vane, Gilbert Gerard, and John Pim. Did they remember when they gave this warrant, how odious it was to Parliaments, and some of themselves, to have the pockets of men searched? When my pockets had been sufficiently ransacked, I rose and got my clothes about me, and so half ready, with my gown upon my shoulders, he held me in the search till past nine of the clock in the morning. He took from me twenty and one bundles of papers, which I had prepared for my defence; the two letters before named, which came to me from his gracious Majesty about Chartham and my other benefices; the Scottish Service Book, with such directions as accompanied it; a little book, or Diary, containing all the occurrences of my life; and my book of private devotions; both these last written through with my own hand Nor could I get him to leave this last; but he must needs see what passed between God and me:—a thing, I think, scarce ever offered to any Christian. The last place which he rifled was a trunk which stood by my bed side. In that he found nothing but about forty pounds in money for my necessary expenses, which he meddled not with, and a bundle of some gloves. This bundle he was so careful to open, as that he caused each glove to be looked into. Upon this I tendered him one pair of the gloves; which he refusing, I told him he might take them and fear no bribe, for he had already done me all the mischief he could, and I asked no favour of him. So he thanked me, took the gloves, bound up my papers, left two sentinels at my door, which were not dismissed till the next day noon, and went his way. I was somewhat troubled to see myself used in this manner; but knew no help but in God, and the patience which He had given me. And how His gracious Providence over me, and His goodness to me, wrought upon all this, I shall in the end discover, and will magnify, however it succeed with me.

June 10. There came out an Ordinance against me to take all my temporalities into the Parliament's hands; that so they might give not only Chartham, but all things else which fell into my gift. This Ordinance was laid as a great punishment upon me. But I humbly thank both Houses for it, as for the greatest benefit they have bestowed on me since my troubles; especially since the sequestration of my jurisdiction. Nov. 2, 1641. For it appears before in this history, how ever since that time I have been troubled for every benefice which hath fallen in my gift; disenabled to prefer any friend or chaplain of my own, were he never so worthy; and, which is worse by much, forced to admit such men, how unworthy soever, as were by them nominated to me, or else fall under a contempt of their ordinances, and such arbitrary punishment as they shall thereupon load me with. Whereas now I am freed both from the trouble and the sin of admitting unworthy persons into the Church Service, and leave them to the business, and the account for it.—June 11, Sunday. One came and preached at the Tower, (his name I could not learn.)   In his sermon, after he had liberally railed on me, he told the auditory, that Mr. Prynne had found a book in my pocket, which would discover great things:—this to inflame the people against me; et, si non satis insanirent sua sponte, instigare.   This is zealous preaching! God forgive their malice.

June 12, Monday. An Ordinance passed, that the Synod of Divines, formerly named by both Houses, (not chosen by the Clergy,) should begin to sit on the first of July following; and they did begin to sit that day; Dr. Twiss in the chair; and he made the Latin Sermon.   The names of these synodical men are to be seen in the Ordinance printed June 12; where any man that will may see a great, if not the greater, part of them, Brownists or Independents or New England ministers, if not worse, or at the best refractory persons to the doctrine or discipline or both of the Church of England established by law, and now brought together to reform it.   An excellent conclave!   But I pray God, that befal not them, which Tully observes fell upon Epicurus, *Si quæ corrigere voluit, deteriora fecit;* He made every thing worse that he went about to mend. I shall for my part never deny, but that the Liturgy of the Church of England may be made better; but I am sure withal it may easily be made worse. And howsoever, it would become this Synod well to remember, that there is a Convocation of the English Prelates and Clergy, lawfully chosen and summoned, and by no supreme or legal authority as yet dissolved: and can there be two national Synods at one time, but that one must be irregular? Belike we shall fall to it in the Donatists' way: they set up *altare contra altare* in Africa; and these will set up *synodum contra synodum* in England. And this, without God's infinite mercy, will bring forth a schism, fierce enough to rend and tear religion out of this kingdom: which God, for the merits and mercies of Christ, forbid!

A Committee of the House of Commons

sent Mr. Dobson my comptroller to me to the
Tower, to require me to send them word
under my hand, what originals I had of the
Articles of Religion established 1562, and
1571. This was on Wednesday, July 12.
And I returned by him the same day this
answer in writing, with my name to it.
" The original Articles of 1571, I could
never find in my paper-study at Lambeth, or
any where else: and whether any copy of
them were ever left there, I cannot tell. The
original Articles of 1562, with many hands
to them, I did see, and peruse there: but
whether the Bishops' hands were to them or
not, I cannot remember." This answer satisfied them; but what their aim was I cannot
tell, unless they meant to make a search about
the two first lines in the twentieth Article, concerning the power of the Church; in these
words, " The Church hath power to decree
Rites and Ceremonies, and authority in Controversies of Faith;" which words are left
out in divers printed copies of the Articles,
and are not in the one and twentieth Article

of Edw. VI. nor in the Latin copy of the
Articles 1571.   But in the original Articles of
1562, the words are plain and manifest,
without any interlining at all.   If this were
their aim, it is probable we shall see somewhat, by what their Synod shall do concerning that Article*.

On Tuesday, August 3, my servant Mr.
Edward Lenthrop came to me, and told me,
that the day before he met with Sir K. Digby, who had the leave to go out of prison,
(by the suit of the French Queen,) and to
travel into France.   But before he took his
journey, he was to come before a Committee,

* This was a notable point in the early stages of the
Puritan controversy; respecting which may be found
facts in Strype, inaccuracy in Fuller, and, as usual, no
lack of noise in Neal (l. 190.).   Heylin expressly says,
that he examined the Convocation Books, and that the
contested clause was there.   In the arbitrary reign of
Elizabeth it was a point of much importance, as going
a great way towards fixing a limit to the prevalent
Erastianism.   It is now a merely antiquarian question,
the clause having been recognized and confirmed at the
review in the reign of Charles the Second.

and there (he said) he had been. It seems it
was some Committee about my business; for
he told Mr. Lenthrop, and wished him to tell
it me, that the Committee took special notice
of his acquaintance with me, and examined
him strictly concerning me and my religion,
whether he did not know, that I was offered
to be made a Cardinal; and many other such
like things. That he answered them, that
he know nothing of any Cardinalship offered
me: and for my religion, he had reason to
think, I was truly and really as I professed
myself; for I had laboured with him against
his return to the Church of Rome: (which is
true, and I have some of my papers yet to
shew.) But he farther sent me word, that
their malice was great against me; though
he saw plainly, they were like men that
groped in the dark, and were to seek what to
lay to my charge. But soon after mutterings
arose, that Mr. Prynne in his search had found
great matters against me, and that now I
should be brought to trial out of hand.

Some men now, it seems, made overture

for peace, and some good hopes of it began
to shew themselves (as it was then said) in
both Houses. This was on Saturday, Aug. 5.
But there wanted not those which made
themselves ready for battle: for on Sunday,
Aug. 6, printed bills were pasted up in
London, to animate the people to go to Westminster against peace; and the like bills
were read in some churches. Excellent
church-work! And on Monday, Aug. 7,
some thousands, men and women, went to
the Parliament, and clamorously petitioned
against peace; and the next day five or six
hundred women, and these were as earnest
for peace: but ye may observe it is but hundreds for thousands that came against it. Yet
on Wednesday, Aug. 9, the number of women
increased, when it seems men durst not appear. But their desire for peace was answered by some troops of horse which were
sent for, by which some of the women were
killed, and divers of them shrewdly wounded.
God of His mercy set an end to these bloody
distractions! In the midst of this fury of

the people, on Thursday, Aug. 10, came out
Rome's Master-Piece. This book Mr. Prynne
sets forth in print, upon occasion of some
papers which he had in his search taken
from me: and it was done to drive the
people headlong into mischief, whose malice
against me needed not his setting on. After
this, the Diurnal and other pamphlets began
to mention me, and that now a charge was
drawing up against me.

Upon Friday, Aug. 11, Sir Robert Har-
lowe was made Lieutenant of the Tower,
in the room of Sir John Conniers. And on
Tuesday, Aug. 15, he removed Mr. Bray,
who had been my Warder from my first
commitment to the Tower, and put Mr.
Cowes, another of the Warders, to be my
keeper. The cause of this change I could
never learn. The 19th of Aug. after, being
Saturday, Alderman Pennington, then Lord
Mayor of London, was made Lieutenant of
the Tower, and took possession of it. The
next day, being Sunday, in the afternoon, one
preached in the Tower-church, in a buff

coat and a scarf, but had a gown on. He told the people, they were all blessed that died in this cause, with much more such stuff. His name (as I there heard) was Kem, Parson or Vicar of Low-Layton in Essex, and then Captain of a troop of horse. Quam bene conveniunt! But the next Sunday, Aug. 27, during the afternoon Sermon, a Letter, subscribed John Browne, was thrust under the door of my prison. When I opened it, I found it a most bitter libel. God forgive the author of it! On Monday, Sept. 11, the new Lieutenant, the Lord Mayor, changed my Warder again, removed Mr. Cowes, and put Mr. Spencer to attend me. And when I moved him, that I might not have such often change put upon me, as no other prisoner had; his answer was, that if he did not remove Mr. Cowes, the Committee would. So I know not how to help myself, but by patience.

Then came the Covenant, that excellent piece of . . . . . from Scotland, and was sworn by the Parliament and the Synod, in St.

Margaret's Church in Westminster, on Monday, Sept. 25. The effects which followed, were as strict as the Covenant: for on Monday, Oct. 3, the order made that time twelve month, was renewed, and all prisoners locked up, and no man suffered to speak with them, but by leave from the Lieutenant, and in the presence of their several Warders respectively.

By this time Mr. Prynne's malice had hammered out something; and on Tuesday, Oct. 24, an order was brought me from the Lords, dated Oct. 23, with a copy of ten additional Articles, brought up by the Commons against me. This order required me to make my answer in writing by the 30th of the same month. Though [Mr. Prynne] had promised me a faithful restitution of [my papers] within three or four days, yet to this day (being almost five months after) I had received but three bundles of the twenty and one, which he had from me. I petitioned the Lords again on Saturday, Oct. 28, and then Mr. Dell, my secretary, was assigned me for my solicitor; and I was allowed two servants more to go about my business. And the House of Commons by their order agreed to the Lords, that I should have copies of any of the papers taken from me; but it should be at my own charge. Wonderful favour this, and as much justice! My estate all taken from me, and my goods sold, before ever I came to hearing; and then I may take copies of my papers at my own charge!

On Tuesday, Oct. 31, I humbly petitioned the Lords for direction of my counsel, how to carry themselves towards me and my defence: and that they would honourably be pleased, in regard the Articles charged me with treason and misdemeanour, and were intermixed one with another, to distinguish which were for treason, and which for misdemeanour; as also for longer time to put in my answer. The Lords upon this gave an order, that I should have time till Nov. 13, but would declare no opinion touching the distinguishment of the Articles, but left me to my counsel to advise as they pleased. My counsel told me plainly, I were as good have no counsel, if the Articles were not distinguished; for they were so woven one within another, and so knit up together in the conclusion, that they might refer all to treason, and so they be suffered to give me no counsel at all in matter of fact. Hereupon they drew me another petition to the same effect, which I caused to be delivered Nov. 6. But it received the same answer. Then, Nov. 7, being Wednesday, I petitioned the House of Commons to the same purpose; and Nov. 8, this my petition was read in the House of Commons, and after a short debate the resolution was, that they being my accusers would not meddle with any thing, but left all to the order of the Lords, before whom the business was, and my counsels' own judgment thereupon. This seemed very hard, not only to myself and my counsel, but to all indifferent men that heard it. In the meantime I could resort no whither but to patience and God's mercy.

Nov. 13. I appeared in the Parliament House according to the order, and was at the bar. And, my answer being put in, I humbly besought their Lordships to take into their honourable consideration my great years, being threescore and ten complete, and my memory and other faculties, by age and affliction, much decayed:—my long imprisonment, wanting very little of three whole years, and this last year very little better than close imprisonment; my want of skill and knowledge in the laws to defend myself; the generality and uncertainty of almost all the Articles, so that I cannot see any particulars against which I may provide myself, &c. While I was speaking this, the Lords were very attentive, and two of them took pen and paper at the table, and took notes; and it was unanimously granted, that my counsel should be heard, and so they were. And the order then made upon their hearing was, that they should advise me, and be heard themselves in all things concerning matter of law, and in all things, whether of *law* or *fact*,

Y

that were not charged as treason; and that
they would think upon the distinguishment
in time convenient. This was all I could
get, and my counsel seemed somewhat better
content, that they had gotten so much. Not
long after this I heard from good hands, that
some of the Lords confessed I had much
deceived their expectation; for they found
me in a calm, but thought I would have been
stormy. And this being so, I believe the
two Lords, so careful at their pen and ink,
made ready to observe any disadvantages to
me, which they thought choler and indignation might thrust forth. But I praise God
the Giver, I am better acquainted with patience than they think I am.

On Thursday, Dec. 28, which was Innocents' day, one Mr. Wells, a New-England
Minister, came to me, and in a boisterous
manner demanded to know whether I had
repented or not? I knew him not till he told
me he was suspended by me, when I was
Bishop of London, and he then a Minister in
Essex. I told him, if he were suspended, it

was doubtless according to law. Then upon a little further speech, I recalled the man to my remembrance, and what care I took in conference with him at London House to recall him from some of his turbulent ways; but all in vain. And now he inferred out of the good words I then gave him, that I suspended him against my conscience. In conclusion he told me, I went about to bring popery into the kingdom, and he hoped I should have my reward for it. When I saw him at this height, I told him, he and his fellows, what by their ignorance and what by their railing and other boisterous carriage, would soon actually make more papists by far, than ever I intended; and that I was a better Protestant than he or any of his followers. So I left him in his heat.

By this time something was made ready again in my great business: and Wednesday at night, Jan. 3, I received an order for my appearance on the Monday following. I was on Sunday, Jan. 7, ordered again to appear in Mr. Smart's suit [Prebendary of Durham,

against Dr. Cosin, Chaplain to Bishops Over-
all and Neile, and Charles I. afterwards
Bishop of Durham, Ed.] the next day.   The
warrant bare date a fortnight before: yet
partly to sanctify the Sabbath, and partly to
shew his great civility to me in giving me
warning, I was not served with it till Sunday
night at seven of the clock.   The next morning I went to Westminster as I was commanded.   But I was sent back, and not so
much as called upon.   So, beside the charge
I was at, that day was lost and taken from
me and my business, as short time as I had
given me.

Jan. 22. At this day and time I appeared
as I was ordered to do; but could not obtain
of the Lords, either to take my former answer
off from the file, if I must put in another;
nor to distinguish the Articles, which were
treason and which misdemeanor; nor leave
for my counsel to speak to the generality and
uncertainty of the original Articles, which
they professed were such as no man living
could prepare answer for.   But I must put

in my answer presently, [which the Archbishop did,] or be taken pro confesso. This day the Thames was so full of ice, that I could not go by water. It was frost and snow, and a most bitter day. I went therefore with the Lieutenant in his coach, and twelve Warders with halberts went all along the streets. I could not obtain either the sending of them before, or the suffering them to come behind, but with the coach they must come; which was as good as to call the people about me. So from the Tower-gate to Westminster, I was sufficiently railed on and reviled all the way. God of His mercy forgive the misguided people! My answer being put in, I was for that time dismissed; and the tide serving me, I made a hard shift to return by water.

And now, notwithstanding all this haste made to have my answer in, Mr. Prynne cannot make this broken business ready against me. Therefore to fill up some time, I was ordered to be at the House again, Monday, Jan. 29, about Mr. Smart's business. But being put to this trouble and charge, and shewed to the people for a farther scorn, I was sent back again, and had nothing said to me.

All February passed over, and Mr. Prynne not yet ready. He had not yet sufficiently prepared his witnesses.

And now (Saturday, March 9,) being ready to enter upon the hearing and the trial itself, I hold it necessary for me to acquaint the reader with some general things before that begin: partly to the end he may see the course of this trial, and the carriage which hath been in it; and partly to avoid the often and tedious repetition, which else must necessarily be of some of them; and especially that they may not be mingled, either with the evidence, or my answer to it, to interrupt the current, or make any thing more obscure.

1. The Committee appointed by the House of Commons, to manage and press the evidence against me, were Serjeant Wilde, Mr. Browne, Mr. Maynard, Mr. Nicholas, Mr. Hill: but none spake at the bar, but the first four; Mr. Hill was Consul-Bibulus; Mr.

Prynne was trusted with the providing of all the evidence, and was Relater and Prompter and all: never weary of any thing, so he might do me mischief. And I conceive in future times, it will not be the greatest honour to these proceedings, that he, a man twice censured in the High Court of Star-Chamber, set in the pillory twice; once for libelling the Queen's Majesty, and other Ladies of great honour; and again for libelling the Church, and the government and governors of it, the Bishops, and that had his ears there cropped; should now be thought the only fit and indifferent man to be trusted with the witnesses and the evidence against me, an Archbishop, and sitting at his censure.

2. Mr. Prynne took to him two young men to help to turn his papers, and assist him; Mr. Grice, and Mr. Beck. Mr. Grice was son to Mr. Tho. Grice, Fellow of St. Jo. Bapt. College in my time, and after beneficed near Staines. I knew not what the matter was, but I could never get his love. But he is dead, and so let him rest. And

now his son succeeds, and it seems he inherits his father's disposition towards me; for I hear his tongue walks liberally over me in all places. For Mr. Beck, he had received some courtesy from me, and needed not in this kind to have expressed his thankfulness. But I leave them both to do the office which they have undertaken, and to grow up under the shadow of Mr. Prynne; God knows to what.

3. It was told me by a man of good credit, that was present and heard it, that my name coming in question among some gentlemen, after divers had spoken their thoughts of me, and not all one way, a Parliament-man being there, was pleased to say, That I was now an old man, and it would be happy, both for me and the Parliament, that God would be pleased to take me away. And yet I make no doubt, but that if age, or grief, or faintness of spirit, had ended my days, many of them would have done as Tiberius did in the case of Asinius Gallus; that is, incusarent casus, qui reum abstulissent, ante-

quam coram convinceretur. They would cry out against this hard chance, that should take away so guilty a person from public trial, when they were even ready for it. After this, when a friend of mine bemoaned my case to another Parliament-man, (of whom I had deserved very well,) and said, he knew I was a good man; the Parliament-man replied, Be he never so good, we must now make him ill for our sakes. What the meaning of these speeches is, let understanding men judge. And even during my trial, some citizens of London were heard to say, that indeed I answered many things very well; but yet I must suffer somewhat for the honour of the House.

4. So all my hopes now, under God, lay wholly on the honour and justice of the Lords. Yet seeing how fierce many of the people were against me, and how they had clamoured in other cases, and that Mr. Prynne was set up at once both to mischief and to scorn me; and foreseeing how full of reproaches my trial was likely to be; I had a

strong temptation in me, rather to desert my defence, and put myself into the hands of God's mercy, than endure them. But when I considered what offence I should commit therein against the course of justice, that that might not proceed in the ordinary way; what offence against my own innocency, and my good name, which I was bound both in nature and conscience to maintain by all good means, which by deserting my cause could not be; but especially, what offence against God, as if He were not able to protect me, or not willing, in case it stood with my eternal happiness, and His blessed will of trial of me in the mean time: I say, when I considered this, I humbly besought God for strength and patience, and resolved to undergo all scorns, and whatsoever else might happen to me, rather than betray my innocency to the malice of any.

5. And though my hopes, under God, were upon the Lords, yet when my trial came on, it did somewhat trouble me, to see so few Lords in that great House. For at the great-

est presence that was any day of my hearing, there were not above fourteen, and usually not above eleven or twelve. Of these, one third part, at least, each day took, or had occasion to be gone, before the charge of the day was half given. I never had any one day the same Lords all present at my defence in the afternoon, that were at my charge in the morning. Some leading Lords scarce present at my charge, four days of all my long trial, nor three at my defence; and, which is most, no one Lord present at my whole trial, but the Right Honourable the Lord Gray of Wark, the Speaker, without whose presence t could not be a House. · In this case I stood n regard of my honourable judges. ·

6. When my hearing came on, usually my charge was in giving till almost two of the lock. Then I was commanded to withdraw; and upon my humble petition for ime to answer, I had no more given me han till four the same afternoon, scarce time nough advisedly to peruse the evidence. My counsel not suffered to come to me till

I had made my answer, nor any friend els
but my solicitor Mr. Dell, to help to turn m
papers; and my Warder of the Tower to
by to look to this. And this was not th
least cause, why I was at first accused of r
less than treason; ne quis necessarioru
juvaret periclitantem majestatis crimina sul
debantur, as it fell out in Silanus's cas
who had more guilt about him (yet not
treason) than (God be thanked) I have; be
was prosecuted with like malice, as appea
in that story. At four o'clock, or after, th
House sate again; and I made my answe
and if I produced any witness, he was no
suffered to be sworn; so it was but like
testimony at large, which the Lords migh
the more freely believe or not believe,
they pleased. After my answer, one or mo
of the Committee replied upon me. By th
time all was done, it was usually half a
hour past seven. Then in the heat of th
year (when it overtook me) I was presentl
to go by water to the Tower, full of weari
ness, and with a shirt as wet to my bac

with sweat, as the water could have made it, had I fallen in: yet I humbly thank God for it, He so preserved my health, as that though I were weary and faint the day after, yet I never had so much as half an hour's headache, or other infirmity, all the time of this comfortless and tedious trial.

7. Now for the method, which I shall hold in this history of my trial, it shall be this. I will set down the evidence given on each day by itself, and my answer to it. But whereas all the evidence was given together, and so my whole answer after; to avoid all looking back, and trouble of turning leaves to compare the answer with the evidence, I will set down each particular evidence, and my answer to it, and so all along, that the indifferent reader may, without farther trouble, see the force of the one, and the satisfaction given in the other, and how far every particular is from treason. And if I add any thing to my answers in any place, either it is because in the shortness of time then given me to make my answer, it came not to my

present thoughts; or if it did, yet I forbare
to speak it with that sharpness; holding it
neither fit nor safe in my condition, to pro-
voke either my accusers or my judges. And
whatsoever is so added by me, in either of
these respects, the reader shall find it thus
marked in the margin, as here it stands
in this [" "].

8. Nor did I wrong Mr. Prynne, where
I say, that for all the haste to put in my
answer, Jan. 22, he could not make this
broken business so soon ready against me:
for it is well known, he kept a kind of
school of instruction for such of the witnesses
as be durst trust, that they might be sure to
speak home to the purpose he would have
them. And this an utter barrister, a man
of good credit, knows; who, in the hearing
of men beyond exception, said, The Archbishop is a stranger to me, but Mr. Prynne's
tampering about the witnesses is so palpable
and foul, that I cannot but pity him, and cry
shame of it. When I heard this, I sent to
this gentleman, to know if he tendered my

case so far, as to witness it before the Lords. The answer I received was, that the thing was true, and that very indignation of it made him speak: but heartily prayed me, I would not produce him as a witness; for if I did, the times were such, he should be utterly undone: and it is not hard to guess by whom. Upon this I consulted some friends; and upon regard of his safety on the one side, and my own doubt, lest if forced to his undoing, he might, through fear, blanch and mince the truth to my own prejudice, who produced him; I forbare the business, and left Mr. Prynne to the bar of Christ, Whose mercy give him repentance, and amend him. But upon my Christianity, this story is truth.

FIRST DAY OF THE TRIAL.

Now I come to Tuesday, March 12, the day appointed for my trial to begin; and begin it did. When I was come and settled at the bar, Serjeant Wilde made a solemn speech for introduction.

[After Wilde's speech, the Archbishop continues.]

I was much troubled to see myself, in such an honourable Assembly, made so vile; yet seeing all men's eyes upon me, I recollected myself, and humbly desired of the Lords two things. " One, that they would expect proof, before they gave up their belief to these loud but loose assertions; especially, since it is an easy thing for men so resolved to conviciate, instead of accusing; when, as the rule given by Optatus holds firm, quum intenditur crimen, when a crime is objected, (especially so high a crime as this charged on me,) it is necessary that the proof be manifest, which yet against me is none at all. The other, that their Lordships would give me leave, not to answer this gentleman's particulars, (for that I shall defer till I hear his proofs,) but to speak some few things concerning myself, and this grievous impeachment brought up against me."

Which being yielded unto me, I then spake as follows:

" My Lords,

" My being in this place, and in this condition, recalls to my memory that which I
long since read in Seneca; Tormentum est,
etiamsi absolutus quis fuerit, causam dixisse.
It is not a grief only, no, it is no less than a
torment, for an ingenuous man to plead
criminally, much more capitally, at such a
bar as this; yea, though it should so fall out,
that he be absolved. The great truth of this
I find at present in myself: and so much
the more, because I am a Christian; and not
that only, but in Holy Orders; and not so
only, but by God's grace and goodness preferred to the greatest place this Church
affords; and yet now brought, causam dicere,
to plead, and for no less than life, at this
great bar. And whatsoever the world thinks
of me, (and they have been taught to think
more ill than, I humbly thank Christ for it,
I was ever acquainted with,) yet, my Lords,
this I find, tormentum est, it is no less than
torment to me to appear in this place to such
an accusation. Nay, my Lords, give me

z

leave, I beseech you, to speak plain truth:
no sentence, that can justly pass upon me,
(and other I will never fear from your Lordships) can go so near me as causam dixisse,
to have pleaded for myself, upon this occasion, and in this place. For as for the sentence,
(I thank God for it,) I am at St. Paul's ward:
if I have committed any thing worthy of death,
I refuse not to die: for I bless God, I have so
spent my time, as that I am neither ashamed
to live, nor afraid to die. Nor can the world
be more weary of me, than I am of it: for
seeing the malignity which hath been raised
against me by some men, I have carried my
life in my hands these divers years past. But
yet, my Lords, if none of these things,
whereof those men accuse me, merit death by
law; though I may not in this case, and
from this bar, appeal unto Cæsar; yet to
your Lordships' justice and integrity, I both
may and do appeal; not doubting, but that
God of His goodness will preserve my innocency. And as Job in the midst of his affliction said to his mistaken friends, so shall I

to my accusers; "God forbid, I should justify you; till I die I will not remove my integrity from me; I will hold it fast, and not let it go; my heart shall not reproach me, as long as I live."

"My Lords, I see by the Articles, and have now heard from this gentleman, that the charge against me is divided into two main heads; the laws of the land, and the religion by those laws established.

"For the laws, first, I think I may safely say, I have been, to my understanding, as strict an observer of them all the days of my life, so far as they concern me, as any man hath; and since I came into place, I have followed them, and been as much guided by them, as any man that sat where I had the honour to sit. And for this I am sorry I have lost the witness of the Lord Keeper Coventry, and of some other persons of honour, since dead. And the learned counsel at law, which attended frequently at the Council Table, can witness, (some of them,) that in references to that Board, and in debates

arising at the Board, I was usually for that
part of the cause where I found law to be:
and if the counsel desired to have their
client's cause referred to the law, (well I
might move in some cases for charity, or
conscience, to have admittance, but) to the
law I left them, if thither they would go.
And how such a carriage as this through the
whole course of my life, in private and
public, can stand with an intention, nay a
practice, to overthrow the law, and to introduce an arbitrary government, which my soul
hath always hated, I cannot yet see.   And it
is now many years since I learned of my
great master (in humanis) Aristotle, pericu-
losum esse; that it is a very dangerous thing
to trust to the will of the judge rather
than the written law.   And all kingdoms
and commonwealths have followed his judgment ever since; and the School-disputes
have not dissented from it.   Nay more, I
have ever been of opinion, that human laws
bind the conscience, and have accordingly
made conscience of observing them.   And

this doctrine I have constantly preached, as occasion hath been offered me. And how is it possible I should seek to overthrow those laws, which I held myself bound in conscience to keep and observe? Especially, since an endeavour to overthrow law, is a far greater crime than to break or disobey any particular law whatsoever; all particulars being swept away in that general. And, my Lords, that this is my judgment, both of Parliaments and laws, I beseech your Lordships that I may read a short passage in my book against Fisher the Jesuit, which was printed and published to the world before these troubles fell on me, and before I could so much as suspect this charge could come against me; and therefore could not be purposely written to serve any turn. [I had leave, and did read it; but for brevity's sake, refer the reader to the book itself.] Conf. 26. xiv. p. 176. Oxf. edit.

" As for religion, I was born and bred up in and under the Church of England, as it yet stands established by law. I have by

God's blessing, and the favour of my Prince, grown up in it to the years which are now upon me, and to the place of preferment which I yet bear: and in this Church, by the grace and goodness of God, I resolve to die. I have, ever since I understood ought in divinity, kept one constant tenor in this my profession, without variation or shifting from one opinion to another, for any worldly ends: and if my conscience would have suffered me to shift tenets in religion with time and occasion, I could easily have slid through all the difficulties which have pressed upon me in this kind. But, of all diseases, I have ever hated a palsy in religion; well knowing, that too often a dead palsy ends that disease, in the fearful forgetfulness of God and His judgments. Ever since I came in place, I laboured nothing more, than that the external public worship of God (too much slighted in most parts of this kingdom) might be preserved, and that with as much decency and uniformity, as might be; being still of opinion, that unity cannot long continue in the Church, where uniformity is shut out at the church-door. And I evidently saw, that the public neglect of God's service in the outward face of it, and the nasty lying of many places dedicated to that service, had almost cast a damp upon the true and inward worship of God; which while we live in the body, needs external helps, and all little enough to keep it in any vigour. And this I did to the uttermost of my knowledge, according both to law and canon, and with the consent and liking of the people; nor did any command issue out from me against the one, or without the other, that I knew of.

"Farther, my Lords, give me leave, I beseech you, to tell you this also: that I have as little acquaintance with recusants of any sort, as I believe any man of place in England hath: and for my kindred, no one of them was ever a recusant, but Sir William Webb, grandchild to my uncle Sir William Webb, sometime Lord Mayor of London; and him, with some of his children, I reduced back again to the Church of England, as is well known, and I as able to prove.

" One thing more I humbly desire may be thought on; it is this: I am fallen into a great deal of obloquy in matter of religion, and that so far, as that it is charged in the Articles, that I have endeavoured to advance and bring in Popery. Perhaps, my Lords, I am not ignorant, what party of men have raised this scandal upon me; nor for what end; nor perhaps by whom set on: but, however, I would fain have a good reason given me, (if my conscience lead me that way, and that with my conscience I could subscribe to the Church of Rome,) what should have kept me here (before my imprisonment) to endure the libels, and the slanders, and the base usage in all kinds, which have been put upon me, and these to end in this question for my life: I say; I would fain know a good reason of this. For first, my Lords, is it because of any pledges I have in the world to sway me against my conscience? No sure.

For I have nor wife nor children*, to cry out
upon me to stay with them; and if I had,
I hope the call of my conscience should be
heard above them. Or, secondly, is it,
because I was loth to leave the honour and
the profit of the place I was risen unto?
Surely no: for I desire your Lordships, and
all the world else, should know, I do much
scorn honour and profit, both the one and
the other, in comparison of my conscience.
Besides, it cannot be imagined by any reasonable man, but that if I could have complied
with Rome, I should not have wanted either
honour or profit. And suppose I could not
have so much of either, as here I had; yet

---

* Laud wrote Strafford a serious letter on his third
and secret marriage, which seems to have been taken
amiss. Laud in his reply, after wishing his friend and
his lady all mutual content that may be, thus writes:
" For myself, I must needs confess to your Lordship
my weakness, that having been married to a very
troublesome and unquiet wife before, (the Church?) I
should be so ill advised as now, being about sixty, to go
marry another of a more wayward and troublesome
generation."

sure would my conscience have served me that way, less of either with my conscience would have prevailed with me, more than greater against my conscience.

" Or, thirdly, is it because I lived here at ease, and was loth to venture the loss of that? Not so, neither. For whatsoever the world may be pleased to think of me, I have led a very painful life, and such as I could have been very well content to change, had I well known how. And had my conscience led me that way, I am sure I might have lived at far more ease ; and either have avoided the barbarous libellings, and other bitter and grievous scorns which I have here endured, or at the least been out of the hearing of them. Nay, my Lords, I am as innocent in this business of religion, as free from all practice, or so much as thought of practice, for any alteration to Popery, or any way blemishing the true Protestant Religion established in the Church of England, as I was when my mother first bare me into the world. And let nothing be spoken against me but truth,

and I do here challenge whatsoever is between heaven and hell, to say their worst
against me in point of my religion: in which,
by God's grace, I have ever hated dissimulation; and had I not hated it, perhaps it
might have been better for me for worldly
safety, than now it is. But it can no way
become a Christian Bishop to halt with God.

" Lastly, if I had any purpose to blast the
true Religion established in the Church of
England, and to introduce Popery, sure I
took a very wrong way to it. For, my Lords,
I have stayed as many that were going to
Rome, and reduced as many that were already gone, as (I believe) any Bishop or
other Minister in this kingdom hath done;
and some of them men of great abilities, and
some of them persons of great place. And is
his the way, my Lords, to introduce Popery?
beseech your Lordships consider it well.
For surely, if I had blemished the true Pro-
estant Religion, I could not have settled such
men in it: and if I had purposed to intro-
luce Popery, I would never have reduced

such men from it. And though it please the
author of the Popish Royal Favourite to say,
that scarce one of the swaying Lord Prelates
is able to say, that ever he converted one
Papist to our religion; yet how void of charity
this speech of his is, and how full of falsehood, shall appear by the number of those
persons, whom, by God's blessing upon my
labours, I have settled in the true Protestant
Religion established in England. And, with
your Lordship's leave, I shall name them,
that you may see both their number and their
condition; though I cannot set them down in
that order of time, in which I either converted or settled them. -

"1. And first; Hen. Birkhead, of Trinity
Coll. in Oxford, was seduced by a Jesuit, and
brought up to London to be conveyed beyond
the seas. His friends complained to me: I
had the happiness to find him out, and the
blessing from God to settle his conscience. So
he returned to Oxford, and there continued[f].

[f] This furnishes another painful instance of the malignant temper and conduct of the Puritan faction. See

" 2, 3. Two daughters of Sir Rich. Lechford in Surrey, were sent to sea to be carried to a Nunnery. I heard of it, and caused them to be brought back, before they were got out of the Thames. I settled their consciences, and both of them sent me great thanks, since I was a prisoner in the Tower.

" 4, 5. Two scholars of St. John's Coll. in Cambridge, Topping and Ashton, had slipped away from the College, and here at London had got the French Embassador's pass, (I

Wharton's note. " Rushworth, p. 632, relateth, that when some of the Lords, hearing the name of Birkenhead, and imagining him to be the author of the Oxford Aulicus, smiled at it. The Archbishop taking notice of it, stopped and assured the Lords, that he meant not him, but another person of like name. Yet after all, Prynne, in publishing this speech, hath the impudence to affirm in the margin of his book, that this convert of the Archbishop's was " the author of all the libellous Popish Oxford Aulicus;" although he knew full well, that his name was John Birkenhead; and adds, that at the naming of this convert, most of the Lords and auditors smiled; but saith not one word of the Archbishop's correction of their mistake."

have the pass to shew :) I found means to get them to me, and I thank God settled both their minds, and sent them back to their College. Afterwards hearing of Topping's wants, I allowed him means till I procured him a Fellowship: and he is at this time a very hopeful young man, as most of his time in that University, a Minister, and Chaplain in house at this present to the Right Honourable the Earl of Westmorland.

" 6, 7, 8. Sir William Web my kinsman, and two of his daughters; and the better to secure them in religion, I was at the charge (their father being utterly decayed) to marry them to two religious Protestants ; and they both continued very constant. And his eldest son I took from him, placed him with a careful Divine, maintained him divers years, and then settled him with a gentleman of good worth.

" 10, 11. The next, in my remembrance, was the Lord Maio of Ireland, who, with another gentleman, (whose name I cannot recal,) was brought to me to Fulham, by

Mr. Jefford, a servant of his Majesty's, and well known to divers of your Lordships.

" 12. The Right Honourable the Lord Duke of Buckingham was almost lost from the Church of England, between the continual cunning labours of Fisher the Jesuit, and the persuasions of the Lady his mother. After some miscarriages, King James, of ever-blessed memory, commanded me to that service. I had God's blessing upon me so far, as to settle my Lord Duke to his death.

13. And I brought the Lady his mother to the Church again ; but she was not so happy as to continue with us.

14. The Lady Marchioness Hamilton was much solicited by some priests, and much troubled in mind about it. My Lord spake with me of it; and though at that present I was so overlaid with business, that I could not (as I much desired) wait upon that honourable person myself; yet I told my Lord, I would send one to his Lordship, that should diligently attend that service, and that I would give him the best direction I

could. And this I did, and God be thanked,
she died very quietly, and very religiously,
and a good Protestant: and my Lord Marquess told me, he had acknowledged this
service of mine to an honourable Lord, whom
I now see present.

"15. Mr. Chillingworth's ('*a desperate apos-
tate papist.*' W. Prynne.) learning and abilities
are sufficiently known to all your Lordships.
He was gone, and settled at Douay. My
letters brought him back; and he lived and
died a defender of the Church of England.
And that this is so, your Lordships cannot
but know: for Mr. Prynne took away my
letters, and all the papers which concerned
him, and they were examined at the Committee[s].

[s] Besides the well-known passage about Chillingworth's orthodoxy, in Clarendon, (Life, i. 62, 63.) there
is a very instructive one in the Autobiography (ch. iii.
p. 79, 80.) of the *infidel* Gibbon, lately edited and illus-
trated by the *Revd.* Mr. Milman, who quotes with apparent approbation the boast of Sir James Mackintosh,
(Monthly Review, N. S. xx. 87.) that " the Chris-

"16, 17. Mr. Digby was a Priest, and Mr. James Gentleman, a schoolmaster in a recusant's house. This latter was brought to me by a Minister, (as far as I remember,) in Buckinghamshire. I converted both of them, and they remain settled.

"18. Dr. Hart, a Civilian, son to a neighbour of mine at Fulham. He was so far gone, that he had written part of his motives which wrought (as he said) that change in

tianity of Chillingworth is certainly not altogether in dogma, and not at all in spirit, the same with that of (Bp.) Horsley: but perfectly coincident, both in doctrine and spirit, with the Christianity of Locke and Clarke, of Watson and Paley." Gibbon's words (omitting some blasphemous language about Chillingworth's disbelief of the Catholic doctrine of the Holy Trinity) are as follows: "His frequent changes proceeded from too nice an inquisition into truth. His doubts grew out of himself; he assisted them with all the strength of his reason: he was then too hard for himself; but finding as little quiet and repose in those victories, he quickly recovered by a new appeal to his own judgment: so that in all his sallies and retreats, he was in fact his own convert."

him.   I got sight of them; shewed him
wherein he was deceived; had God's blessing
to settle his conscience; and then caused an
able Divine to answer his motives, and give
him the copy.

"19, 20. There were beside these, Mr.
Christopher Seburne, a gentleman of an
ancient family, in Herefordshire; and Sir
William Spencer, of Yarnton in Oxfordshire.
The sons and heirs of Mr. Wintchome, and
Mr. Williscot, whom I sent with their friends'
good liking to Wadham College in Oxford;
and I received a certificate, Anno 1638, of
their continuing in conformity to the Church
of England: nor did ever any of these relapse
again to Rome, but only the old Countess of
Buckingham, and Sir William Spencer, that
ever I heard of. And if any of your Lordships doubt of the truth of any of these
particulars, I am able and ready to bring full
proof of them all. And by this time I hope
it appears, that one of the swaying Prelates
of the time is able to say, he hath converted
one Papist to the Protestant religion. And

let any Clergyman of England come forth, and give a better account of his zeal to this present Church.

" And now, my Lords, with my most humble thanks for your Lordships' favour and patience in hearing me, I shall cease to be farther troublesome for the present; not doubting but I shall be able to answer whatever shall be particularly objected against me."

After I had ended this speech, I was commanded to withdraw. As I went from the bar, there was Alderman Hoyle of York, and some other, which I knew not, very angry, and saying, it was a very strange conversion that I was like to make of them; with other terms of scorn. I went patiently into the little Committee-chamber at the entering into the House. Thither Mr. Peters followed me in great haste, and began to give me ill language, and told me that he, and other Ministers, were able to name thousands, that they had converted. I knew him not, as having never seen him (to my remembrance) in my life, though I had heard enough of him. And as I was going to answer him, one of my counsel, Mr. Hearn, seeing how violently he began, stepped between us, and told him of his uncivil carriage towards me in my affliction: and indeed he came as if he would have struck me. By this time, some occasion brought the Earl of Essex into that room, and Mr. Hearn complained to him of Mr. Peters's usage of me; who very honourably checked him for it, and sent him forth. Not long after, Mr. Hearn was set upon by Alderman Hoyle, and used as coarsely as Peters had used me, and (as far as I remember) only for being of counsel with such a one as I; though he was assigned to that office by the Lords. What put them into this choler, I know not; unless they were angry to hear me say so much in my own defence; especially for the conversion of so many, which I think they little expected. For the next day a great Lord met a friend of mine, and grew very angry with him about me; not forbearing to ask what I meant, to name the particulars, which I had mentioned in the end of my speech, saying many godly Ministers had done more. And not long after this, (the day I now remember not,) Mr. Peters came and preached at Lambeth, and there told them in the pulpit, that a great Prelate, their neighbour, (or in words to that effect,) had bragged in the Parliament House, that he had converted two and twenty; but that he had wisdom enough, not to tell how many thousands he had perverted; with much more abuse. God of his mercy relieve me from these reproaches, and lay not these men's causeless malice to their charge!

After a little stay, I received my dismission for that time, and a command to appear again the next day at nine in the morning: which was my usual hour to attend, though I was seldom called into the House in two hours after.

A. D. 1644.

[The impossibility of finding Archbishop Laud guilty of treason by any even obsolete law, or even, as Guizot expresses it, (ii. 84. Engl. Trans.) by "the tyrannical traditions of

Parliament," made his trial a weary and complicated process, which would soon have weighed down a "weak old man" with a less stout heart than Laud. There were two sets of Articles put in against him, styled, Original and Additional Articles; and on March 28, 1644, they had only reached the 5th and 6th Original and the 9th Additional Article. Although the meekness and wonderful wisdom of the Archbishop are shewn more especially in his defence, yet this volume must confine itself, *mainly* at least, to the few hints of his state of mind and circumstances which are given from time to time in his History of his Troubles and Trial. Ed.]

On Thursday, April 4, I was again brought to the House, made a sufficient scorn and gazing-stock to the people; and after I had waited some hours, was sent back, by reason of other business, unheard: but ordered to appear again Monday, April 8. Then I appeared again, and was used by the basest of the people as before. I did not

)pear any day, but it cost me six or seven
)unds. I grew into want. This made my
)unsel and other friends to persuade me, the
:xt time I had admittance to speak, to move
e Lords again for some necessary allowance;
)twithstanding my former petition had been
jected. This advice I meant to have fol-
wed that day. But after some hours at-
ndance, I was sent back again unheard, and
dered to come again on Thursday, April 11.
his day I did not come to the House; a
arrant being sent to. the Tower, which
ayed me till Tuesday, April 16. This day
us ended, I was ordered to appear again
 Monday, April 22. I came, and my former
iswer having taken off the edge of many
en, (for so I was told by good hands,) the
orns put upon me at my landing and else-
here were somewhat abated, though when
was at best I suffered enough. After I had
tended the pleasure of the House some
)urs, I was remitted without hearing, and
mmanded to attend again upon Thursday,
pril 25. But sent back again then also,

and ordered to appear on Tuesday, April 30
And when I came, I was sent away once
more unheard: no consideration had of my
self, or the great charge which this frequen
coming put me to, I was then ordered to
appear again on Saturday, May 4. Then I
was heard again; and the day proceeded
[His eighth day of hearing.]

At my parting from the House, I was
ordered to appear again on Thursday, May 9
But then fairly put off by an order (sent to
the Lieutenant of the Tower) to Monday
May 13. So the scorn and charge of that
day was scaped. But then I appeared ac
cording to this order, and had scorn plenty,
for what I escaped the day before. And,
after long attendance, was dismissed again
unheard, and had Thursday, May 16, assigned unto me. That day held; and proceeded. [His ninth day of hearing.]

The 16th of May I had an order from the
Lords, for free access of four of my servants
to me. On Friday, May 17, I received a
note from the Committee, that they intended

to proceed upon part of the sixth Original Article remaining, and upon the seventh.

This day, May 20, [his tenth day of hearing,] Mr. Serjeant Wilde undertook the business against me. And at his entrance he made a speech, being now to charge me with matter of religion. In his speech he spake of a tide which came not in all at once. And so he said it was in the intended alteration of religion. First a connivance, then a toleration, then a subversion. Nor this, nor that. But a tide it seems he will have of religion. And I pray God His truth (the true Protestant religion here established) sink not to so low an ebb, that men may with ease wade over to that side, which this gentleman seems most to hate. He fears both ceremonies and doctrine. But in both he fears where no fear is; which I hope shall appear.

June 11. [His thirteenth day of hearing.] The first charge of this day, was the opinion which was held of me beyond the seas. The first witness was Sir Henry Mildmaye, who (as is before related) told me without asking,

that I was the most hateful man at Rome,
that ever sate in my See since the Reformation.   Now he denied not this; but being
helped on by good preparation, a flexible
conscience, and a fair leading interrogatory,
by Mr. Nicholas, (Mr. Serjeant Wilde was
sick, and came no more till the last day, when
I made my recapitulation,) he minced it.
And now he says, that there were two factions at Rome, and that one of them did indeed speak very ill of me, because they
thought I aimed at too great a power here in
England; but the other faction spake as well
of me, because they thought I endeavoured
to bring us in England nearer to the Church
of Rome.   But first, my Lords, this gentleman's words to me were round and general.
That I was hated at Rome; not of a party or
faction there.   And my servants heard him at
the same time, and are here ready to witness
it, that he then said the Pope was a goodly
gentleman, and did use to ride two or three
great horses in a morning; and, but that he
was somewhat taller, he was as like Auditor

Philips (who was then at dinner with me) as could be. But I pray mark what wise men he makes them at Rome. One faction hates me, because I aim at too much power; and the other loves me, because I would draw England nearer Rome: why, if I went about to draw England nearer Rome, can any among them be such fools as to think my power too great? For if I used my power for them, why should any there condemn me? and if I used it against them, why should any here accuse me? Non sunt hæc bene divisa temporibus. These things suit not with the times, or the dispositions of Rome; but the plain truth is, I do not think that ever he was at Rome. I after heard a whisper, that he only stepped into France for another cure, not to Rome for curiosity, which was the only cause he gave the Lords of his going thither.

2. The second witness was Mr. Challoner. He says not much of his own knowledge, but of fame, that tattling gossip; yet he told the Lords, I was a very obscure man, till within

these fifteen years. Be it so, if he please. Yet I have been a Bishop above three and twenty years. And it is eighteen years since I was first Dean of his Majesty's Chapel Royal. He says, that after this time there was a strong opinion of reconciliation to Rome. A strong opinion, but a weak proof. For it was an opinion of enemies, and such as could easily believe what they overmuch desired. He farther said, that some of them were of opinion, that I was a good Roman Catholic, and that I wrought cunningly to introduce that religion by inches. And that they prayed for me. First, my Lords, the opinion of enemies is no proof at all, that I am such as they think me. And, secondly, this is a notable and no unusual piece of cunning, for an enemy to destroy by commending. For this was the ready way, and, I doubt not, but it hath been practised to raise a jealousy against me at home, thereby either to work the ruin of my person, or utterly to weaken and disable me from doing harm to them, or good for the Church of

England. Besides, if the commendation of enemies may in this kind go for proof, it shall be in the power of two or three practising Jesuits, to destroy any Bishop or other Churchman of England when they please. At last, he told a story of one Father John, a Benedictine; that he asked him how Church Livings were disposed in England, and whether I had not the disposing of those which were in the King's gift; and concluded, that he was not out of hope to see England reduced to Rome. Why, my Lords, this is not Father John's hope alone; for there is no Roman Catholic, but hath some hope alive in him to see this day. And were it not for that hope, there would nqt have been so many, some desperate, all dangerous, practices upon this kingdom to effect it, both in Queen Elizabeth's time and since. But if this I-know-not-what Father John hope so, what is that to me?

3. The third witness was Mr. Anthony Mildmaye. A man not thought on for a witness, till I called for his brother Sir Henry.

But now he comes laden with his brother's language. He says just as Sir Henry did before, that there were two factions in Rome, the Jesuits, and they abhorred me; but the other, the Secular Priests, they wished me well, as he was informed. First, this is so one and the same testimony, that any man that will may see, that either he informed his brother, or his brother him. Secondly, here is nothing affirmed; for it is but as he was informed. And he doth not tell you by whom. It may be, my Lords, it was by his brother. Then he says, This was to make myself great, and tells a tale of Father Fiston, as much to the purpose as that which Mr. Challoner told of Father John. But whatsoever either of these fathers said, it was but their own opinion of me, or hearsay; neither of which can prove me guilty of any thing. Thus much Mr. Anthony made a shift to say by five of the clock at afternoon, when I came to make my answer. And this (as I have sufficient cause to think) only to help to shore up his brother's testimony. But in the morning, when he should have come, as his brother did, he was by nine in the morning so drunk, that he was not able to come to the bar, nor to speak common sense, had he been brought thither.

June 20. [Fifteenth day of hearing.] This day I came again to the House. A day or two before, as now also, the landing-place at Westminster was not so full of people; and they which were there much more civil towards me than formerly. My friends were willing to persuade me, that my answer had much abated the edge of the people, saving from the violent and factious leaders of the multitude, whom, it seems, nothing would satisfy but my life, (for so I was after told in plain terms, by a man deeply interested in them;) when I presently saw Quarterman coming towards me, who, so soon as he came, fell to his wonted railing, and asked aloud, " What the Lords meant, to be troubled so long and so often with such a base fellow as I was? they should do well to hang me out of the way." I heard the words with grief enough, and so left them and him in the hands of God. My servants were earnest to have me complain to the Lords. I remembered my late complaint about the pamphlets had no redress; and so forbare it. They, notwithstanding, out of their zeal, complained to Mr. Lieutenant of the Tower; who presently went forth, and said he would school him. But I hearkened no more after it.

When I came to the bar, Mr. Nicholas began with great violence, and told the Lords, "the business grew higher and higher against me." What the business did will after appear. But I am sure he grew higher and higher, and from this time forward, besides the violence of expression, gave me such language as no Christian would give a Jew. But God, I humbly thank Him, blessed me with patience; and so I made my ears obedient. That which made him say the business grew higher and higher, was this. Upon my often calling to have the oaths at the coronations of King James and King Charles compared, some of them repaired again to my

study at Lambeth, to search for all such
copies of coronation books as could there be
found. In this diligent and curious search (for
Mr. Prynne's malice made it) they found some
papers concerning Parliaments, no other (I
praise God for it) than such, as with indifferent construction might, I hope, well pass,
especially considering what occasion led me,
and what command was upon me. And, as
I have been told by able and experienced
men, they would have been nothing, had
they been found in any but this troublesome
and distracted time about the rights of Parliaments, (as it is said.) Howsoever I was
most unfortunate they should be now found,
and I had not left them a being, but that I
verily thought I had destroyed them long
since. But they were unhappily found among
the heaps of my papers.

July 17. [Eighteenth day of hearing.]
The first charge was, that I deny them (the
French and Dutch Reformed Congregations)
to be a Church: for they say that I say
plainly in my book against Fisher, that

No Bishop, no Church.   Now it is well known they have no Bishops, and therefore no Church.   The passage in my book is an inference of St. Jerom's opinion, no declaration of my own.   And, if they or any other be aggrieved at St. Jerom for writing so, they may answer him.   But they have now left me never a book in my study; so I cannot make them any fuller answer, without viewing the place, than themselves help me to by their own confession.   Which is, that he adds this exception, " that none but a Bishop can ordain, but in casu necessitatis," which is the opinion of many learned and moderate Divines.   Yet this is very considerable in the business, whether an inevitable necessity be cast upon them, or they pluck a kind of necessity upon themselves.

[Secondly,] they say, " I disliked the giving of this title Antichrist to the Pope." No, I did not simply dislike it, but I advised Bishop Hall, if he thought it good, not to affirm it so positively.   Here Mr. Nicholas fell extreme foul upon me, in so much that I could not but wonder at their patience which heard him. Among other titles bestowed upon me, many and gross, he called me over and over again, *Pander to the Whore of Babylon.* I was much moved; and humbly desired the Lords, that if my crimes were such, as that I might not be used like an Archbishop, yet I might be used like a Christian: and that were it not for the duty which I owe to God and my own innocency, I would desert my defence, before I would endure such language in such an honourable presence.

The third charge was out of a paper, which Bishop Hall, about the time when he wrote his book in defence of Episcopacy, sent unto me, containing divers propositions concerning Episcopal government. In which, either he or I or both say, (for that circumstance I remember not,) " That Church government by Bishops is not alterable by human law." To this I answered, that Bishops might be regulated and limited by human laws, in those things which are but incidents to their calling. But their calling, so far as it is Jure Divino, by divine right, cannot be taken away. They charge farther, that I say this is the doctrine of the Church of England. And so I think it is. For Bishop Bilson set out a book in the Queen's time, intituled, the Perpetual Government. And, if the government by Bishops be perpetual, as he there very learnedly proves through the whole book, it will be hard for any Christian nation to out it. Nor is this his judgment alone, but of the whole Church of England. For in the Preface to the Book of Ordination are these words. " From the Apostles' time, there have been three Orders of Ministers in the Church of Christ, Bishops, Priests, and Deacons." Where it is evident, that in the judgment of the Church of England, Episcopacy is a different, not *Degree* only, but *Order*, from Priesthood, and so hath been reputed from the Apostles' times. And this was then read to the Lords. And the law of England is as full for it, as the Church. For the Statute in the eighth of the Queen, absolutely confirms all and every part of this

Book of Ordination. Where also the law calls it the high estate of Prelacy. And Calvin, (if my old memory do not fail me,) upon those words of St. John, As My Father sent Me, so send I you, &c, says thus upon that place, Eandem illis imponit Personam ac idem Juris assignat. And, if our Saviour Christ put the same person upon the Apostles, and assigned to them the same right, which His Father gave Him, it will prove a sour work to throw their successors the Bishops out of the Church after sixteen hundred years' continuance: and in the mean time cry out against innovation. For either Christ gave this power to His Apostles only; and that will make the Gospel a thing temporary, and confined to the Apostles' times; or else He gave the same *power*, though not with such eminent *gifts*, to their successors also, to propagate the same Gospel to the end of the world, as St. Paul tells us He did, Ephes. iv. 11. Now all the primitive Church all along gives Bishops to be the Apostles' successors, and then it would be well thought on, what right any Christian State hath (be their absolute power what it will) to turn Bishops out of that right in the Church, which Christ hath given them[1].

[1] In opposition to this statement, it is not a little curious to contrast the opinions of a Tudor Courtier as to the source of Episcopal power with those of one of the celebrated Parliamentary leaders in the great rebellion. They illustrate the conveniently moveable character of Erastian views. Sir Francis Knollys said to Archbishop Whitgift, on occasion of Dr. Bancroft's famous Sermon at St. Paul's Cross, Jan. 12, 1588,— " I do not deny that Bishops may have lordly authority and dignity, *provided* they claim it not from a higher authority than her MAJESTY's Grant. If Bishops are not undergovernors to her *Majesty* of the Clergy, but superior governors over their brethren by God's ordinance, it will then follow that her *Majesty* is not supreme governor over her Clergy." Neal, Hist. Par. i. 322. Forty-one years later, the notable John Pym, in a speech of very considerable power, in Charles's third Parliament, thus states his view of the question. " Howsoever it is alleged that the PARLIAMENT are not judges in matters of faith, yet ought they to know the established and fundamental truths, and the contrary to them ; for *Parliaments* have confirmed acts of

Then followed the charge of Sancta Clara's Book, alias Monsieur St. Giles: so they expressed it; and I must follow the way they lead me. First then, they charge that I had often conference with him, while he was writing his book intituled Deus, Natura, Gratia. No, he never came to me, till he was ready to print that book. Then some friends of his brought him to me. His suit then was, that he might print that book here. Upon speech with him, I found the scope of his book to be such, as that the Church of England would have little cause to thank him for it: and so absolutely denied it. Nor did he ever come more at me after this, but twice

General Councils, which have not been received until they have been so authorized. The Convocation cannot meet these mischiefs, (i. e. countenancing of heretics,) because it is but a provincial Synod, only of the jurisdiction of Canterbury, and the power thereof is not adequate to the whole kingdom; while the Convocation of York may, perhaps, not agree with that of Canterbury. It is in short reserved for the judgment of the *Parliament*, that being the judgment of the King and of the three estates of the kingdom."

or thrice at most, when he made great friends to me, that he might print another book, to prove that Bishops are by divine right. My answer then was, that I did not like the way which the Church of Rome went, in the case of Episcopacy. And however, that I would never give way, that any such book should be printed here from the pen of a Romanist; and that the Bishops of England were able to defend their own cause and calling, without calling in aid from Rome; and would in due time. Maintenance he never had any from me, nor did I then know him to be a Priest. Nor was there any proof so much as offered in contrary to any of this.

At last came in the last charge of this day. That a Cardinal's hat was offered unto me. My Diary quoted for this, at Aug. 4, and 21, 1633. I could hinder no offer, unless I could prophesy what each man came about, and so shun them. But why is not my answer, there set down, expressed too? My answer was, that somewhat dwelt in me, which would not suffer me to accept that, till Rome were other than now it is. Besides, I went presently to his Majesty, and acquainted him with it : which is all that the law requires at my hands. And his Majesty very prudently and religiously (yet in a calm way, the persons offering it, having relation to some Embassador) freed me speedily of that both trouble and danger. They urged further out of the papers of Andreas ab Habernfield, (which Mr. Prynne took from me in his search,) that Signior Con had power to offer me a Cardinal's hat. The words which they cite are, (for I could never get sight of those papers since,) Mandatum habuit offerre, sed non obtulit. What power he had to make me such an offer, I know not ; but themselves confess he did not offer it. Nor had I ever any speech with him, during all the time he stayed here. I was solicited as much by honourable friends to give him admittance to me at Lambeth, with assurance he should speak nothing about religion, as ever I had about any thing in my life. I still refused, and could not persuade myself to do other, and yet could not but inwardly (In verbo Sacerdotis, this is true) condemn myself of gross incivility for refusing. For which yet now I see I am much bound to God for that unmannerliness. Had I held a correspondence with him, though never so innocent, where had I now been? Besides, I would not have it forgotten, that if to offer a Cardinal's hat, or any like thing, shall be a sufficient cause to make a man guilty of treason, it shall be in the power of any Romanist to make any English Bishop a traitor when he pleases: a mischief not to be endured. And thus this long and tedious day ended; and I had order to attend again on July 24, which I did accordingly.

July 29. This last day of my trial.

Aug. 23. I received an order from the Lords, that if I had a mind to make a recapitulation of my long and various charge, I should provide myself for it.

Then came Monday, Sept. 2; and, according to the order from the Lords, I made the

capitulation of my whole cause. But, so
on as I came to the bar, I saw every Lord
esent with a new thin book in folio in a
ue coat. I heard that morning that Mr.
rynne had printed my Diary, and published
to the world to disgrace me. Some notes
his own are made upon it. The first and
st are two desperate untruths[k], beside some
hers. This was the book then in the Lords'
nds, and I assure myself that time picked
r it, that the sight of it might damp me,

[k] Some of the initials and secret entries in the Diary
rynne had chosen to explain, on the supposition they
plied the secret sins of the writer. That they did
note sins is in many cases clear, as they were days
hamiliation throughout his life. But Fuller well
ys, (ap. Lawson,) " An exact diary is a window into
i heart who maketh it, and therefore pity it is that
y should look therein, but either the friends of the
rty, or such ingenuous foes as will not (especially in
ings doubtful) make conjectural comments to his dis-
ace. But, be E. B. male or female, and the sin
mmitted of what kind soever, his fault whispers not
much to his shame, as his solemn humiliation sounds
his commendation."

and disenable me to speak.   I confess I was
a little troubled at it.   But after I had gathered up myself, and looked up to God, I
went on to the business of the day.   And thus
I spake.

[Here follows the Archbishop's recapitulation.]

Here ended my recapitulation, and with it
the work of that day.   I was ordered to
appear again the Saturday following to hear
Mr. Brown sum up the whole charge against
me.   But upon Tuesday, Sept. 3, this was
put off, to give Mr. Brown more time, to
Wednesday, Sept. 11.

On Wednesday, Sept. 4, as I was washing
my face, my nose bled, and something plentifully, which it had not done, to my remembrance, in forty years before, save only once,
and that was just the same day and hour,
when my most honourable friend the Duke
of Buckingham was killed at Portsmouth,
myself being then at Westminster.—And upon
Friday, as I was washing after dinner, my
nose bled again.   I thank God I make no

superstitious observation of this or any thing else; yet I have ever used to mark what and how any thing of note falls to me. And here I after came to know, that upon both these days in which I bled, there was great agitation in the House of Commons to have me sentenced by Ordinance; but both times put off, in regard very few of that House had heard either my charge or defence. On Wednesday, Sept. 11, Mr. Brown made in the Lords' House, a sum or brief of the charge which was brought against me, and touched by the way at some things in my recapitulation. But in regard I might not answer him, I took no perfect notes, but stood still, and possessed my soul in patience; yet wondering at the bold, free, frequent, and most false swearing, that had been against me. When Mr. Brown had ended, I humbly desired again, that my counsel might be heard in point of law. And they were hereupon ordered to deliver in writing under their hands, what points of law they would insist upon, and that by Saturday, Sept. 14.

My counsels' queries having been formally sent down to the House of Commons, they were there referred to a Committee of Lawyers to consider of; and on Friday, September 27, they were earnestly called upon to hasten their report. And on Friday, Oct. 4, Mr. Nicholas made a great noise about me in the House, and would have had me presently censured in the House; and no less would serve his turn, but that I must be hanged, and was at Sus. per Coll. till upon the reasons before given, that if they went on this way, they must condemn me unheard, this violent clamour ceased for that time. And a message was sent up to the Lords for my counsel to be heard, as touching the first question concerning treason; but not concerning any exception that they shall take against the Articles in point of certainty. This message the Lords took into present consideration, and ordered it accordingly; and appointed the Friday following, being Octob. 11, for my counsel to be heard, and myself to be present.

This day according to this order of the Lords, I and my counsel attended. My counsel were Mr. Hern and Mr. Hales of Lincoln's Inn, and Mr. Gerrard of Gray's Inn. When we were called into the House, and the Lords settled in their places, Mr. John Hern (who was the man that spake what all had resolved on) delivered his argument very freely and stoutly, proving that nothing which I have either said or done according to this charge is treason, by any known established law of this kingdom.

This day ended, I had a few days rest. But on Tuesday, Oct. 22, being a day made solemn for humiliation, my chamber at the Tower was searched again for letters and papers; but nothing found.

After this, there went up and down, all about London and the suburbs, a petition for the bringing of delinquents to justice; and some preachers exhorted the people to be zealous in it, telling them it was for the glory of God, and the good of the Church. By this means they got many hands of men which little thought what they went about. In this petition none were named but myself and the Bishop of Ely (Wren), so their drift was known to none but their own party, and was undoubtedly set on foot to do me mischief. Whose design this was, God knows; but I have cause to suspect Mr. Prynne's hand in it. This barbarous way of the people's clamouring upon great courts of justice, as if they knew not how to govern themselves and the causes brought before them, is a most unchristian course, and not to be endured in any well-governed State. This petition, with a multitude of hands to it, was delivered to the House of Commons on Monday, Oct. 28. Concerning which I shall observe this, that neither the Lord Mayor nor the Sheriffs made any stop of this illegal and blood-thirsty course, though it were publicly known, and the people exhorted to set hands to it in the parish churches. What this, and such like courses as these, may bring upon this city, God alone knows, Whom I humbly pray to shew it mercy.

Nov. 1. This day, being All-hallows day, a warrant came to the Lieutenant, from the House of Commons, to bring me to their bar, to hear the evidence formally summed up, and given against me in the Lords' House. I knew no law nor custom for this; for though our votes, by a late Act of Parliament, be taken away, yet our Baronies are not: and so long as we remain Barons, we belong to the Lords' House, and not to the Commons. Yet how to help myself I knew not; for when the warrant came to me, the Lords' House was risen; and I was commanded to the House of Commons the next morning, before the Lords came to sit: so I could not petition them for any privilege. And had I done it, I doubt it would have been interpreted for an endeavour to make a breach between the Houses. And should I have under any pretence refused to go, Mr. Lieutenant would have carried me.

Therefore, on Saturday, Nov. 2, I went, according to the warrant, to the House of Commons. So soon as ever I was come to

the bar, Mr. Speaker told me, there was an
Ordinance drawn up, to attaint me of high
treason; but, that they would not pass it,
till they had heard a summary of the charge
which was laid against me; and, that I was
sent for to hear it also. I humbly besought
them that my counsel and my solicitor (who
were always present with me in the Lords'
House) might stand now by me; but it
would not be granted. Then Mr. Brown, by
order from the Speaker, delivered the collection and sum of the charge against me;
much at one with that which he formerly
made in the Lords' House. Now I took notes
of it as exactly as I could. He had no sooner
done, but Mr. Speaker pressed me to make
answer presently. I humbly besought the
House I might not be put to that, the charge
being long and various; but that I might
have time; and, that my counsel might be
heard for matter of law. I was commanded
to withdraw. And when I was called in
again, I received an order peremptory to
answer the Monday sevennight after, to such

things as the Reporter was mistaken in; but not a word of hearing my counsel. I returned to my prison.

This Wednesday, Nov. 6, I got my Prayer-Book, by the help of Mr. Hern and Mr. Brown, out of Mr. Prynne's hands, where it had been ever since the last of May, 1643.

Monday, Nov. 11. I came to the House of Commons again; and, according to their peremptory order, made my answer to the summary charge which Mr. Brown made against me. But here I shall advertise the reader, that, to avoid troublesome and tedious repetition, I shall not set down my answer at large as there I spake it; because there is nothing in it but what is in my former answers, the beginning and the end only excepted. But it was necessary for me then to make a whole and an entire answer, because the House of Commons had then heard no part of my defence. But, I presume, the charitable reader will look upon my answers in their proper place, rather than be troubled a second time with the same thing. Yet because Mr. Brown went a different way in his summary from the charge largely given, I shall represent a skeleton of my answer, with all the limbs of it entire, that it may be seen, as it were, together; though I report nothing which hath been already said. And thus I began:

"Mr. Speaker,

"I was here November 2. It was the first time that ever I came within these doors; and here then you gave me the most uncomfortable breakfast that ever I came to; namely, that this Honourable House had drawn up an Ordinance against me of high treason; but that before they would proceed farther, I should hear the sum of the charge which was against me; which was the cause I was sent for then. And to give my answer to that which was then said, or rather mistaken in saying and inferring, is the cause of my coming now.

"And first, Mr. Speaker, I give thanks to this Honourable House, that they have given me leave to speak for myself. Secondly, I do humbly desire, if any word or thing should be mistaken, or unadvisedly expressed, by me, (which shall be sore against my will,) I may have liberty to recal and expound myself. Thirdly, That you will favourably consider into what straits I am cast, that, after a long and tedious hearing, I must now come to answer to a sum, or an epitome of the same charge, which, how dangerous it may be for me, all men that know epitomes cannot but understand.

" Mr. Speaker, I am come hither to make a brief of my answer to a sum of my charge, wherein I may receive as much detriment by my own brief, for want of larger expression, as by the other of my charge by omission or mistake. Yet since your command is upon me, I shall without further preface (which, I conceive, would be as tedious to you, as to me troublesome) address myself, and with as much brevity, as the many heads of the charge will bear. And that my answer may be the clearer, both to this Honourable House, and to the gentleman who reported the charge, I shall follow every thing in the same order he proceeded in. So far forth, at least, as an old slow hand could take them, a heavy heart observe them, and an old decayed memory retain them.

" This worthy gentleman hath pressed all things as hardly against me, as the cause can any way bear; that was his duty to this Honourable House, and it troubles me not. But his carriage and expressions were civil towards me in this my great affliction; and for this I render him humble and hearty thanks; having from other hands pledged my Saviour in gall and vinegar, and drunk up the cup of the scornings of the people to the very bottom."

[The Archbishop spoke on the particulars of his charge, and thus concluded :]

" Mr. Speaker, I shall draw towards an end. Yet not forgetting what Ordinance you told me was drawn up against me. If that which I have now said may any way satisfy this Honourable House to make stay of it, or to mitigate it, I shall bless God and you for it. And I humbly desire you to take into consideration, my calling, my age, my former life, my fall, my imprisonment, long and strict; that these considerations may move with you. In my prosperity, (I bless God for it!) I was never puffed into vanity, whatever the world may think of me. And in these last full four years' durance, I thank the same God, gravem fortunam constanter tuli, I have with decent constancy borne the weight of a pressing fortune; and I hope God will strengthen me unto and in the end of it.

"Mr. Speaker, I am very aged, considering the turmoils of my life; and I daily find in myself more decays than I make shew of; and the period of my life, in the course of nature, cannot be far off. It cannot but be a great grief unto me, to stand at these years thus charged before you, yet give me leave to say thus much without offence: whatsoever errors or faults I may have committed by the way, in any my proceedings, through human infirmity; (as who is he that hath not offended, and broken some statute-laws too by igno-

rance, or misapprehension, or forgetfulness,
at some sudden time of action?) yet if God
bless me with so much memory, I will die
with these words in my mouth: that I never
intended, much less endeavoured, the subversion of the laws of the kingdom; nor the
bringing in of Popish superstition upon the
true Protestant religion, established by law in
this kingdom.

"And now, Mr. Speaker, having done
with the fact, I have but this one thing to
put to the consideration of this Honourable
House.   My charge hath been repeated, I
confess, by a very worthy and a very able
gentleman.   But ability is not absolute in
any.   The evidence given against me before
the Lords was (as by the law it ought to be)
given in upon oath; but the evidence now
summed up, and presented to this Honourable House, is but upon the collection and
judgment of one man, how able or entire
soever; and what he conceived is proved
against me, is but according to his judgment
and memory; which perhaps may differ

much from the opinion and judgment of the judges themselves, who heard the evidence at large: nor was this gentleman himself present every day of my hearing; and then for those days in which he was absent, he can report no more here, than what others have reported to him. So for so much, his repetition here is but a report of a report of evidence given: and at the best but a report of evidence, and not upon oath. And, I suppose, never any jurors, who are triers of the fact in any case, civil or criminal, did ever ground their verdict upon an evidence only reported before them, and which themselves heard not.

" And if this manner of proceeding shall be thought less considerable in my person; yet I humbly desire it may be thoroughly weighed in the prudent judgment of this Honourable House, the great preserver of the laws and liberties of the subjects of England, how far it doth or may trench upon these in future consequences, if these great boundaries be laid loose and open.

" And because my infirmities are many and great, which age and grief have added to those which are naturally in me, I most humbly desire again, that my counsel may be heard for point of law, according to the former concession of this Honourable House: for I assure myself, upon that which hath been pleaded to the Lords, that no one, nor all of the things together which are charged against me, if proved, (which I conceive they are not,) can make me guilty of high treason, by any known established law of this kingdom.

" The sum of all is this: upon an impeachment arising from this House, I have pleaded Not guilty.   Thereupon issue hath been joined, and evidence given in upon oath. And now I must humbly leave it to you, your wisdom and justice, whether it shall be thought fit, and just, and honourable, to judge me here only upon a report, or a hearsay, and that not upon oath." --

Here ended the heavy business of this day. I was exceeding faint with speaking so long;

nd I, had great pain and soreness in my reast for almost a fortnight after; then, I iank God, it wore away. I was commanded) withdraw, and to attend the House again n Wednesday, Nov. 13, which I did. Then [r. Brown made a reply to my answer. The ·ply had some great mistakes in it; but else as, for the most part, but a more earnest firming of what he had delivered. And I)nceived I was not to answer to his reply, ut that he was to have the last speech; for) it was always carried, during my hearing in ie Lords' House. Therefore, being dismissed, went away: and I was no sooner gone, but ie House called for the Ordinance which ·as drawn up against me, and without hear- ig my counsel, or any more ado, voted me uilty of high treason. And yet, when I ime that day to the House, all men, and iany of the House themselves, did much iagnify my answer before given. I will rbear to set down in what language, because was high; and as no time can be fit for anity, so least of all was this time for me;

and vain I must needs be thought, should
here relate what was told me from many a
good hands. But it seems the clamour pr
vailed against me.

On Saturday, Nov. 16, this Ordinance w
passed the House of Commons suddenly, ar
with so great deliberation, as you have hea
was transmitted to the Lords; and by the
the debate concerning it put off to Frida
Nov. 22. Then the Earl of Pembroke beg
more fully to shew his cankered humo
against me; how provoked, I protest I kno
not, unless by my serving him far beyond h
desert. There, among other coarse languag
he bestowed (as I am informed) the rasc
and the villain upon me; and told the Lord
they would put off giving their consent to tl
Ordinance, till the citizens would come dow
and call for justice, as they did in my Lor
Strafford's case. Was there not justice an
wisdom in his speech? Hereupon the bus
ness was put off to Saturday, Nov. 23, an
then to Friday, Nov. 29. But then upo
Thursday, Nov. 28, Mr. Stroud came up wit

a message from the Commons, to quicken
the Lords in this business; and at the end of
his message he let fall, That they should do
well to agree to the Ordinance, or else the
multitude would come down and force them
to it. At this, some Lords very honourably
took exception; and Mr. Stroud durst not
bide it, that this was any part of the message
delivered him by the House of Commons.
But the matter was passed over, and Mr.
Stroud not so much as checked. This, it may
be, was thought seasonable by some, to
hearten on the violence of the Earl of Pembroke.

The business, not long heard on Friday,
was put off again to Monday, Dec. 2, and the
House of Lords put into a Committee, to
examine particulars by their notes; the
Earl of Northumberland on the Woolsack
during the debate, which continued, more
or less, some days. Where their own notes
failed, they called to Mr. Brown, Clerk of
their House, for his. But at last, finding
him very ready and quick for any thing that

was charged against me, but loth to be
known what answer I gave to any point,
some Lords observed it. And it did after
appear, that the notes which he put to the
Lords, were not the notes which himself
took, but that he had a copy given him,
(whether by Mr. Prynne or any other, I
know not,) and I was informed that the Earl
of Warwick had another copy of the very
same. This is marvellous just and honourable in that Earl, and most Christian-like in
Mr. Brown. It may be, he learned it out
of the notes which his father-in-law takes at
sermons.

Upon Monday, Dec. 16, there was (the
times considered) a very full House of Lords;
about twenty present, and my business largely
debated, and ready to come to the question.
I wish with all my heart it had, while the
House was so full. But the Earl of Pembroke
fell again into his wonted violence: and
asked the Lords what they stuck at? and
added, What, shall we think the House of
Commons had no conscience in passing this

Ordinance? Yes, they know well enough
what they did. One of the wits hearing this
excellent passage of the Earl's, protested,
If ever he lived to see a Parliament in Bedlam, this prudent Earl should be Speaker, if
he were able to procure him the place.

In the mean time, this unhappy clamour of
his put the business off again to the next day,
being Tuesday; then there were but fourteen
Lords in the House. My business was assumed, and proposed in the questions, and I
was voted guilty of the fact in all three:
namely, guilty of endeavouring to subvert
the laws; to overthrow the Protestant Religion; and that I was an enemy to Parliaments. Then it being put to the judges,
whether this were treason or no; the judges
unanimously declared, that nothing which
was charged against me was treason, by any
known and established law of the land, with
many things to and fro concerning this business.

On Tuesday, Christmas-eve, the Lords had
a conference with the Commons about it. In

which they declared, that they had diligent
weighed all things that were charged again
me, but could not by any one of them, or a
find me guilty of treason. And therefore d
sired that the argument made by my couns
might be answered. And if it could be mad
appear unto them by any law to be treason
they would then proceed farther, as in h
nour and justice they should find fit. The
came Christmas-day, the last Wednesday i
the month, and a most solemn Fast kept on it
with as solemn an ordinance for the du
observance of this Fast, and against th
manner of keeping of that day in forme
superstitious times. A Fast never befor
heard of in Christendom. After this conference, Mr. Serjeant Wild, speaking free t
some friends about this business, told them
he wondered the Lords should so much dis
trust their judgments, as to desire a conference about it. To see how good wits agree
Surely, I believe he was of the Earl of Pembroke's council, or the Earl of his, they
jump so together. It seems in there men'

opinions, the House of Commons can neither err in conscience nor judgment. Howsoever, that House thought it fit the Lords should be satisfied, that I was by law guilty of high treason. And to that end sent up a Committee, Jan. 2, 1644, to make proof of it to their Lordships. At this meeting two Judges were present, Justice Reeves, and Judge Bacon. The managers of the business against me were three lawyers, Mr. Brown, Serjeant Wild, and Mr. Nicholas. Neither myself nor any of my counsel there. What this will effect upon the Lords, time must discover, as it doth the effects of other eclipses. And thus far I had proceeded in this sad history by Jan. 3, 1644. The rest shall follow as it comes to my knowledge.

[H. W. Next day, the Archbishop receiving the news, that the Bill of Attainder had passed in the House of Lords, broke off his history, and prepared himself for death. I shall therefore supply the history from the accounts of Mr. Rushworth, and Mr. Heylin.]

THE

ACTS OF THE MARTYRDOM

OF

WILLIAM,

ARCHBISHOP OF CANTERBURY.

———

ARCHBISHOP LAUD was kept for more than
four years a prisoner and Confessor in the
Tower of London[1]; an old man, " for judgment thrown aside," yet never among all the
distractions and great events without, forgotten by the fear and hatred of the enemies
who had mercilessly hunted him to death.
It was in 1640, that Pococke, the Oriental
Scholar, arrived in London, and found his
patron in the Tower. In Paris, Laud's imprisonment had made a great sensation, espe-

[a] These Acts are compiled from Heylin, Fuller,
Antony Wood, Rushworth, Clarendon, and other
sources. ED.

cially among the learned, and Pococke was
made the bearer of a message to him from
Grotius—"that it was his humble request
and advice, that his Grace would find out
some way, if possible, to escape out of the
hands he was now in, and pass to some place
beyond seas, there to preserve himself till
better times; at least to obtain some present
security from the malice of his bitter enemies,
and the rage of a deluded people." " I thank
my good friend, Hugo Grotius," was the
Archbishop's reply, " for the care he has
thus expressed of my safety, but I can by
no means be persuaded to comply with his
advice. An escape, indeed, is feasible enough;
yea, it is, I believe, the very thing which my
enemies desire; for every day an opportunity
for it is presented to me, a passage being left
free, in all likelihood for this very purpose,
that I should endeavour to take advantage of
it; but they shall not be gratified by me in
what they appear to long for. I am almost
seventy years old, and shall I now go about
to prolong a miserable life, by the trouble

and shame of flying? And were I willing to
be gone, whither should I fly? Should I go
to France, or any other Popish country, it
would be to give some seeming ground to
that charge of Popery they have endeavoured
with so much industry, and so little reason,
to fasten upon me. But if I should get into
Holland, I should expose myself to the in-
sults of those sectaries there, to whom I am
odious, and have every Anabaptist come and
pull me by the beard. No; I am resolved
not to think of flight, but, continuing where
I am, patiently expect and bear what a good
and wise Providence hath appointed for me,
of what kind soever it may be."

We have elsewhere followed him through
his long and weary trial; in which, as his
enemy Prynne confesses, he made as full, as
gallant, as pithy a defence, and spake as
much for himself, as was possible for the wit
of man to invent; and that with so much art,
vivacity, oratory, audacity, and confidence,
that he shewed not the least acknowledgment
of guilt in any of the particulars which were

charged upon him. If we compare his demeanour during this latter part of his life
with the character given of him by Lord
Clarendon, we may see that suffering had
done somewhat of its sanctifying work upon
him. " He was a man of great parts and
very exemplary virtues, and discredited by
some popular natural infirmities; the greatest
of which was, (besides a hasty, sharp way of
expressing himself,) that he believed innocence of heart and integrity of manners, was
a guard strong enough to secure any man in
his voyage through this world, in what company soever he travelled, and through what
ways soever he was to pass: and sure never
any man was better supplied with that provision. He was always maligned and persecuted by those who were of the Calvinian
faction, which was then very popular, and who,
according to their usual maxim and practice,
call every man they do not love, *Papist;* and
under this senseless appellation they created
him many troubles and vexations. He was a
man of great courage and resolution, and being

most assured within himself, that he proposed
no end in all his actions and designs but what
was pious and just, (as sure no man had ever
a heart more entire to the King, the Church,
or his country,) he never studied the easiest
ways to those ends; he thought, it may be,
that any art or industry that way would dis-
credit, at least make the integrity of the end
suspected, let the cause be what it will. He
did court persons too little; nor cared to
make his designs and purposes appear as
candid as they were, by shewing them in any
other dress than their own natural beauty,
though perhaps in too rough a manner; and
did not consider enough what men said,
or were like to say of him. No man was a
greater or abler enemy to popery; no man a
more resolute and devout son of the Church
of England. He was prosecuted by lawyers
assigned to that purpose, out of those, who
from their own antipathy to the Church and
Bishops, or from some disobligations received
from him, were sure to bring passion, animosity, and malice enough of their own;

what evidence soever they had from others. And they did treat him with all the rudeness, reproach, and barbarity imaginable; with which his judges were not displeased. He defended himself with great and undaunted courage, and less passion than was expected from his constitution; answered all their objections with clearness and irresistible reason; and convinced all impartial men of his integrity, and his detestation of all treasonable intentions. So that though few excellent men have ever had fewer friends to their persons, yet all reasonable men absolved him from any foul crime that the law could take notice of, and punish. However, when they had said all they could against him, and he all for himself that need to be said, and no such crime appearing, as the Lords, as the supreme court of judicatory, would take upon them to judge him to be worthy of death, they resorted to their legislative power, and by Ordinance of Parliament, as they called it, that is, by a determination of those members who sat in the Houses, (whereof in the House of Peers there were not above twelve,) they appointed him to be put to death as guilty of high treason. The first time that two Houses of Parliament had ever assumed that jurisdiction, or that ever Ordinance had been made to such a purpose; nor could any rebellion be more against the law, than that murderous act. Much hath been said of the person of this great Prelate before, of his great endowments, and natural infirmities; to which shall be added no more in this place, (his memory deserving a particular celebration,) than that his learning, piety, and virtue, have been attained by very few, and the greatest of his infirmities are common to all, even to the best men."

When the trial was over, and the Ordinance passed for his execution, he was called and asked, " what he could say more, why he should not suffer death?" Now the King, seeing the great danger this faithful Bishop was in, had sent him secretly from Oxford, which holy and hospitable city was to the last a sanctuary for the loyal subjects of the

King, a full pardon, signed and sealed with
the Great Seal of England. The Archbishop
had received it with great joy, as it was a
testimony of the King's great affection to him,
and care of him. And at this, when he was
questioned, "What he could say more, why
he should not suffer death?" he made answer, "that he had the King's gracious pardon, which he pleaded, and tendered to
them, and desired that it might be allowed."
Whereupon they sent back to the Tower,
and, with no long debate, set the Royal
pardon aside, as without power in this judgment: as though it had been ordered, that
each fresh step they took in this cruel business should have a new weight of sin to bear;
which, God knows, it need not.

On the 6th of January, six Peers, and it
was strange to find so many in the English
peerage, to wit, Philip Earl of Pembroke,
Henry Earl of Kent, William Earl of Salis-
bury, Oliver Earl of Bolingbroke, Dudley
Lord North, and William Lord Gray of
Wark, all of them Presbyterians, condemned

the Archbishop to be *hung* on the 10th of
January next. On the same day with this
unrighteous sentence, Parliament abolished
the Book of Common Prayer. Which made
Antony Wood to say, speaking of " the King's
and the Church's martyr," that he was " a
man of such integrity, learning, devotion, and
courage, as, had he lived in the primitive
times, would have given him another name;
whom, though the cheated multitude were
taught to misconceive, (for those honoured
him most who best knew him,) yet impartial posterity will know how to value him,
when they hear that the rebels sentenced him
on the same day they voted down the Liturgy
of the Church of England."

Meanwhile the manner of his death troubled
the good Archbishop not a little; and with a
deeply Christian magnanimity and largeness
of heart, whatever some poor, unworthy
minds have thought or said about it, he was
not above petitioning his malicious enemies,
that, considering he was a Bishop in the
Church, he might die by beheading rather

than by the gibbet.   Which request the Commons at first violently refused, but did afterwards assent unto.

The passing of the Ordinance being signified to him by the then Lieutenant of the Tower, he neither entertained the news with a stoical apathy, nor wailed his fate with weak and womanish lamentations, (to which extremes most men are carried in this case,) but heard it with so even and so smooth a temper, as shewed he neither was ashamed to live, nor afraid to die.   The time between the sentence and execution he spent in prayers and applications to the Lord his God ; having obtained, though not without some difficulty, his chaplain Dr. Sterne, who afterwards sat in the Chair of York, to attend upon him.   His chaplains, Drs. Heywood and Martin, he much wished might be with him. But it seems it was too much for him to ask. So instead, two violent Presbyterians, Marshall and Palmer, were ordered by Parliament to give him religious consolations : which consolations his Grace quietly declined.   Indeed, little preparation was needed to receive that blow, which could not but be welcome, because long expected. For so well was he studied in the art of dying, especially in the last and strictest part of his imprisonment, that by continual fastings, watchings, prayers, and such like acts of Christian humiliation, his flesh was rarified into spirit, and the whole man so fitted for eternal glories, that he was more than half in heaven, before death brought his bloody but triumphant chariot, to convey him thither. He, that had so long been a Confessor, could not but think it a release of miseries to be made a Martyr.

On the evening of the 9th, Sheriff Chambers, of London, brought the warrant for his execution. In preparation to so sad a work, he betook himself to his own, and desired also the prayers of others, and particularly of Dr. Holdsworth, fellow-prisoner in that place for a year and a half; though all that time there had not been the least converse betwixt them. This evening before his passover, the night before the dismal combat betwixt him and death, after he had refreshed his spirits with a moderate supper, he betook himself unto his rest, and slept very soundly till the time came, in which his sevants were appointed to attend his rising. A most assured sign of a soul prepared.

The 10th of January came, on which the Archbishop completed his life of seventy-one years, thirteen weeks, and four days. His death was the more remarkable, in falling on St. William's day, as if it did design him to an equal place in the English Calendar, with that which William, Archbishop of Bourges, had obtained in the French: who, (being as great a zealot in his time against the spreading and increase of the Albigenses, as Laud was thought to be against those of the Puritan faction, and the Scottish Covenanters,) hath ever since been honoured as a Saint and Confessor in the Gallican Church; the tenth of January being destined for the solemnities of his commemoration, on which day our Laud ascended from the scaffold to a throne of glory.

In the morning he was early at his prayers; at which he continued till Pennington, Lieutenant of the Tower, and other public officers, came to conduct him to the scaffold; which he ascended with so brave a courage, such a cheerful countenance, as if he had mounted rather to behold a triumph, than be made a sacrifice; and came not there to die, but to be translated. And though some rude and uncivil people reviled him, as he passed along, with opprobrious language, as loth to let him go to the grave in peace, yet it never discomposed his thoughts, nor disturbed his patience. For he had profited so well in the school of Christ, that " when he was reviled, he reviled not again; when he suffered, he threatened not; but committed his cause to Him that judgeth righteously."

And, as he did not fear the frowns, so neither did he covet the applause of the people; and therefore rather chose to read what he had to speak, than to affect the ostentation either of memory or wit in that dreadful agony: whether with greater mag-

nanimity than prudence can hardly be sa:
And here it followeth from the copy, pi
sented very solemnly by Dr. Sterne to I
sorrowing master, the good King Charle
at Oxford.

The Archbishop's Speech upon the Scaffold.

Good People,

This is an uncomfortable time to preacl
yet I shall begin with a text of Scriptur
Hebrews xii. 2. " Let us run with patien
the race which is set before us : lookir
unto Jesus, the Author and Finisher of o
faith, Who, for the joy that was set befo
Him, endured the Cross, despising the sham
and is set down at the right hand of tl
throne of God."

I have been long in my race ; and how
have looked unto Jesus, the Author an
Finisher of my faith, He best knows. I a
now come to the end of my race, and here
find the Cross, a death of shame. But th
shame must be despised, or no coming to th

right hand of God. Jesus despised the shame for me, and God forbid that I should not despise the shame for Him.

I am going apace, as you see, towards the Red sea, and my feet are upon the very brink of it: an argument, I hope, that God is bringing me into the Land of Promise; for that was the way through which He led His people.

But before they came to it, He instituted a passover for them. A lamb it was, but it must be eaten with sour herbs[a]. I shall obey, and labour to digest the sour herbs, as well as the lamb. And I shall remember it is the Lord's passover. I shall not think of the herbs, nor be angry with the hands that gathered them; but look up only to Him who instituted that, and governs these: for men can have no more power over me than what is given them from above[b].

I am not in love with this passage through the Red sea, for I have the weakness and infirmity of flesh and blood plentifully in me.

[a] Exodus xii. 18.   [b] St. John xix. 11.

And I have prayed with my Saviour, *Ut transiret calix iste*, that this cup of red wine might pass from me[d]. But if not, God's will, not mine, be done. And I shall most willingly drink of this cup as deep as He pleases, and enter into this see, yea, and pass through it, in the way that He shall lead me.

But I would have it remembered, good people, that when God's servants were in this boisterous sea, and Aaron among them, the Egyptians which persecuted them, and did in a manner drive them into that sea, were drowned in the same waters, while they were in pursuit of them.

I know my God, Whom I serve, is as able to deliver me from this sea of blood, as He was to deliver the Three Children from the furnace[e]. And (I most humbly thank my Saviour for it) my resolution is, as theirs was: they would not worship the image which the king had set up, nor will I the imaginations which the people are setting up. _Nor will I forsake the temple and the truth of God, to

d St. Luke xxii. 42.   e Daniel iii.

follow the bleating of Jeroboam's calves in Dan and in Bethel.

And as for this people, they are at this day miserably misled: God of His mercy open their eyes, that they may see the right way. For at this day the blind lead the blind; and if they go on, both will certainly fall into the ditch[f].

For myself, I am (and I acknowledge it in all humility) a most grievous sinner many ways, by thought, word, and deed: and yet I cannot doubt but that God hath mercy in store for me, a poor penitent, as well as for other sinners. I have now upon this sad occasion ransacked every corner of my heart; and yet I thank God I have not found among the many, any one sin which deserves death by any known law of this kingdom.

And yet hereby I charge nothing upon my judges: for if they proceed upon proof by valuable witnesses, I or any other innocent may be justly condemned. And I thank God, though the weight of the sentence lie heavy

f St. Luke vi. 39.

upon me, I am as quiet within as ever I was in my life.

And though I am not only the first Archbishop, but the first man, that ever died by an Ordinance in Parliament, yet some of my predecessors have gone this way, though not by this means: for Elphegus was hurried away and lost his head by the Danes; Simon Sudbury in the fury of Wat Tyler and his fellows. Before these, St. John Baptist had his head danced off by a lewd woman; and St. Cyprian, Archbishop of Carthage, submitted his head to a persecuting sword. Many examples great and good; and they teach me patience. For I hope my cause in heaven will look of another dye, than the colour that is put upon it here.

And some comfort it is to me, not only that I go the way of these great men in their several generations; but also that my charge, as foul as it is made, looks like that of the Jews against St. Paul; (Acts xxv. 8.) for he was accused for the law and the temple, i. e. religion; and like that of St. Stephen, (Acts

vi. 14.) for breaking the ordinances which Moses gave, i. e. law and religion, the holy place and the law. (verse 13.)

But you will say, Do I then compare myself with the integrity of St. Paul and St. Stephen? No: far be that from me. I only raise a comfort to myself, that these great saints and servants of God were laid at in their times, as I am now. And it is memorable that St. Paul, who helped on this accusation against St. Stephen, did after fall under the very same himself.

Yea, but here is a great clamour that I would have brought in Popery. I shall answer that more fully by and by. In the mean time, you know what the Pharisees laid against Christ Himself, " If we let him alone, all men will believe on Him, *et venient Romani*, and the Romans will come; and take away both our place and nation. Here was a causeless cry against Christ, that the Romans would come: and see how just the judgment of God was. They crucified Christ

5 St. Luke xi. 48.

for fear lest the Romans should come; and His
death was it which brought in the Romans
upon them, God punishing them with that
which they most feared. And I pray God
this clamour of *venient Romani*, (of which I
have given no cause,) help not to bring them in.
For the Pope never had such an harvest in
England since the Reformation, as he hath
now upon the sects and divisions that are
amongst us. In the mean time, " by honour
and dishonour, by good report and evil report,
as a deceiver and yet true[b]," am I passing
through this world.

Some particulars also I think it not amiss
to speak of.

1. And first, this I shall be bold to speak
of the King, our gracious Sovereign. He
hath been much traduced also for bringing in
of Popery: but on my conscience (of which I
shall give God a present account) I know him
to be as free from this charge as any man
living. And I hold him to be as sound a
Protestant, according to the religion by law

[b] 2 Corinthians vi. 8.

established, as any man in his kingdom; and that he will venture his life as far and as freely for it. And I think I do or should know both his affection to religion, and his grounds for it, as fully as any man in England.

2. The second particular is concerning this great and populous city, (which God bless.) Here hath been of late a fashion taken up to gather hands, and then go to the great court of the kingdom, the Parliament, and clamour for justice, as if that great and wise court, before whom the causes come which are unknown to the many, could not or would not do justice but at their appointment; a way which may endanger many an innocent man, and pluck his blood upon their own heads, and perhaps upon the city's also.

And this hath been lately practised against myself; the magistrates standing still, and suffering them openly to proceed from parish to parish without check. God forgive the setters of this; with all my heart I beg it: but many well-meaning people are caught by it.

In St. Stephen's case, when nothing else would serve, they stirred up the people against him. (Acts vi. 12.) And Herod went the same way: when he had killed St. James, yet he would not venture upon St. Peter, till he found how the other pleased the people. (Acts xii. 3.)

But take heed of having your hands full of blood; (Isaiah i. 15.) for there is a time best known to Himself, when God above other sins makes inquisition for blood. And when that inquisition is on foot, the Psalmist tells us, that God remembers; but that is not all; He remembers, and forgets not the complaint of the poor[1], i. e. whose blood is shed by oppression[2].

Take heed of this: "it is a fearful thing to fall into the hands of the living God[3];" but then especially when He is making inquisition for blood. And with my prayers to avert it, I do heartily desire this city to remember the prophecy that is expressed in Jer. xxvi. 15.

3. The third particular is, the poor Church

[1] Psalm ix. 12.　　[2] Ver. 9.　　[3] Hebrews x. 31.

of England. It hath flourished, and been a shelter to other neighbouring Churches, when storms have driven upon them. But, alas! now it is in a storm itself, and God only knows whether or how it shall get out. And which is worse than a storm from without, it is become like an oak cleft to shivers with wedges made out of its own body; and at every cleft, profaneness and irreligion is entering in. While (as Prosper says[a]) men that introduce profaneness are cloked over with the name *religionis imaginariæ*, of imaginary religion: for we have lost the substance, and dwell too much in opinion. And that Church, which all the Jesuits' machinations could not ruin, is fallen into danger by her own.

4. The last particular (for I am not willing to be too long) is, myself. I was born and baptized in the bosom of the Church of England, established by law: in that profession I have ever since lived, and in that I come now to die.

What clamours and slanders I have en-

[a] Lib. ii. de Vitæ Contempt. c. 4.

dured for labouring to keep an uniformity in
the external service of God, according to the
doctrine and discipline of this Church, all men
know, and I have abundantly felt. Now at
last I am accused of high treason in Parliament, a crime which my soul ever abhorred.
This treason was charged to consist of two
parts, an endeavour to subvert the laws of the
land; and a like endeavour to overthrow the
true Protestant religion, established by law.

Besides my answers to the several charges,
I protested mine innocency in both Houses.
It was said, Prisoners' protestations at the bar
must not be taken. I must, therefore, come
now to it upon my death, being instantly to
give God an account for the truth of it.

I do therefore here, in the presence of God
and His holy Angels, take it upon my death,
that I never endeavoured the subversion either
of law or religion. And I desire you all to remember this protest of mine for my innocency
in this, and from all treasons whatsoever.

I have been accused likewise as an enemy
to Parliaments. No: I understand them, and

the benefit that comes by them, too well to
be so. But I did dislike the misgovernments
of some Parliaments many ways, and I had
good reason for it; for *corruptio optimi est
pessima.* And that being the highest court,
over which no other hath jurisdiction, when it
is misinformed or misgoverned, the subject is
left without all remedy.

But I have done. I forgive all the world,
all and every of those bitter enemies which
have persecuted me; and humbly desire to
be forgiven of God first, and then of every
man. And so I heartily desire you to join in
prayer with me.

O eternal God and merciful Father, look
down upon me in mercy, in the riches and
fulness of all thy mercies. Look upon me,
but not till Thou hast nailed my sins to the
Cross of Christ, not till Thou hast bathed me in
the blood of Christ, not till I have hid myself
in the wounds of Christ; that so the punishment due unto my sins may pass over me.
And since Thou art pleased to try me to the

uttermost, I most humbly beseech Thee, give me now in this great instant, full patience, proportionable comfort, and a heart ready to die for Thine honour, the King's happiness, and this Church's preservation.   And my zeal to these (far from arrogancy be it spoken) is all the sin (human frailty excepted, and all incidents thereto) which is yet known to me in this particular, for which I come now to suffer; I say, in this particular of treason. But otherwise, my sins are many and great; Lord, pardon them all, and those especially (whatever they are) which have drawn down this present judgment upon me.   And when Thou hast given me strength to bear it, do with me as seems best in Thine own eyes. Amen.

And that there may be a stop of this issue of blood in this more than miserable kingdom, O Lord, I beseech Thee give grace of repentance to all blood-thirsty people.   But if they will not repent, O Lord, confound all their devices, defeat and frustrate all their designs and endeavours upon them, which are or shall be contrary to the glory of Thy great Name, the truth and sincerity of religion, the establishment of the King, and his posterity after him, in their just rights and privileges; the honour and conservation of Parliaments in their just power; the preservation of this poor Church in her truth, peace, and patrimony; and the settlement of this distracted and distressed people, under their ancient laws, and in their native liberties. And when Thou hast done all this in mere mercy for them, O Lord, fill their hearts with thankfulness, and with religious dutiful obedience to Thee and Thy commandments all their days. So, Amen, Lord Jesu, Amen. And receive my soul into thy bosom. Amen.

Our Father, which art in heaven, Hallowed be thy Name. Thy kingdom come. Thy will be done in earth, As it is in heaven. Give us this day our daily bread. And forgive us our trespasses, As we forgive them that trespass against us. And lead us not into temptation; But deliver us from evil:

For thine is the kingdom, The power, and the glory, For ever and ever. Amen.

After these devotions, the Martyr rose, and gave his papers to Dr. Stern, his chaplain, who went with him to his Martyrdom, saying, "Doctor, I give you this, that you may shew it to your fellow-chaplains, that they may see how I went out of the world; and God's blessing and mercy be upon you and them." Then turning to a person named Hinde, whom he perceived busy writing the words of his address, he said, "Friend, I beseech you, bear me. I cannot say I have spoken every word as it is in my paper, but I have gone very near it, to help my memory as well as I could, but I beseech you, let me have no wrong done me:" intimating that he ought not to publish an imperfect copy. "Sir," replied Hinde, "you shall not. If I do so, let it fall upon my own head. I pray God have mercy upon your soul." "I thank you," answered the holy Martyr; "I did not speak with any jealousy as if you would do so, but only, as a poor man going out of the world, it is not possible for me to keep to the words of my paper, and a phrase might do me wrong."

This said, he next applied himself to the fatal block, as to the haven of his rest. But finding the way full of people, who had placed themselves upon the theatre to behold the tragedy, he said, " I thought there would have been an empty scaffold, that I might have had room to die. I beseech you, let me have an end of this misery, for I have endured it long." Hereupon room was made for him to die. While he was preparing himself for the axe, he said, " I will put off my doublet, and God's will be done. I am willing to go out of the world; no man can be more willing to send me out, than I am willing to be gone."

But there were broad chinks between the boards of the scaffold: and he saw that some people were got under the very place where the block was seated. So he desired either that the people might be removed, or dust brought to fill up the crevices, lest, said he, "my innocent blood should fall upon the heads of the people."

The holy Martyr was now ready for death, and very calmly waiting for his crown. It was like a scene out of primitive times. His face was fresh and ruddy, and of a cheerful countenance. But there stood, to look on and rail, one Sir John Clotworthy, an Irishman, and follower of the Earl of Warwick. He was a violent and wrong-headed man, an enthusiast, and very furious as a demagogue. Being irritated that the revilings of the people moved not the strong quiet of the holy Martyr, or sharpened him into any show of passion, "he would needs put in and try what he could do with his sponge and vinegar." So he propounded questions to him, not as if to learn, but rudely and out of ill nature, and to expose him to his associates. "What," asked he, "is the comfortablest saying which a dying man would have in his mouth?" To which the holy Martyr with very much meekness answered, "Cupio dissolvi et esse cum Christo." "That is a good

desire," said the other, " but there must be a
foundation for that divine assurance." " No
man can express it," replied the Martyr, " it
is to be found within." The busy man still
pursued him, and said, " It is founded upon
a word, nevertheless, and that word should
be known." " That word," said the Martyr,
" is the knowledge of Jesus Christ, and that
alone." But he saw that this was but an
indecent interruption, and that there would
be no end to the trouble, and so he turned
away from him to the executioner, as the
gentler and discreeter person: and, putting
some money into his hand, without the least
distemper or change of countenance, he said,
" Here, honest friend, God forgive thee, and
do thine office upon me in mercy." Then did
he go upon his knees; and the executioner
said that he should give a sign for the blow
to come; to which he answered, " I will, but
first let me fit myself." After that he prayed.

THE ARCHBISHOP'S PRAYER,

AS HE KNEELED BY THE BLOCK.

Lord, I am coming as fast as I can. I know I must pass through the shadow of death, before I can come to see Thee. But it is but *umbra mortis*, a mere shadow of death, a little darkness upon nature: but Thou by Thy merits and passion hast broke through the jaws of death. So, Lord, receive my soul, and have mercy upon me; and bless this kingdom with peace and plenty, and with brotherly love and charity, that there may not be this effusion of Christian blood amongst them, for Jesus Christ His sake, if it be Thy will.

Then he bowed his head upon the block "down, as upon a bed," and prayed silently awhile. No man heard what it was he prayed in that last prayer. After that he said out loud, "Lord, receive my soul;" which was the sign to the executioner; and at one blow he was beheaded.

There was no malice which was too great for his miserable enemies. They said he had purposely painted his face, to fortify his cheeks against discovery of fear in the paleness of his complexion. But, as if for the confutation of this poor malice, his face, ruddy in the last moment, instantly after the blow turned white as ashes.

Multitudes of people went with his body to the grave, which was borne in a leaden coffin to the church of All Hallows, Barking, a church of his own patronage and jurisdiction. It was noted of many as extraordinary, that, although the Liturgy had been by human law abolished, he the great champion of the Church and her Ceremonies was buried by his brave friends according to the old ritual, which it was high treason to use. So that it went to its grave with him. Both only for a while.

" For my faith," saith the holy Martyr, in in his last Will and Testament*, " I die as I

* Where also he says, " I take the boldness to give to my dread and dear Sovereign King Charles, (whom

have lived, in the true orthodox profession of the Catholic Faith of Christ, foreshewed by the Prophets, and preached to the world by Christ Himself, His blessed Apostles, and their successors; and a true member of His Catholic Church, within the Communion of a living part thereof, the present Church of England, as it stands established by law.

" I leave my body to the earth, whence it was taken, in full assurance of the resurrection of it from the grave at. the last day. This resurrection I constantly believe my dear Saviour Jesus Christ will make happy unto me His poor and weary servant. And for my burial, though I stand not much upon the place, yet if it conveniently may be, I desire to be buried in the Chapel of St. John

God bless,) £1000, and I do forgive him the debt which he owes me, being £3000, and require that the tallies for it be delivered up." Then, with many worldly gifts, he prays, that on his College there may rest God's everlasting blessing; and he gives a paten of gold for the young Duke of Buckingham, to use in his Chapel for a memorial of him.

Baptist's College in Oxford, underneath the Altar or Communion Table there. And should I be so unhappy as to die a prisoner; yet my earnest desire is, I may not be buried in the Tower. But wheresoever my burial shall be, I will have it private, that it may not waste any of the poor means which I leave behind me to better uses."

So on the 24th of July, being St. James's Eve, 1663, the remains of the holy Martyr were translated to Oxford, and laid in one of the four brick vaults beneath the Altar of St. John's. And he has no monument, except his own city of Oxford, and the present English Church.

So the dead which he slew at his death were more than they which he slew in his life.

COMMUNE UNIUS MARTYRIS.

EXTRA TEMPUS PASCHALE.

Ad Vesperas.

Deus, Tuorum militum
Sors, et corona, præmium:
Laudes canentes Martyris
Absolve nexu criminis.

Hic nempe mundi gaudia,
Et blanda fraudum pabula,
Imbuta felle deputans
Pervenit ad cœlestia.

Pœnas cucurrit fortiter,
Et sustulit viriliter,
Fundensque pro Te sanguinem,
Æterna dona possidet.

Ob hoc precatu supplici
Te poscimus piissime;
In hoc triumpho Martyris
Dimitte noxam servulis.

Laus et perennis gloria
Patri sit atque Filio,
Sancto simul Paraclito,
In sempiterna sæcula.

APPENDIX.

A.

*Things which I have projected to do, if God
bless me in them.*

[The poor not always is forgot,
Nor yet the meek man's longing thought
For ever gone and past.

PSALM IX. Oxford.]

1. Blotted out.

2. To build at St. John's in Oxford, where I was bred up, for the good and safety of that College. Done.

3. To overthrow the Feoffment, dangerous both to the Church and State, going under the specious pretence of buying in Impropriations. Done.

4. To procure King Charles to give all the Impropriations, yet remaining in the Crown, within the Realm of Ireland, to that poor Church. Done, and settled there.

5. To set upon the repair of St. Paul's Church in London. Done.

6. To collect and perfect the broken, crossing, and imperfect Statutes of the University of Oxford; which had lain in a confused heap some hundred of years. Done.

7. Blotted out.

8. To settle the Statutes of all the Cathedral Churches of the new foundations; whose Statutes are imperfect, and not confirmed. Done for Canterbury.

9. To annex for ever some settled Commendams, and those, if it may be, sine cura, to all the small Bishoprics. Done for Bristol, Peterborough, St. Asaph, Chester, Oxford.

10. To find a way to increase the stipends of poor Vicars.

11. To see the tithes of London settled, between the Clergy and the City.

12. To set up a Greek press in London and Oxford, for printing of the Library Manuscripts; and to get both letters and matrices. Done for London.

13. To settle £80 a year for ever, out of Dr. Fryar's lands, (after the death of Dr. John Fryar the son,) upon the fabric of St. Paul's, to the repair till that be finished, and to keep it in good state after.

14. To procure a large Charter for Oxford, to confirm their ancient privileges, and obtain new for them, as large as those of Canterbury, which they had gotten since Henry VIII. which Oxford had not. Done.

15. To open the great square at Oxford between St. Mary's and the Schools, Brasennose and All Souls.

16. To settle an Hospital of Land in Reading, of 100 pounds a year, in a new way. I have acquainted Mr. Barnard, the Vicar of Croydon, with my project. He is to call upon my executors to do it; if the surplusage of my goods (after debts and legacies paid)

come to three thousand pounds. Done to the value of 200 pounds per annum.

17. To erect an Arabic Lecture in Oxford, at least for my lifetime, my estate not being able for more. That this may lead the way, &c. Done. I have now settled it for ever. The Lecture began to be read Aug. 10, 1636.

18. The Impropriation of the Vicarage of Cuddesden to the Bishop of Oxford, finally sentenced Wednesday, April 19, 1637. And so the house built by the now Bishop of Oxford, Dr. John Bancroft, settled for ever to that Bishopric. Done.

19. A book in vellum fair written, containing the records which are in the Tower, and concern the Clergy. This book I got done at my own charge, and have left it in my study at Lambeth for posterity, July 10, 1637. Ab anno 20 Ed. I. ad annum 24 Ed. IV. Done.

20. A new Charter for the College near Dublin to be procured of his Majesty; and a body of new Statutes made, to rectify that government. Done.

21. A Charter for the town of Reading, and a Mortmain of, &c. Done.

22. If I live to see the repair of St. Paul's near an end, to move his Majesty for the like grant from the High Commission, for the buying in of Impropriations, as I have now for St. Paul's. And then I hope to buy in two a year at least.

23. I have procured for St. John Baptist's College in Oxford the perpetual inheritance and patronage of, &c.

B.

The Testimony of the Reverend Mr. Jonathan Whiston, concerning the opinion had of the Archbishop at Rome; and with what joy the news of his death and suffering was there received.

I do remember, that being Chaplain to the Honourable Sir Lionel Tolmach, Baronet, about the year 1666, I heard him relate to some person of quality, how that in his younger days he was at Rome, and well acquainted with a certain Abbot; which

Abbot asked him, Whether he had heard any news from England? He answered, No. The Abbot replied, I will tell you then some; Archbishop Laud is beheaded. Sir Lionel answered, You are sorry for that, I presume. The Abbot replied again, that they had more cause to rejoice, that the greatest enemy of the Church of Rome in England was cut off, and the greatest CHAMPION of the Church of England silenced: or in words to that purpose. In witness whereof, I have hereunto set my hand, this 28th day of September, 1694.

JONA. WHISTON,
Vicar of Betheraden in Kent.

The Testimony of the learned and worthy John Evelyn, Esq. Fellow of the Royal Society, concerning the same matter.

I was at Rome in the company of divers of the English Fathers, when the news of the Archbishop's suffering, and a copy of his Sermon made upon the scaffold, came thither. They read the Sermon, and commented upon it with no small satisfaction and contempt; and looked upon him as one that was a great enemy to them, and stood in their way; whilst one of the blackest crimes imputed to him was his being Popishly affected.

JOHN EVELYN.

C.

Some of the illustrious men brought forward or patronized by Archbishop Laud.

Archbishop Usher.	Archbishop Sheldon.
Bishop Morton.	Bishop Hall.
Bishop Montague.	Bishop Taylor.
Archbishop Juxon.	Bishop Sanderson.
Dr. Pococke.	Lord Clarendon.
Somner the Antiquary.	Sir Henry Spelman.
John Hales.	Selden.

———

Chillingworth,
cum multis aliis.

D.

An attempt to shew the shares of the Universities in the popular movement of the Great Rebellion.

1. Oliver Cromwell	..	Sydney	Cambridge
2. Fairfax	...	St. John's ..	Cambridge
3. Sir Edw. Coke	..	Trinity ..	Cambridge
4. Sir Robert Cotton	..	Trinity ..	Cambridge
5. Hugh Peters ..	..	Trinity ..	Cambridge
6. Sir John Eliot	..	Exeter ..	Oxford
7. Pym ..	.. ..	Pembroke ..	Oxford
8. Hampden	.. ..	Magdalen ..	Oxford
9. Vane the Younger		Magdalen ..	Oxford
10. Marten the Regicide		Univ. Coll. ..	Oxford
11. Prynne ..	.. ..	Oriel	Oxford
12. Harrington	.. ..	Trinity ..	Oxford
13. Fiennes, (W. Lord Say and Sele)		New Coll. ..	Oxford
14. Fiennes, Nathaniel		New Coll. ..	Oxford
15. Essex, (Lord)	..	Merton	Oxford
16. Selden ..	.. ..	Hart Hall ..	Oxford
17. Whitelock	.. ..	St. John's ..	Oxford
18. Lenthall ..	.. ..	St. Alban's ..	Oxford
19. Ludlow ..	.. ..	Trinity	Oxford
20. Sir W. Waller	..	Magdalen ..	Oxford
21. Ireton ..	.. ..	Trinity	Oxford
22. Sir B. Rudyard	..	St. John's ..	Oxford
23. Strode ..	.. ..	St. Mary Hall	Oxford
24. Dr. Twisse, Prolocutor of the Westminster Assembly		New Coll. ..	Oxford

ص ٣٣٦

Milton Keynes UK
Ingram Content Group UK Ltd.
UKHW020730291223
435170UK00006B/330